Melissa Stewart & Nancy Chesley

Perfect Pairs

Using Fiction & Nonfiction Picture Books to Teach Life Science, K-2

Stenhouse Publishers
Portland, Maine

Stenhouse Publishers
www.stenhouse.com

Copyright © 2014 by Melissa Stewart and Nancy Chesley

Credits on page 339.

Library of Congress Cataloging-in-Publication Data
Stewart, Melissa.
    Perfect pairs : using fiction & nonfiction picture books to teach life science, K–2 / Melissa Stewart, Nancy Chesley.
        pages cm
    ISBN 978-1-57110-958-3 (paperback)—ISBN 978-1-62531-021-7 (ebook) 1. Life sciences—Study and teaching (Elementary) 2. Life sciences—Study and teaching—Activity programs. 3. Picture books for children—Educational aspects. I. Chesley, Nancy. II. Title.
    QH315.S82 2014
    570.71—dc23

                                                        2014010235

Cover design, interior design, and typesetting by Martha Drury

Manufactured in the United States of America

PRINTED ON 30% PCW
RECYCLED PAPER

20 19 18 17 16 15 14   9 8 7 6 5 4 3 2 1

For Nancy Chesley, who understood my vision and helped me shape it and bring it to fruition.

—M.S.

For Jenny and Todd, with love.

—N.C.

Contents

Acknowledgments   *ix*

Introduction   1
How *Perfect Pairs* Can Help You
Not All Nonfiction for Children Is Created Equal
Why Combine Science and Children's Books?
Why Pair Fiction and Nonfiction?
From Idea to Book
Who Is This Guide For?

Getting Started   7
Obtaining the Books
Starting with a Wonder Statement
The Investigative Process
Reinforcing the Concept
ELA Links
The Wonder Journal
Science Dialogues and Science Circles

Meeting the Standards   15
Addressing the Next Generation Science Standards
Supporting the Common Core State Standards for
    English Language Arts

Lessons for Kindergarten   23

Lesson K.1:   What Plants and Animals Need to Survive   25
The Salamander Room by Anne Mazer & *From Seed to Pumpkin*
by Wendy Pfeffer

Lesson K.2: **What Animals Eat** 36
Gobble It Up! A Fun Song About Eating! by Jim Arnosky & *Time to Eat*
by Steve Jenkins and Robin Page

Lesson K.3: **How Animals Depend on Their Environment** 45
Just Ducks! by Nicola Davies & *Hip-Pocket Papa* by Sandra Markle

Lesson K.4: **How Animals Can Change an Environment** 54
Mole's Hill by Lois Ehlert & *At Home with the Gopher Tortoise*
by Madeleine Dunphy

Lesson K.5: **How People Can Change an Environment** 62
On Meadowview Street by Henry Cole & *Wangari's Trees of Peace:
A True Story from Africa* by Jeanette Winter

Lesson K.6: **How to Reduce Our Impact on Creatures in
Land Environments** 72
Where Once There Was a Wood by Denise Fleming &
A Place for Butterflies by Melissa Stewart

Lesson K.7: **How to Reduce Our Impact on Creatures in
Water Environments** 80
Big Night for Salamanders by Sarah Marwil Lamstein &
Turtle, Turtle, Watch Out! by April Pulley Sayre

Picture Books for Kindergarten Lessons 87

Lessons for Grade 1   91

Lesson 1.1: **How an Animal's Body Parts Help It Survive** 93
The Snail's Spell by Joanne Ryder & *What Do You Do with a Tail
Like This?* by Steve Jenkins

Lesson 1.2: **How Animals Find and Catch Food** 103
A Frog in the Bog by Karma Wilson & *Just One Bite* by Lola Schaefer

Lesson 1.3: **How Animals Protect Themselves** 112
Swimmy by Leo Lionni & *What Do You Do When Something Wants
to Eat You?* by Steve Jenkins

Lesson 1.4: **How a Plant's Parts Help It Survive** 119
Jack's Garden by Henry Cole & *Plant Secrets* by Emily Goodman

Lesson 1.5: **Mimicking Plant and Animal Body Parts
to Solve Problems** 128
Iggy Peck, Architect by Andrea Beaty & *Winter's Tail: How One
Little Dolphin Learned to Swim Again* by Juliana Hatkoff,
Isabella Hatkoff, and Craig Hatkoff

Lesson 1.6: **How Animal Parents and Young Interact**   **138**
What Dads Can't Do by Douglas Wood & *Little Lost Bat*
by Sandra Markle

Lesson 1.7: **How Young Animals Are Like Their Parents**   **147**
Just Like My Papa by Toni Buzzeo & *What Bluebirds Do*
by Pamela F. Kirby

Lesson 1.8: **How Adult Animals of the Same Species Can
Be Different**   **156**
Dogs by Emily Gravett & *No Two Alike* by Keith Baker

Picture Books for Grade 1 Lessons   **163**

Lessons for Grade 2   167

Lesson 2.1: **How Wind, Water, and Animals
Disperse Seeds**   **169**
Miss Maple's Seeds by Eliza Wheeler & *Planting the Wild Garden*
by Kathryn O. Galbraith

Lesson 2.2: **Understanding Habitats**   **178**
A House for Hermit Crab by Eric Carle & *Song of the Water Boatman
& Other Pond Poems* by Joyce Sidman

Lesson 2.3: **Understanding Biomes**   **188**
The Great Kapok Tree by Lynne Cherry & *Here Is the
Southwestern Desert* by Madeleine Dunphy

Lesson 2.4: **Life in Wetlands**   **200**
Catfish Kate and the Sweet Swamp Band by Sarah Weeks &
Frog in a Bog by John Himmelman

Lesson 2.5: **Life in Grasslands**   **214**
Water Hole Waiting by Jane Kurtz and Christopher Kurtz &
Out on the Prairie by Donna M. Bateman

Lesson 2.6: **How Plants Change as They Grow**   **224**
Plantzilla by Jerdine Nolen & *A Seed Is Sleepy*
by Dianna Hutts Aston

Lesson 2.7: **How Butterflies Change as They Grow**   **231**
Clara Caterpillar by Pamela Duncan Edwards &
Where Butterflies Grow by Joanne Ryder

Picture Books for Grade 2 Lessons   **239**

Appendix A: *Tables of Next Generation Science Standards (NGSS) and Common Core State Standards for English Language Arts (ELA) Addressed in* Perfect Pairs *Lessons*   243

Appendix B: *Reproducibles for* Perfect Pairs *Lessons*   257

Bibliography of Picture Books in Perfect Pairs *Lessons*   329

Professional References   337

Credits   339

Index   343

Acknowledgments

We gratefully acknowledge kindergarten teacher Kathi Hardy, first-grade teacher Jamie Palmer, and second-grade teacher Ann Slattery of Pownal Elementary School in Pownal, Maine, for helping us field test the lessons in this book. Their suggestions and insights were invaluable.

We would also like to thank Lisa Demick, Principal of Pownal Elementary School, for her enthusiasm for our project and for welcoming us into her school. A special thank you, also, to primary educational technician Kim Ordway, who was always there when we needed her assistance. This book benefited greatly from the eager and dedicated community of K–2 student scientists at Pownal Elementary and their supportive parents and guardians. Thanks for teaching us so much and for allowing us to illustrate this book with photos of you participating in the activities as well as samples of your student work.

We also deeply appreciate the efforts of kindergarten teacher Ann Witham, first-grade teacher Trish Curtis, and second-grade teacher Sarah Otterson of Hebron Elementary School in Hebron, Maine, who taught some of our early draft lessons to their students.

Thank you to our editor Toby Gordon for acquiring this book and guiding us seamlessly through the editorial process and the entire Stenhouse staff, including Jill Cooley, Chris Downey, and Jay Kilburn. We would also like to acknowledge the contributions of Erin Trainer. And finally we would like to extend a heart-felt thank you to the children's book authors, illustrators, and publishers (Abrams, Boyds Mills, Candlewick, Charlesbridge, Chronicle, Disney-Hyperion, HarperCollins, Holt, Houghton Mifflin Harcourt, Peachtree, Penguin Random House, Scholastic, and Simon & Schuster) who allowed us to use the cover images of books free of charge.

Introduction

How *Perfect Pairs* Can Help You

In recent years, most elementary science programs have focused on hands-on lessons that emphasize direct observations and firsthand experiences. These lessons are ideal for teaching some science concepts. For example, it's very easy for children to see and experience current weather conditions, properties of matter, and light and sound in the world around them. But when it comes to life science, hands-on lessons aren't always feasible, effective, safe, or environmentally sound.

Young children can't directly experience predator-prey relationships or habitat loss. They can't develop a true understanding of the interdependence of living things through hands-on activities. And they can't observe a range of animals or fully explore habitats from the confines of a classroom. *Perfect Pairs: Using Fiction & Nonfiction Picture Books to Teach Life Science, K–2* addresses this conundrum by offering an alternative form of instruction that is both fun and effective.

Because high-quality, science-themed children's picture books can bring a whole world of plants, animals, ecosystems, and natural processes to life, *Perfect Pairs* succeeds where science programs emphasizing hands-on activities fall short. *Perfect Pairs* allows students to fully explore science topics that can't be adequately taught through direct experiences.

As a teacher, you know that finely crafted children's books have the ability to motivate, engage, and delight children. And the good news is that today's children's authors are creating science-themed titles that are more innovative, more intriguing than ever before.

A first grader observes the inside of a bean with a hand lens.

But you also know that most children can't build a solid understanding of key science concepts simply by reading about them. They need more support, more guidance. Students learn best by participating in a broad range of experiences that introduce and reinforce scientific ideas. Then they can move beyond the lesson, applying their new knowledge to a variety of situations.

Perfect Pairs marries the wonderful array of science-themed children's fiction and nonfiction picture books currently available with authentic, engaging minds-on activities and investigations.

Each lesson begins by inviting students to wonder about a life science idea and uses two finely crafted children's books to guide the class through an investigative process that explores the idea. The lessons address the Performance Expectations outlined in the Next Generation Science Standards and support the goals of the Common Core State Standards for English Language Arts.

Even if you are the most science-shy elementary teacher, *Perfect Pairs* can transform the way you teach science. Over time, you can become a more confident and competent teacher whose classroom buzzes with curious students eager to explore their world. Instead of approaching science instruction with apprehension, you'll look forward to it.

Not All Nonfiction for Children Is Created Equal

Once upon a time, nonfiction books for children were lifeless assemblages of facts with a few scattered images decorating the pages. These books conveyed information, but that's about it.

Today's young readers expect more. Much more. And today's nonfiction authors have risen to the challenge. In recent years, a new kind of children's nonfiction has emerged. These innovative titles are remarkably creative and compelling. Their purpose is to delight as well as inform.

Kindergarten students participate in an activity that ties into the wonderful repetition in *Turtle, Turtle, Watch Out!* by April Pulley Sayre.

The very best nonfiction books—the books your students should be reading—are written by dedicated authors with true passion for their topics. These authors search far and wide for the freshest, most fascinating information. Then they carefully craft language that will engage young readers and appeal to their natural curiosity. The publishers of these books invest considerable resources in high-quality artwork and visually dynamic design that echo and enrich the text. As a result, the final products are a pleasure to read and explore.

Some of the critically acclaimed nonfiction titles we've selected for *Perfect Pairs* read like stories. Others offer lovely lyrical language that pleases readers with alliteration, rhythm, and repetition or a lively, playful style that amuses readers with unexpected word choices, puns, or internal rhyme. Still others have a game-like quality that invites participation. All of the books are short enough to read in one sitting and have strong read-aloud potential.

We have seen firsthand that when children are exposed to finely crafted, beautifully illustrated science-themed children's nonfiction, the authors' techniques begin to reappear in student writing assignments. As a result, these titles can and should be used as mentor texts during language arts instruction. In addition, reading and working with these titles gives students experience that prepares them to read and respond to similar passages on standardized tests.

More than anything else, though, our hope is that the beauty and craftsmanship of these texts will inspire your students, fueling their own journeys of scientific discovery.

Why Combine Science and Children's Books?

Make no mistake about it. The purpose of *Perfect Pairs* is to teach science. It's not a reading program that includes science content simply because children love to read about insects and dinosaurs and sharks.

In each lesson, the featured fiction and nonfiction picture books do much more than launch students into the topic. They are an integral part of the science instruction.

Why do we advocate this approach? Because it works.

Melissa began pairing the science books she's written with popular children's fiction titles in 2006. While visiting schools as an author-in-residence, she noticed that some students connect more strongly to fiction than to nonfiction. With the understanding that different children learn in different ways, Melissa developed a broad range of innovative activities that reinforce the key science concepts highlighted in the fiction-nonfiction book pairs. Because she firmly believes that writing (and drawing, for early elementary students) is the best way for the majority of students to synthesize ideas and make sense of new content, many of her activities included a strong writing (and/or drawing) component.

Melissa was thrilled to discover that students were actively learning science concepts when they used her lessons, and she was delighted by the enthusiasm of teachers, who eagerly asked for more lessons.

Why did teachers like the lessons so much? Because they were easy and inexpensive to implement, and because they were comfortable to teach.

Many elementary teachers do not have a strong science background. Some even report being intimidated by their school's science curriculum and feel ill equipped to teach basic science concepts. Building science lessons around children's books enables many elementary educators to approach science instruction with greater confidence.

But that's not the only reason that the lessons work so well. In recent years, many schools have scaled back on science education, and teachers have been asked to devote more time to language arts and math in an effort to improve student scores on assessment tests. As a result, many elementary students receive limited science instruction, and many middle school students are sorely lacking in basic science knowledge and skills. Because Melissa's initial lessons emphasized reading and writing skills, they allowed teachers to expose students to science without compromising language arts instruction time.

Why Pair Fiction and Nonfiction?

Some students love reading fiction. Others would rather delve into richly-illustrated, fact-filled nonfiction titles. Because different children enjoy different kinds of books and learn in different ways, pairing fiction and nonfiction titles is an effective way to introduce science concepts.

When these book pairs are presented in conjunction with innovative, minds-on activities and investigations that appeal to a wide variety of learning styles, students are even more likely to remember the experience—and the content.

Bringing high-quality science-themed fiction and nonfiction picture books into the classroom engages a broad range of students and supports the goals of the Common Core State Standards for English Language Arts. All of the picture books we've selected for *Perfect Pairs* feature stellar writing, tremendous visual appeal, high production quality, and close attention to even the most minute details. They are individually crafted by authors, illustrators, editors, art directors, and graphic designers who are passionate about what they do. And students can absolutely tell the difference.

From Idea to Book

When we met in 2008, Nancy was concerned with the way she saw teachers trying to use books to teach science. As a retired elementary teacher and science, math, and literacy specialist for the Maine Mathematics and Science Alliance, she was working with classroom teachers to integrate science-themed children's books into inquiry-based lessons. She was intrigued with Melissa's ideas, and we began a series of conversations about the most useful and practical way to combine the magic of children's books with the wonders of the natural world.

With the publication of the Next Generation Science Standards (NGSS), we knew the time was right to create *Perfect Pairs*. By bringing together Nancy's tremendous experience as an educator and Melissa's knowledge of children's books, we have created a resource that makes science easy to teach and fun to learn. Why are we so confident that the lessons included in this book will appeal to a broad range of students and teachers?

- They are inexpensive and easy to implement.
- They offer innovative activities and investigations that help students understand life science concepts included in the NGSS.
- They showcase the eight science and engineering practices incorporated into the NGSS.
- They support the Common Core State Standards for English Language Arts.
- They help students prepare for critical reading and open response questions on standardized tests.
- They respect and reinforce students' natural curiosity, sense of wonder, and feelings of connectedness to the natural world.

- They focus on concepts that are not accessible through hands-on experiences, extending the students' world beyond the classroom.

Who Is This Guide For?

This teaching resource is intended for elementary educators who

- have limited time and expertise to develop science units.
- have limited resources to teach science.
- are excited to teach science, but need additional guidance or are looking for fresh ideas.
- enjoy sharing wonderful children's books with students.
- recognize that science lessons that incorporate reading and writing activities will enhance students' achievement in language arts as well as in science.

Perfect Pairs contains a wealth of ideas for connecting science and English language arts, allowing you to integrate more science into your limited instruction time. Because each *Perfect Pairs* lesson directly addresses the Next Generation Science Standards and supports the Common Core State Standards for English Language Arts, you can be confident that you are teaching students the critical concepts and skills they need to know.

Getting Started

Obtaining the Books

At the time of publication, all of the children's books included in *Perfect Pairs* were in print. Going forward, the introduction of print-on-demand technology and e-books means that out-of-print books will become less of a problem. For now, however, children's books go in and out of print frequently. If you find that one of the books you'd like to use is no longer in print, don't worry. There are still many ways that you can locate copies for your class:

- Check your school and public libraries. Even if they don't own the book, you may be able to obtain it through interlibrary loan.
- Check your local bookstore. Even if it's not in stock, the staff may be able to help you track it down.
- Try AbeBooks (http://www.abebooks.com), an online marketplace that can locate new, used, rare, and out-of-print books through a community of independent booksellers around the world.
- Check Alibris (http://www.alibris.com), which connects people with new, used, and hard-to-find books and other media from thousands of independent sellers located all over the world.
- Search Amazon (http://www.amazon.com) to connect with sellers of used books. Enter the title of the book you seek and see if any used copies are available.
- Check Powell's Books (http://www.powells.com), which offers an extensive list of both new and used books.

Starting with a Wonder Statement

Authentic science always begins with a question, with a fleeting thought, with a curious person. That curious person has an idea, wonders if it is valid, and then tries to find out. Because wondering is at the heart of scientific discovery, each *Perfect Pairs* lesson starts with a Wonder Statement that we've carefully crafted to address one Next Generation Science Standards Performance Expectation. It is followed by a Learning Goal, which clearly specifies the new knowledge and essential understanding students will gain from the lesson. Together, the Wonder Statement, Learning Goal, and fiction-nonfiction book pair launch students into a fun and meaningful investigative process.

A grade 2 Wonder Statement with illustrated vocabulary cards

The Investigative Process

Because an instructional model is helpful in organizing an effective science experience for children, we have developed an Investigative Process that draws on elements of the popular 5-E Learning Cycle model (Bybee, Taylor, Gardner, Scotter, Powell, Westbrook, and Landes 2006) as well as the four-step Stages of Inquiry model espoused by the Education Development Center (EDC) in Waltham, Massachusetts (Worth, J. Winokur, Crissman, M. Winokur, and Davis 2009). In each lesson, our three-step model (Engaging Students, Exploring with Students, Encouraging Students to Draw Conclusions) guides teachers and

Teaching Tip

Some of the vocabulary included in the NGSS Performance Expectations will be challenging for early elementary students, and yet student assessment tests may include these difficult terms. To help students feel comfortable with the domain-specific language, we have used a teaching strategy called scaffolding. We begin by using words students will be familiar with and gradually introduce domain-specific vocabulary in context. We recommend that you employ the same technique as you work through the lessons with your class.

A sample data table from Lesson 1.4

Plant Part	Secret
Seed	Tiny Plant Inside
Stem	Keeps it upright, carries water, and grows leaves
Flower	Makes the fruit
Fruit	Seeds Inside
Leaf	Collects Sun

students through a series of activities that bring science to life. Our model effectively integrates the NGSS science and engineering practices and offers specific opportunities for students to record, organize, model, and analyze information.

Engaging Students

At the beginning of the investigative process, students participate in a common experience that will generally require one thirty- to forty-five-minute block of time. This part of the lesson is designed to pique their interest in the Wonder Statement and prepare them for a science investigation. In some cases, students have an opportunity to generate content vocabulary that will help them communicate their ideas and discoveries. The common experience may also provide a basis for predictions as the lesson progresses. Often during this phase, students' misconceptions surface, providing the teacher with insight into their current understanding.

Exploring with Students

This is the heart of the investigative process. Teachers guide students in developing and carrying out a plan to find, collect, and organize information that addresses the Wonder Statement. As students delve into the featured books, they use models, diagrams, and especially data tables to focus on the information most critical to the investigation. Because early elementary students with limited reading skills may have difficulty keeping track of information included in the data tables, we have provided review activities that reinforce the data the class has compiled in each table as well as key points discussed in the related section of the lesson. This part of the lesson will generally require two thirty- to forty-five-minute blocks of time—one block for each of the featured children's books.

Encouraging Students to Draw Conclusions

During the first two stages of the investigative process, you and your class will participate in a broad and extensive learning experience initiated by the Wonder Statement. This final step of the investigative process, which will generally require two thirty- to forty-five-minute blocks of time, helps students refocus their thinking on the key ideas in the NGSS Performance Expectation (PE) by rephrasing the Wonder Statement in the form

A kindergarten student makes a visual model that communicates a solution to a problem.

of a question. Then, as students respond to the question, they review, integrate, analyze, interpret, and evaluate the data they've collected and use it to draw conclusions. Finally, students demonstrate their understanding by participating in an activity that emphasizes the connection between the two featured books and thoroughly addresses the targeted science practice embedded in the lesson's PE.

Reinforcing the Concept

Following the Investigative Process, each lesson includes suggestions for innovative activities that reinforce the Learning Goal. With differential learning styles in mind, these activities often involve kinesthetic experiences or the arts. This section also lists additional fiction and nonfiction book pairs that are well suited for further exploration of the same Wonder Statement.

ELA Links

In the Next Generation Science Standards, each Performance Expectation (PE) is accompanied by a list of Common Core standards that the NGSS developers believe can be addressed through a science investigation related to that PE. Whenever possible, *Perfect Pairs* investigative processes support those standards. The ELA (English Language Arts) Links sections offer additional opportunities for making connections to

Common Core reading and writing standards and can be addressed during the Investigative Process or integrated into your class's ELA block. Each one begins with a question that asks students to compare the writing, art, and design styles of the two featured books. Subsequent questions call attention to interesting or unique literary aspects of the books so that students can begin to probe the intricacies of the writing process.

The Wonder Journal

All professional scientists keep notebooks. But they have little in common with the structured student notebooks found in most elementary classrooms. A scientist's notebook should be a place to keep track of ideas, thoughts, questions, observations, sketches, diagrams, claims, evidence, and insights about the workings of the natural world. And sometimes it can even include personal, diary-like entries.

The notebooks kept by Nobel Prize-winning American chemist Linus Pauling contain everything from shopping lists to philosophical musings about life. Leonardo da Vinci's notebooks include thoughts, ideas, and tips from an amazing thinker as well as thousands of scientific drawings, providing a fascinating glimpse into the mind of one of history's greatest figures.

Ideally, students' science notebooks should have the same kind of richness and creativity. But reaching this level of proficiency takes time and practice. In the early elementary grades, students need a certain amount of guidance and structure. That's why we recommend that children keep a Wonder Journal—a science notebook that emphasizes a balance between modeled instruction and open-ended opportunities.

One of our goals in *Perfect Pairs* is to lay the groundwork necessary for students to consistently produce rich, thoughtful science notebook entries. At the early elementary level, Wonder Journals give young scientists the freedom to ask questions and to explore and think. They allow students to record their journey through productive investigative processes that

- lead to content knowledge.
- nurture curious young minds.
- build enthusiasm for the way the world works.

A Wonder Journal is a place for students to record what they've observed and experienced *and* to freely express their sense of wonder.

A Wonder Journal's fluid format encourages creative problem solving. It allows young scientists to think deeply and rigorously. And it gives them practice organizing, synthesizing, and communicating their ideas and insights as they travel down the path of discovery and understanding. This kind of exploration is what makes young minds come alive.

But Wonder Journals won't work without guidance. Early elementary students need assistance focusing their wonderings into effective and useful records of their scientific journey. That's why we recommend that during *Perfect Pairs* lessons, students make guided entries as well as open-ended entries in their Wonder Journals.

Guided Entries

In an ideal world, students would work in the same way as professional scientists—developing their own questions about the world and pursuing them independently. But an elementary classroom isn't an ideal world. Because time for science instruction is at such a premium, teachers must steer students toward investigations that are age appropriate and will lead to an understanding of science concepts deemed essential by the Next Generation Science Standards.

With this goal in mind, we have designed the lessons in this book so that teachers model and guide some Wonder Journal entries. For instance, students should always include the Wonder Statement in their journals. During the Exploring with Students phase of the Investigative Process, you will provide your class with formatted data tables. These visual models will help students collect and organize the information they'll need during the Drawing Conclusions stage of the investigation. These guided entries will increase productive instructional time. They will also decrease confusion and frustration as students work their way through the Investigative Process.

Open-ended Entries

As students move through the Investigative Process, encourage them to record their predictions, ideas, questions, and perspectives with drawings and creative language. By giving students the opportunity to imagine and wonder, create and improvise, probe and explore, these open-ended entries will fuel the imagination, curiosity, and perceptions of young scientists.

Our hope is that the finely crafted language and beautiful illustrations of the books featured in each *Perfect Pairs* lesson will inspire students and serve as models for their own writing and artwork. A Wonder Journal should be a place where students

In this Wonder Journal entry, a first grader wonders why octopus mothers die after they watch their children swim away.

I WONDr WI OCTOPUS MOTHr Die Artr ThAe WOCh ThAr chiLDriN SWiM A WAe.

Teaching Tip

Because elementary-aged children have a limited amount of energy to write, it's important that Wonder Journal entries be productive. They should contribute directly to (1) student understanding of key science concepts or (2) building student enthusiasm for exploring the world around them, or both.

- Avoid writing Wonder Statements or data table structures on the board and asking students to copy them. Instead, create preprinted labels and handouts that students can add to their journals.
- Student writing should be legible, but let your class know that correct spelling, sentence structure, and mechanics are not a priority.

feel free to record their scientific insights and experiences as well as communicate their discoveries visually and verbally.

Setting Up a Wonder Journal

There are no set rules for Wonder Journals. You should choose the materials and format you think will work best in your classroom. To keep things simple and inexpensive, try folding several pieces of $8\frac{1}{2}$-by-14-inch paper in half and stapling them along the fold to create a booklet. You can use blank white paper, lined paper, graph paper, story paper, or any combination. Students can draw and color on the cover.

Commercial-grade composition books are also a fairly inexpensive option. Students may wish to personalize the covers by gluing on letters made of construction paper, images cut out of magazines, or natural materials they have collected.

To promote the idea that a Wonder Journal is a special place for each student to record his or her own unique journey of scientific discovery, it is important to respect the integrity of the student entries. If you wish to provide feedback, write your notes in a friendly color (not red) on a sticky note. When possible, phrase your comments in the form of questions. Instead of telling students they are wrong, ask them to consider other possibilities. Most important, be sure to encourage creative thinking and praise their statements of wonder.

The Wonder Journal is a critical component of the *Perfect Pairs* lessons. It is also a place where students will apply and reinforce the reading and writing skills that they learn during their language arts instruction. Experience has shown us that these journals can become prized possessions for students and equally treasured indications for parents of their child's earliest scientific achievements.

A proud first grader shows her Wonder Journal.

Science Dialogues and Science Circles

The critical role of discourse in science cannot be overstated. As students talk with their classmates and teacher, ideas and questions—as well as understanding—evolve. *Perfect Pairs* includes a variety of opportunities for students to talk and share ideas. During the Engaging stage of the lessons, conversations can expose student misconceptions. Brainstorming can reveal links between prior knowledge and the concepts students are about to learn. Informal Turn and Talk chats with classmates as well as guided class discussions can enhance both the Exploring and the Drawing Conclusions stages of lessons.

The lessons also feature two innovative teaching strategies that encourage young scientists to speak their minds. During Science Dialogues and Science Circles, young scientists have the opportunity to share their ideas with one another and to agree or disagree with ideas presented by classmates.

A Science Dialogue is a method for introducing a new concept that builds on an idea students have recently learned. As students share with their classmates, they are expected to provide rationale for their thoughts. Science Dialogues give you an opportunity to assess your students' evolving understanding and identify potential misconceptions.

A Science Circle (adapted from Worth et al. 2009) is a technique for synthesizing information and assessing student understanding of a key science concept. Students review and process what they've learned by drawing on evidence gathered during earlier stages of an investigation.

During Science Dialogues and Science Circles, the entire class sits in a circle. In some cases, you begin with a question, observation, or information that fosters a discussion. In other cases, student volunteers share ideas or Wonder Journal entries and classmates provide feedback. In both cases, students practice exchanging ideas as if they were scientific colleagues. Your role is to act as a facilitator, keeping the discussion focused, clarifying student responses, and asking questions that model true scientific discourse.

You may find this form of teaching difficult at first, but keep trying. You'll be thrilled by the results. After the conversation is over, you may wish to work with the class to recount the main points and record them on chart paper. Later, you may choose to develop the ideas into a handout for students to add to their Wonder Journals. The entire class will benefit from the permanent record of the conversation, but it will be especially helpful to English language learners.

Meeting the Standards

Addressing the Next Generation Science Standards

The Next Generation Science Standards (NGSS) provide educators with Performance Expectations (PEs) for students to meet at each grade level. These PEs are statements that describe what students should know and be able to do at the completion of instruction. The PEs address critical content in four domains:

- Life Sciences
- Earth and Space Sciences
- Physical Sciences
- Engineering, Technology, and Applications of Science

PEs draw upon three dimensions originally outlined in *A Framework for K–12 Science Education*, which was published by the National Research Council in 2012:

1. Content-rich statements called Disciplinary Core Ideas (DCIs)
2. Science and engineering practices that describe behaviors scientists and engineers engage in as they carry out their work.
3. Crosscutting concepts (patterns, cause and effect, structure and function, etc.) that have applications across all domains of science and engineering.

Here's an example. For kindergarten, one PE associated with the Life Sciences domain is K-LS1-1. According to this PE, students should be able to "Use observations to describe [*practice*] patterns [*crosscutting concept*] of what plants and animals (including humans) need to survive [*DCI*]" (NGSS Lead States).

The NGSS also provide PE Clarification Statements that describe parameters for instruction and assessment. For example, the Clarification Statement for K-LS1-1 is: "Examples of patterns could include that animals need to take in food but plants do not; the different kinds of foods needed by different types of animals; the requirement of plants to have light; and, that all living things need water." Clarification Statements like this one helped us determine the focus of instruction for *Perfect Pairs* lessons.

The lessons in *Perfect Pairs* have been designed to address the Disciplinary Core Idea(s), the science and engineering practice, and the crosscutting concept incorporated into each NGSS Performance Expectation. Because the goal of *Perfect Pairs* is to focus on concepts that cannot be directly experienced or fully explored through hands-on activities, most of the lessons address PEs in the NGSS Life Sciences (LS) domain. In some cases, concepts traditionally thought of as life science topics (interactions among living things, human impact on land and water, etc.) are included in the NGSS Earth and Space Science (ESS) domain. *Perfect Pairs* also includes lessons that explore these PEs. For your convenience, Tables 1–3 in Appendix A list the PE featured in each *Perfect Pairs* lesson.

A Closer Look at Performance Expectations (PEs)

In reviewing Tables 1–3 in Appendix A, you will notice that some PEs are the focus of two or more lessons. In these cases, we felt that a series of related learning experiences would make it possible for young children to more fully explore all three dimensions (DCIs, practices, crosscutting concepts) of the PE as well as the broad range of suggestions sometimes included in Clarification Statements. Thus, we recommend that you share all related lessons with your students.

In some cases, *Perfect Pairs* lessons include instruction that goes beyond the PE and Clarification Statement. For example, Lesson K.2 addresses the part of the K-LS1-1 Clarification Statement that says, "different kinds of food [are] needed by different types of animals." After exploring this idea with students, the instruction goes a step further by seamlessly introducing the ideas that unrelated animals sometimes eat similar diets and that some animals eat more than one kind of food.

Similarly, 2-LS2-2, one of the grade two Performance Expectations, states that students who demonstrate understanding can "Develop a simple model that mimics the function of an animal in dispersing seeds or pollinating plants." Lesson 2.1 fully addresses this PE, but it also explores the role of wind and water in seed dispersal and explains why seed dispersal is beneficial to plants.

Second graders compare the diversity of life in two grassland biomes.

> Plants on Savannas and Prairies
> 1. Different kinds of plants live on
>   Savannas _____ and _____ prairies .
> 2. There seems to be a greater
>   diversity of [plants] on the prairie.
> 3. There are colorful ____ [flowers]
>   on the prairie, but not on the
>   savanna.
> 4. ____ [grass] ____ grows on savannas
>   and prairies.

According to the NGSS, PE 1-LS3-1 was developed from two separate DCIs, but we felt that the resulting PE statement, "Make observations to construct an evidence-based account that young plants and animals are like, but not exactly like, their parents" left out key ideas in one of the DCIs. So after addressing the PE in Lesson 1.7, we added a second lesson to fully explore the second DCI. Lesson 1.8 investigates the similarities and differences among adult animals of the same species.

PE 2-LS4-1 for grade two states that students should "Make observations of plants and animals to compare the diversity of life in different habitats." We felt that before students could explore this PE in a meaningful way, they needed a learning experience to help them fully understand what a habitat is and why it's important. We developed Lesson 2.2 with that goal in mind. Lesson 2.3 then introduces students to the term *biome* and compares the features and creatures of forest and desert biomes. Lessons 2.4 and 2.5 compare the diversity of life in different types of wetlands and grasslands, respectively.

Incorporating the Eight Science and Engineering Practices

Our knowledge about how students learn science has come a long way since the National Science Education Standards and the Benchmarks for Science Literacy were published in the 1990s (NRC 1996 and AAAS 1993). *Science inquiry* was the buzz term then as educators sought ways to implement the essential content compiled in those two national standards documents.

A Framework for K–12 Science Education (NRC), published in 2012, expanded the meaning and implications of inquiry. Inquiry is now part and parcel of eight science and engineering practices:

1. Asking questions (for science) and defining problems (for engineering)
2. Developing and using models
3. Planning and carrying out investigations
4. Analyzing and interpreting data
5. Using mathematics and computational thinking
6. Constructing explanations (for science) and designing solutions (for engineering)
7. Engaging in argument from evidence
8. Obtaining, evaluating, and communicating information

Science practices like "planning and carrying out investigations" and "analyzing and interpreting data" were common in the days of inquiry. But some of the science practices outlined in *A Framework for K–12 Science Education* weren't a major focus in the past, and the engineering practices were nowhere to be found. NGSS emphasizes the science and engineering practices by incorporating one of them into each PE. And because each *Perfect Pairs* lesson is built around a PE, students engage in the targeted practice as they complete the Encouraging Students to Draw Conclusions stage of the Investigative Process.

But that's not the only way that *Perfect Pairs* incorporates the practices. Because the eight science and engineering practices are so integral to effective science instruction, students authentically participate in a broad range of practices as they do each lesson. For your convenience, Tables 4–6 in Appendix A highlight the practices woven into each *Perfect Pairs* lesson.

Beyond the Next Generation Science Standards

By the end of 2013, many states had begun talking about adapting rather than adopting the NGSS exactly as written. As a result, we decided to include two *Perfect Pairs* lessons that address content that does not directly align with NGSS but has traditionally been part of the K–2 science curriculum. Lesson 2.6 looks at plant life cycles, and Lesson 2.7 focuses on the butterfly life cycle. We suspect that, in most school districts, these topics will continue to be taught in early elementary classrooms.

Supporting the Common Core State Standards for English Language Arts

Because high-quality children's books are an integral part of each *Perfect Pairs* lesson, students will glean much more than an understanding of essential science concepts as they complete the lessons included in this book. As children interact with the language, literary style, and stunning illustrations in each children's book and work through the Investigative Process, they will also improve their reading and writing skills.

The Investigative Process and ELA (English Language Arts) Links sections of each *Perfect Pairs* lesson directly address many of the Common Core English Language Arts Standards for Reading Informational Text, Reading Literature, Writing, and Speaking and Listening. Tables 7–9 in Appendix A indicate the standards that align with the lessons in this book.

How exactly do *Perfect Pairs* lessons support the Common Core State Standards for English Language Arts? Let's look at some examples from Lesson 1.3: How Animals Protect Themselves.

Reading: Literature, Grade 1, Standard 1 (CCSS.ELA-Literacy.RL.1.1): Ask and answer questions about key details in a text.

Lesson Excerpt:

Now return to *Swimmy*. After reading the book, invite students to respond to these questions:

- *How did Swimmy protect himself from the big fish that wanted to eat him?*
- *Did looking different from other fish help him stay safe?*
- *Did Swimmy do what you and your Turn and Talk partner predicted before reading the book?*
- *Did Swimmy use any of the ideas we listed on the chart paper?*
- *Do you think a real fish would be more likely to protect itself the way Swimmy did or the way you suggested in your Wonder Journal?*

Reading: Informational Text, Grade 1, Standard 9 (CCSS.ELA-Literacy.RI.1.9): Identify basic similarities in and differences between two texts on the same topic.

Lesson Excerpt:
- *What do the two books have in common?* (They include information about ways animals protect themselves.)
- *How are the two books different?* (*Swimmy* is a fictional story in which a fish consciously plans an effective protection strategy. The watercolor paintings are beautiful, but not completely realistic. *What Do You Do When Something Wants to Eat You?* is a fun book that discusses the ways many different animals protect themselves. It features clear, straightforward text with realistic and enticing paper-collage art.)

Writing, Grade 1, Standard 8 (CCSS.ELA-Literacy.W1.8): With guidance and support from adults, recall information from experiences or gather information from provided sources to answer a question.

Lesson Excerpt:

When you are done reading, show your students the How Animals Protect Themselves data table that you prepared earlier and read the headings and animal names together. As you read through the list a second time, invite students to explain how each animal protects itself, and record their ideas.

A sample data table might look like this:

How Animals Protect Themselves

Animal	How Animal Protects Itself
Small fish (Swimmy)	Travel in schools to look like a bigger fish
Bombardier beetle	Shoots hot chemicals
Puffer fish	Makes itself bigger
Glass snake	Breaks off its tail
Pangolin	Rolls into an armor-plated ball
Basilisk lizard	Runs away on water
Hog-nosed snake	Plays dead
Clown fish	Hides in a sea anemone
Hover fly	Look like a wasp
Gliding frog	Glides to another tree
Silk moth	Has spots that look like two big eyes
Javanese leaf insect	Looks like a leaf
Flying fish	Leaps out of the water
Blue-tongued skink	Sticks out its large bright-blue tongue

Speaking and Listening, Grade 1, Standard 2 (CCSS.ELA-Literacy.SL.1.2): Ask and answer questions about key details in a text read aloud or information presented orally or through other media.

Lesson Excerpt:

When the children have finished their drawings, ask the class to gather for a Science Dialogue. As you add two new columns (one with the heading "Body Part" and the other with the heading "Behavior") to the classroom data table, introduce students to the idea that some animals use an external body part—a part on the outside of the body—to protect themselves from predators. Others use a behavior to stay safe. And some use both a body part and a behavior to avoid being eaten.

Invite students to share their drawings with the class. As each child presents, the rest of the class should think about whether the animal uses a body part, a behavior, or both to stay safe. When the presenter is done, encourage the class to discuss the best way to fill in the new columns of the data table for the animal. Then allow the children a few minutes to make entries in their Wonder Journals as you record the information in the classroom data table.

During this dialogue, students should feel free to ask their classmates questions and agree or disagree with one another. As children contribute to the conversation, they should provide rationale to support their ideas. To facilitate the discussion, help the students stay focused and restate any unclear comments or ideas.

As these examples from Lesson 1.3 show, *Perfect Pairs* provides students with opportunities to apply the skills and proficiencies outlined in the Common Core State Standards for English Language Arts, making it a fun and meaningful way to integrate science and language arts instruction.

Lessons for Kindergarten

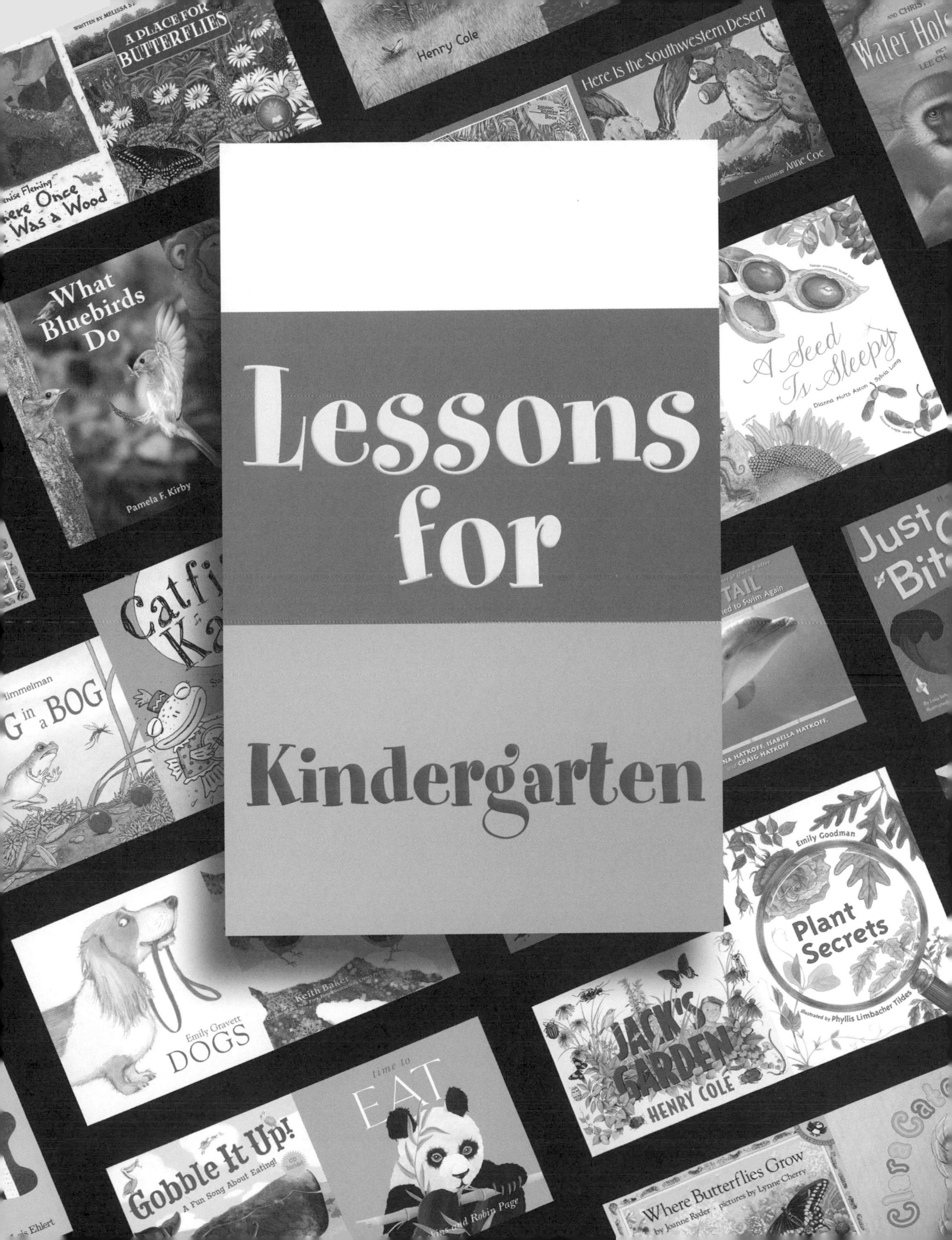

Lesson K.1: What Plants and Animals Need to Survive

The Salamander Room by Anne Mazer   &   *From Seed to Pumpkin* by Wendy Pfeffer

About the Books

The Salamander Room is a gentle tale with an important message. A boy finds a salamander in the woods and asks his mom if he can keep it. Instead of saying no, she asks the boy questions that require him to think about what the salamander needs to survive and, ultimately, to realize that he cannot create an adequate home for the salamander in his bedroom. Lush, shadowy paintings perfectly capture the boy's increasingly elaborate plans for transforming his room into a suitable habitat for the little amphibian.

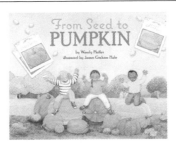

Using clear, simple language, *From Seed to Pumpkin* describes how a pumpkin plant grows through the eyes of three young children. With a level of detail that seems just right for the target audience, the author includes information about how the plant obtains and distributes water and nutrients. Tinted with sunlit colors, the appealing, precise watercolor-and-pencil illustrations help to make the growth process and the passage of time understandable to early elementary students.

Wonder Statement: I wonder what plants and animals need to live and grow.

Learning Goal   In this lesson, students learn that animals need food and water to survive, while plants require water and sunlight. This lesson compares the needs of a salamander (animal) and a pumpkin (plant) as they live and grow.

NGSS Performance Expectation K-LS1-1. Use observations to describe patterns of what plants and animals (including humans) need to survive.

Prep Steps
1. Post the Wonder Statement, *I wonder what plants and animals need to live and grow*, on the wall in the classroom meeting area.
2. Use a brown marker to prepare index cards with the word *animal* for half the students in your class. Use a green marker to prepare index cards with the word *plant* for the other half of your class.

3. Buy a packet of pumpkin seeds at a local garden center. You can also purchase roasted pumpkin seeds at a grocery store, but you will have to explain that these cooked seeds can't grow into plants.

4. Use a green marker to write the words *Pumpkin plant* and *Oak tree* on separate pieces of white paper. Use a brown marker to write the words *Salamander* and *Human* on two additional pieces of white paper. Using a blue marker to write the word *Water*, a black marker to write the word *Food*, and an orange marker to write the word *Sunlight*, create enough index cards for the Venn diagram activity at the end of the lesson.

5. Make copies of the Lesson K.1 Wonder Journal Labels in Appendix B at the back of this book for each child in your class and cut them out. Then make copies of the Lesson K.1 Venn Diagram Template, also in Appendix B.

Engaging Students

Begin the lesson by passing out copies of the Lesson K.1 Wonder Journal Label with the Wonder Statement written on it. After reading the Wonder Statement with the class, ask your students to add it to their Wonder Journals.

Introduce the words *plant* and *animal* by writing them side by side on chart paper. Write *plant* in green marker and *animal* in brown marker. Read the words to your class and invite a few student volunteers to come forward, one at a time, and draw an example of a plant or an animal under the correct word.

Next, place one of the *plant* or *animal* index cards you prepared earlier face down on each student's desk. Pass out white drawing paper and ask students to fold their sheet of paper in half so that it looks like a greeting card.

Invite the students to open up their "greeting cards" and tell them that they are going to make a secret drawing on the right-hand side. Be sure to show them exactly where to draw their secret picture.

Remind the students that the words written in green marker say *plant*, and the words written in brown marker say *animal*. Ask all students with the word *plant* to hold up their cards. Then ask students with the word *animal* to hold up their cards. Encourage students with an animal card to draw an animal that they would like to see in real life. Ask students with a plant card to draw their favorite plant. All students should label their drawings. When the children are done, they should close their "greeting card" so no one else can see their picture.

Now choose three students with animal cards and three students with plant cards to come forward, one at a time, for a modified version of the game Twenty Questions. In this game, the teacher asks the child with the card questions and the rest of the class tries to guess the identity

Teaching Tip

If you are doing this lesson early in the school year, you may want to prefold the sheets of paper to save time.

A student shows her greeting-card drawing of a hummingbird to the class.

of the secret plant or animal. Be sure to include some questions that allow for kinesthetic learning.

- For animals, questions might include: Where does the animal live? Does it have four legs? Can you show us how it moves? Can you show us how it eats? Can you imitate the sounds it makes?
- For plants, questions might include: Can you eat the plant? Can you show us how tall the plant grows? Can you show us the size of the flower and leaves?

When someone guesses the correct plant or animal, the student should open his or her greeting card and show the drawing. After all six children have had a turn, ask the rest of the class to take turns sharing their secret drawings.

Help your students form small groups with classmates whose drawings are similar. For example, all students who have drawn trees might form one group. All students who have drawn large mammals might form a second group. Other groups might include students who drew birds or insects or wildflowers.

Ask the students, *What do you think your plant or animal needs to live and grow?* Encourage each group to think of as many answers as they can. When a group is done brainstorming, its members should return to their seats. Then each child should choose *one* idea and use words or pictures to explain it on the blank left-hand side of his or her greeting card.

Teaching Tip

Preparing a chart with your students' names before the Twenty Questions game and recording each child's secret plant or animal as he or she shares it will make it quicker and easier to help the children form groups.

A greeting card shows one thing a bunny needs to live and grow—carrots.

Teaching Tip

If the idea that a plant is not alive arises, guide a discussion by asking: *Does a plant grow? Does it grow forever? If something dies, was it alive before it died?* Research shows that a child's understanding of whether something is alive develops over time, so don't worry if your kindergartners don't seem to have a firm understanding of the concept (Driver et al. 2001).

Now bring the class back together, and tell the students that you have a secret that you'd like them to try to figure out.

As each child shares the idea described in words and pictures on his or her greeting card, record it on chart paper by placing it in one of three categories (food, water, or sunlight) but *do not* label the categories. Then ask the student to stand in one of three groups, but do not offer any explanation for the sorting scheme yet.

When several students are in each group, pause the sharing activity and encourage the class to guess what each group represents. As additional children share, invite them to guess which group they belong in and why. If they guess correctly, add their ideas to the proper category on the chart paper and invite them to join the group. If they guess incorrectly, encourage their classmates to guide them to the correct group.

After everyone has had a chance to present, ask your students to hold up their greeting cards. Take a photo of each group to document the results of this activity, and then collect the greeting cards. Tell the children that you will share your secret (why they were placed in each group), but first the class is going to read two different books that describe what plants and animals need to live and grow.

Exploring with Students

Introduce *From Seed to Pumpkin* by reading the title and the names of the author and illustrator. Ask your class to explain the role of the author and illustrator in creating a book.

Invite the students to look at the book's front and back cover. What do they think the book will be about? Now show the children the book's title page. Do they have any new ideas?

Next, give each student a pumpkin seed and invite the class to tape the seeds into their Wonder Journals. Explain that their seed could grow into a pumpkin plant that produces pumpkins with more pumpkin seeds inside. But for a pumpkin plant to grow, it needs two things from the natural world. Can they guess what those two things are?

Provide each student with a copy of the Lesson K.1 Wonder Journal Label that says:

A pumpkin plant needs two things to grow. I think they are:

Invite the children to draw and label pictures that show what they think a pumpkin plant needs to live and grow. As the children share their ideas with the class, create a data table to record their thoughts.

A sample data table may look like this:

I think a pumpkin plant needs . . .	I think this because . . .
Water	A plant will dry up without water
Dirt	Dirt holds a plant in place
Sunlight	A plant can't grow in the dark

Now read *From Seed to Pumpkin*. As you finish each page, ask your students to look closely at the art and ask the following questions: *Does the picture show what the text says? If so, can you give an example? Is there anything you see in the picture that I did not mention as I read the text?* Then ask the class if they would like to revise or add to the data table. Be sure to emphasize the two essential needs of growing pumpkin plants (water and sunlight) as they surface in the story.

Your final data table may look like this:

I think a pumpkin plant needs . . .	I think this because . . .
Water	A plant will dry up without water
Dirt	Dirt holds a plant in place
Sunlight	A plant can't grow in the dark
Bees	Bees carry pollen

Ask the students to revisit their previous ideas about what pumpkin plants need to live and grow. They can revise their answers by crossing out or altering their previous drawings or adding new pictures to their Wonder Journals.

Now invite students to gather for a Science Dialogue. Introduce *The Salamander Room* by reading the title and the names of the author and illustrator. Encourage the students to take a close look at the book's cover. Do they think a salamander is a plant or an animal? Why? Once the class agrees that it's an animal, ask your students to consider whether they think plants and animals need the same things to live and grow.

As students discuss this question, encourage them to provide rationale for their ideas. Let the children know that they should feel free to agree or disagree with their classmates. They may also ask questions. To facilitate the discussion, help the students stay focused and restate any unclear comments or ideas.

As the discussion ends, tell the class that Brian, the main character in *The Salamander Room*, is also thinking about what salamanders need to live and grow. After reading the book with your students, work together to create a data table with information from it.

A sample data table may look like this:

What Brian Thinks Salamanders Need	Why
Fresh green leaves and moss	To sleep in
Shiny wet leaves	To move about on
Tree stumps and boulders	To climb on
Insects	To eat
Water	To drink

Now add a third column to the table to help students distinguish between what the salamander really needs to survive and what would just make it more comfortable.

The final table may look like this:

What Brian Thinks Salamanders Need	Why	Real Needs
Fresh green leaves and moss	To sleep in	
Shiny wet leaves	To move about on	
Tree stumps and boulders	To climb on	
Insects	To eat	X
Water	To drink	X

After passing out copies of the Lesson K.1 Wonder Journal Label that says *The Perfect Salamander Room*, invite your students to use information from the data table to make a labeled drawing of a room that contains everything Brian's salamander needs to live and grow. For example, their drawings might include insects for food and a small pool of water for drinking.

This labeled drawing shows a student's idea of The Perfect Salamander Room.

The Perfect Salamander Room

Encouraging Students to Draw Conclusions

Give each child the Lesson K.1 Wonder Journal Label that poses the Wonder Statement as a question: *What do plants and animals need to live and grow?* Then project the documentation photos you took earlier in the lesson on the classroom interactive whiteboard and invite your students to look at them closely. Pass out the students' greeting cards, and ask them to reform the groups you placed them in. Encourage the members of each group to use the information on their greeting cards and what they learned from reading *From Seed to Pumpkin* and *The Salamander Room* to predict why they ended up in their group.

When the groups have generated some ideas, ask them to form a Science Circle and share their thoughts. During the discussion, encourage students to agree, disagree, ask questions of other groups, and offer their own insights. As students contribute to the conversation, remind them to provide evidence for their ideas from the data tables. Facilitate the discussion by helping children stay focused on the topic and restating any unclear comments or ideas.

At the end of the Science Circle session, review the information in the data tables for both the pumpkin plant and the salamander and ask the following questions:

- *What do both the pumpkin plant and the salamander need to live and grow?* (Water.)
- *What does the salamander really need that the pumpkin plant doesn't?* (Food.)

Now ask the students to focus on the remaining needs in the *From Seed to Pumpkin* data table (dirt, sunlight, bees), and select the item that seems to be as important to the pumpkin plant as food is to the salamander. If students struggle to answer this question, reread page ten of *From Seed to Pumpkin*.

To help students understand what pumpkin plants and salamanders need to survive in concrete terms, work with them to create a Venn diagram on the floor of your classroom. If your school owns large hula hoops, place them several feet apart in an open area of your room. Alternately, you can use green and brown yarn to construct the two large nonintersecting circles. Place the *Salamander* label you created earlier in front of the brown yarn circle (or one hula hoop). Place the *Pumpkin plant* label in front of the green yarn circle (or the other hula hoop). Draw and label two nonintersecting circles on chart paper and show students the connection between this visual model and the physical model on the floor.

After giving each student one of the Water or Food or Sunlight index cards you created earlier, invite a few students with Sunlight cards and Food cards to come forward and stand in the circle where they belong. Add the words *Sunlight* and *Food* to the circles you drew on chart paper.

Next, ask a few students with Water cards to come forward and stand where they belong. Give the students a few minutes to realize that they need to stand in both circles. Then guide your class in moving the physical circles so they intersect. Encourage the Water students to place themselves in the area of the Venn diagram that falls within both circles.

Students stand in the Venn diagram physical model.

Then draw a Venn diagram like the one shown below and help your class make a connection between this visual model and their physical model.

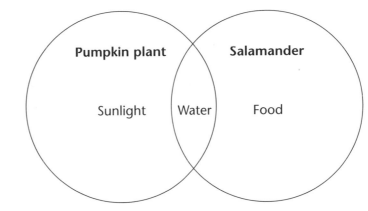

After the students who participated in the activity have returned to their seats, remind your class that a pumpkin is a plant and a salamander is an animal. Then ask the children to identify an oak tree and a human as either a plant or an animal. When you have written these words on a new visual Venn diagram and placed the labels you created earlier in front of the physical model on the floor of your classroom, invite a different group of students to come forward and stand in the correct positions. If there is any disagreement, encourage students to discuss their ideas until the group comes to a consensus. Then add the words *Sunlight, Food,* and *Water* to the visual Venn diagram. Continue this activity, switching labels on the floor Venn model between the *Salamander/Pumpkin plant* pair of cards and the *Oak tree/Human* pair until each child has had a chance to stand in the Venn diagram.

To bring this lesson to a close, provide students with a copy of the Lesson K.1 Venn Diagram Template. Encourage students to use pictures and words to show the needs of the rose and tiger in the diagram. When

This Wonder Journal entry of a Venn diagram compares what a tiger and a rose need to live and grow.

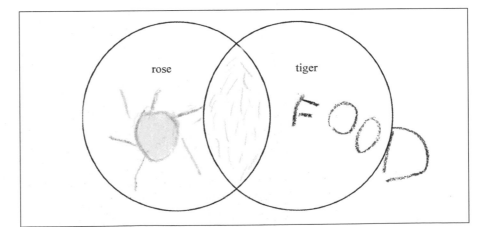

students finish this activity, they should add the diagram to their Wonder Journals.

In this lesson students learned that plants and animals need different things to survive. Animals need food and water, while plants require water and sunlight. With these new insights, students may now begin to wonder how plants and animals survive in deserts (where water is scarce) or if plants can grow deep inside caves (where there is very little light). They should feel free to record these new questions in their Wonder Journals.

Reinforcing the Concept

- You can extend the lesson by reading the following book pairs and discussing the content with the Wonder Statement in mind:
  —*The Snail's Spell* by Joanne Ryder & *Wolfsnail: A Backyard Predator* by Sarah Campbell
  —*Jack's Garden* by Henry Cole & *Seed, Soil, Sun* by Cris Peterson

- Divide the class into five equal-sized groups for an activity called Match Me, which is a variation of the popular game musical chairs. Assign one group to be animals (they can pick which animal), one group to be plants (they can select which plant), one group to be sunlight, one to be water, and one to be food. Provide each child with a name tag that identifies what he or she is.

  The goal of Match Me is to form Live and Grow Teams—trios that include either a plant or an animal and all the elements it needs to survive. Begin to play musical chairs. After the first round, the child left standing should move to the side of the room. Following the second round, the child left standing will look at the first child's name tag. Can he or she be a member of the same Live and Grow Team? If so, the two students link arms. If not, the second child starts a new team. By the end of the activity, the entire class will have sorted themselves into Live and Grow Teams. (Note: If the number of children in your class is not divisible by five, give "extra" students Water name tags. These students can join any team.)

- Invite your students to create visual acrostic poems that reinforce the basic needs of plants and animals. They may choose any of the following as a starter word: *water, sunlight, air,* or *food.* Here's an example:

  W [picture of a wolf]
  A [picture of an apple tree]
  T [picture of a turkey]
  E [picture of an elephant]
  R [picture of a radish]

  When the students are done, you can post their poems on a bulletin board entitled What Plants and Animals Need to Live and Grow.

- Have your students count off by threes. Number ones are members of Team Water. Number twos are members of Team Sunlight. Threes are members of Team Food. When children are "up," they must use sequential letters in the alphabet to name a living thing that needs his or her team name to survive. If Team Sunlight starts, the first player might say "apple tree." If Team Water comes next, the player might say "bat." Then a player from Team Food might say "cheetah." Continue the game until everyone has had a turn.

ELA Links   By now, students have learned that plants and animals have basic needs. Two different books—one fiction, one nonfiction—have played important roles in this lesson. The following questions can help students reflect on the aspects of the featured books that aroused their curiosity, generated and maintained their interest, and enhanced their understanding of the natural world.

- *What do the two books have in common?* (They are both about what a living thing needs to live and grow. Both have illustrations.)
- *How are the two books different?* (*The Salamander Room* is a fictional story that has a main character. It helps us understand all the ways a salamander depends on its surroundings to get the things it needs to live and grow. The art has a magical, imaginary feel to it. *From Seed to Pumpkin* is nonfiction. It explains what a pumpkin plant needs to live and grow and how it changes over time. The art is fun, but realistic.)
- *How does the style of the art in each book seem to match the style of the text?* (The art in *From Seed to Pumpkin* is realistic. It shows exactly what the text describes. The art in *The Salamander Room* is soft and shadowy. That makes sense because it's showing what Brian sees in his imagination.) *Which art do you like better? Why?*

Reference   Driver, R., Squires, A., Rushworth, P. and Wood-Robinson, V. 1994. *Making Sense of Secondary Science: Research into Children's Ideas.* London: Routledge.

Lesson K.2: What Animals Eat

| *Gobble It Up! A Fun Song About Eating!* by Jim Arnosky | & | *Time to Eat* by Steve Jenkins and Robin Page |

About the Books

Fun, simple rhyming text and true-to-life acrylic illustrations encourage children to imagine themselves as animals hunting for prey, emphasizing the role of meat eaters in the natural cycle of life. *Gobble It Up!* is sure to be a winner for its action and facts about the everyday hunt for survival. The catchy song sung by the author on the accompanying CD adds an element of fun.

Time to Eat is an engaging introduction to what animals eat and how they collect, store, and digest their food. The masterfully realistic and charming paper collages are expertly colored and detailed, and the layout nicely spotlights each animal in action.

Wonder Statement: I wonder what kinds of foods different animals eat.

Learning Goal In this lesson, students learn that some animals get the food they need to survive from plants, some get it from other animals, and some get it from both. They also discover that some animals eat more than one kind of food and that unrelated animals may have similar diets.

NGSS Performance Expectation K-LS1-1. Use observations to describe patterns of what plants and animals (including humans) need to survive.

Prep Steps
1. Post the Wonder Statement, *I wonder what kinds of foods different animals eat*, on the wall in the classroom meeting area.
2. Photocopy the Lesson K.2 Animal Cards found in Appendix B on white paper so that each child can have one card. Photocopy the Food Cards (in Appendix B) on colored paper so that each child can have one card. Then laminate the cards and cut them out. (These cards include information from *Time to Eat*.)
3. Write all the words from the Animal Cards on one piece of chart paper and all the words from the Food Cards on a second piece of chart paper.
4. On chart paper, prepare a two-column *Time to Eat* data table with eighteen rows, labeling the left column "Animal" and the right col-

umn "Food." Place double-sided tape in each cell of the table. Be sure to leave extra room to the right of the table, so you can add a third column later.

5. On chart paper, prepare a three-column *Gobble It Up!* data table with six rows, labeling the first column "Animal," the second column "Food," and the third column "Food Group." Place double-sided tape in each cell of the third column.

6. Write *A* on five index cards and *P* on five index cards.

7. Make copies of the Lesson K.2 Wonder Journal Labels in Appendix B for each child in your class and cut them out. Then make a copy of the K.2 Wonder Journal Handout for each child.

Engaging Students

Begin the lesson by passing out copies of the Lesson K.2 Wonder Journal Label with the Wonder Statement written on it. After reading the Wonder Statement with the class, ask your students to add it to their Wonder Journals.

Next, give each student an Animal Card and explain that the word on each student's card is written on chart paper at the front of the room. Read through the words on the chart paper with the class. Then encourage students to help one another read their cards. Clarify any unfamiliar words, such as *anaconda* and *aye-aye*. Read through the list with the students a second time, inviting the children to hold up their cards as the class reads the word aloud.

Students may have some interesting ideas about what animals eat. Provide each child with a copy of the Lesson K.2 Wonder Journal Label that says:

> *My animal is _____. I predict it eats _____.*

Encourage the students to fill in the blanks with words or pictures.

After repeating the activity with the Food Cards, give each student a copy of the Lesson K.2 Wonder Journal Label that says:

> *My food is _____. I predict a _____ eats it.*

Encourage the children to use words or pictures to fill in the blanks. Your students may also use the cards to play games. Here are two suggestions:

- Matching Game
  Give half the class Animals Cards and half the class Food Cards. Ask students with Food Cards to find a partner with the Animal Card they think is most appropriate. It's okay if several students choose the same partner. Guide the children in explaining their

Teaching Tip

If you do this lesson at the beginning of the school year, you may want to simplify this activity by using fewer Animal Cards and having students work in pairs.

Teaching Tip

At each stage of this activity, encourage students to provide verbal explanations for their predictions. Consider recording a few children's explanations with the video setting on a digital camera. These recordings can be replayed later on your interactive whiteboard, allowing students to observe any changes in thinking that take place during the lesson.

decisions to the class. Classmates should feel free to agree or disagree. If they disagree, they may suggest an alternate animal partner.

- Sorting Game

  Create signs that say *I Eat Plants (or something that comes from plants)* and *I Eat Animals (or something that comes from animals)* and place them on opposite sides of the room. After distributing Animal Cards to the entire class, invite students to go to the sign that seems most appropriate. Guide the children in explaining their decision to the class. Classmates may suggest an alternate food choice.

    When the students are satisfied with the classifications, ask them to stand in front of the sign they have chosen and hold up their cards. Then you can take photos to document their thinking.

Exploring with Students

Introduce *Gobble It Up!* by reading the title and the name of the author-illustrator. Ask your class to explain the role of an author-illustrator in creating a book.

Invite the students to look at the book's front and back cover. What do they think the book will be about? (Animals eating one another.) Does the class notice anything unusual in the cover illustration? (Something sticking out of the whale's mouth.) What do they think the whale is eating? Make a list of their guesses on chart paper.

After reading the first page of *Gobble It Up!* ask the students what they think the raccoon is about to eat and record their responses on chart paper. Are they surprised by what the raccoon is shown eating on the next page?

Let your students know that raccoons eat lots of different foods, including nuts, fruits, seeds, frogs, fish, bird eggs, young birds, insects, worms, pet food, human food scraps, and garbage. Look back at your students' responses on the chart paper and discuss with the class which of their ideas are plausible. Put a check mark next to those responses.

As you read the rest of the book, you may want to ask questions like:

- *How do you think a crocodile might fool ducklings with its smile?* (This may expose some anthropomorphic misconceptions, which you can discuss.)
- *What do you think the great white shark will eat?*
- *Do you think all whales eat giant squid? Why or why not?*
- *How is a panda different from the other animals in the book?*

These questions may generate some discussion about the eating habits of various animals.

Teaching Tip

Some of the vocabulary in *Time to Eat* may be unfamiliar to kindergartners, especially English language learners. When an unfamiliar word (*droppings, chisels, wedges, impales*) arises, write it on an index card and encourage your students to guide you in creating a sketch to help them remember what the word means. Then post the card under the Wonder Statement on the wall.

Now introduce *Time to Eat* by reading the title and the names of the author-illustrators. What do the students think the book will be about? Does the book's title page give them any new ideas?

Show your class the *Time to Eat* data table you drew in advance on chart paper. If needed, review the words on the Animal and Food cards. As you read the book, invite students to complete the data table by attaching their Animal and Food cards in the correct spots. This interactive technique for collecting information will help maintain your students' attention.

The completed data table should look like this:

Animal	Food
Panda	Bamboo shoots
Tick	Blood
Shrew	Worm
Woodpecker	Acorn
Chipmunk	Seeds
Bird	Grasshopper
Spider	Insect
Toad	Insect
Anaconda	Jaguar
Ostrich	Leaves
Beetle	Dung
Pelican	Fish
Moth	Nectar
Aye-aye	Beetle
Shark	Fish
Rat	Grain
Baby whale	Milk

When you are done reading the book, add a third column called "Food Group" to the data table. Then tell your class that all the foods can be classified as either a plant (or something that comes from a plant) or an animal (or something that comes from an animal).

After reading the name of each animal in column one of the data table and its corresponding food in column two, ask for a student volunteer to tell you whether that food is a plant (or comes from a plant) or an animal (or comes from an animal). If the rest of the class agrees, place a *P* (*plant*) or an *A* (*animal*) in column three of the data table. If students disagree, discuss the food's classification until the group comes to a consensus. Then add a *P* or an *A* to the data table. Students may need your guidance in identifying the proper classification for blood, dung, and nectar.

Teaching Tip

Providing students with copies of each data table as soon as possible after the class compiles it will allow each child to keep a record of the investigation in his or her Wonder Journal.

The final data table should look like this:

Animal	Food	Food Group
Panda	Bamboo shoots	P
Tick	Blood	A
Shrew	Worm	A
Woodpecker	Acorn	P
Chipmunk	Seeds	P
Bird	Grasshopper	A
Spider	Insect	A
Toad	Insect	A
Anaconda	Jaguar	A
Ostrich	Leaves	P
Beetle	Dung	A
Pelican	Fish	A
Moth	Nectar	P
Aye-aye	Beetle	A
Shark	Fish	A
Rat	Grain	P
Baby whale	Milk	A

Now show your class the *Gobble It Up!* data table you drew on chart paper in advance and explain that, as you page through the book, they should look for information that you can use to complete the first two columns of the table. After completing those columns with your students, place the five *A* cards and five *P* cards you prepared earlier on the floor in front of the table. As you review each row of the data table, invite a student volunteer to come forward, choose the card he or she thinks is correct, and add it to column three of the table. If the rest of the class agrees, move to the next row. If students disagree, discuss the food's classification until the group comes to a consensus. Then add the proper index card to the third column of the table.

The final data table should look like this:

Animal	Food	Food Group
Raccoon	Crawdad	A
Crocodile	Duck	A
Shark	Fish	A
Great whale	Giant squid	A
Panda	Bamboo	P

Encouraging Students to Draw Conclusions

Give each child the Lesson K.2 Wonder Journal Label that poses the Wonder Statement as a question: *What kinds of foods do different animals eat?* Then ask the class to gather for a Science Circle and review the information in the two data tables by reading the name of each animal and its corresponding food.

Encouraging students to look for similarities in the animals' diets will help you introduce two important ideas:

1. Unrelated animals can have similar diets.
2. Some animals eat more than one kind of food.

The following prompts will help you present these ideas to your students:

- *Do you notice anything surprising about the diets of a spider and a toad?* (They both eat insects.)
- *How about the diets of a pelican and a shark?* (They both eat fish.)
- *What do you notice about the diet of a baby whale in* Time to Eat *versus the great whale in* Gobble It Up? (They eat different foods—milk and giant squid). *Why do you think they eat different foods?*

Now ask your students to discuss this question: *Based on what you've observed, can you give evidence that different kinds of animals may eat the same kind of food?* During the discussion, encourage students to agree or disagree with one another. As children contribute to the conversation, remind them to provide evidence to support their ideas.

When the class has offered some examples that satisfy everyone, pass out copies of the Lesson K.2 Wonder Journal Label with the following sentence frame:

A _____ (animal 1) and a _____ (animal 2) are very different, but they both eat _____ (food).

After students have filled in the blanks with words or pictures, ask your class to discuss a second question: *Based on what you've learned, can you give evidence that some animals eat more than one kind of food?* Once again, encourage students to agree or disagree with one another, and remind them to provide evidence to support their ideas.

When the class is ready, pass out copies of the Lesson K.2 Wonder Journal Label with the following sentence frame:

A _____ (animal) eats _____ (food 1), but it also eats _____ (food 2).

Encourage the children to fill in the blanks with words or pictures.

This completed Wonder Journal Handout shows that a butterfly eats plants, a shark eats other animals, and a raccoon eats both.

Lesson K.2 Wonder Journal Handout

I used to wonder what kinds of foods different animals eat.

Now I know that animals eat many different kinds of foods.

Some animals eat plants.

BtFLH

Some animals eat other animals.

SH

Some animals eat both.

RCOИ

To bring the lesson to a close, give each student a copy of the Lesson K.2 Wonder Journal Handout (see Appendix B). Encourage the children to model each category on the handout by drawing sample animals under each of the three statements. This is the evidence that supports their claim.

In this lesson, students have learned that some animals eat plants, some eat other animals, and some eat both. They have also discovered that some animals eat more than one kind of food and that unrelated animals may have similar diets. With these new insights, students may now begin to wonder what other living things eat or have other questions related to animal food choices. They should feel free to record these new questions in their Wonder Journals.

Reinforcing the Concept

- You can extend the lesson by reading the following book pairs and discussing the content with the Wonder Statement in mind:
  —*Pinduli* by Janell Cannon & *What's for Dinner? Quirky, Squirmy Poems from the Animal World* by Katherine B. Hauth

—*Bear Wants More* by Karma Wilson & *Just One Bite* by Lola Schaefer
- *Gobble It Up!* comes with a CD. As your class listens to the song, encourage them to imagine that they are the animals. Divide the class into two groups. Invite one group to act out the part of the raccoon and the other to act out the part of the crawdad. Repeat this process with the crocodile and ducks, shark and smaller fish, whale and squid.
- Guide students as they create an interactive bulletin board with the title *What Kinds of Foods Do Animals Eat?* Ask each student to draw and label two separate pictures—one of an animal and one of the food it eats. Each student must pick a different animal, focusing on the examples included in *Time to Eat, Gobble It Up!, Pinduli, What's for Dinner?, Bear Wants More,* or *Just One Bite.*

  Place the animal pictures in a column on the left-hand side of the board. Scatter the food drawings around the rest of the board. Staple a piece of string to each animal. Each string should be long enough to reach any food on the board. Use a pushpin to attach each food to the board. To match animals with their foods, students should wrap the proper strings around the pushpins.
- Copy the data table below onto chart paper, and let your students know that it compares animal sizes to familiar body parts and classroom objects. The animals in the table are all meat eaters, and their prey is discussed in *Gobble It Up!* or *Time to Eat.*

Predator	Predator Size	Prey	Prey Size
Shrew	Fist	Worm	Finger
Spider	Finger	Insect	Finger
Anaconda	Four tall adults lying down	Jaguar	Adult on hands and knees
Pelican	Child	Fish	Fist
Raccoon	Desk	Crawdad	Finger
Crocodile	Two tall adults lying down	Duck	Football

After reading through the information in the table with your class, invite students to sequence the predators from largest to smallest. Which predators eat animals that are much smaller than themselves? Which predators eat prey that is a little bit smaller than themselves? Are there any animals that eat prey larger than themselves?

ELA Links   By now, students have learned that plants and animals have basic needs. Two different books—one fiction, one nonfiction—have played important roles in this lesson. The following questions can help students reflect on the aspects of the featured books that aroused their curiosity, generated and maintained their interest, and enhanced their understanding of the natural world.

- *What do the two books have in common?* (They both describe what various animals eat. They are both illustrated with art.)
- *How are the two books different?* (*Gobble It Up!* has fun, rhyming text. It was a song before it was a book. *Time to Eat* has straightforward nonfiction text that describes the eating habits of many different animals.)
- *Time to Eat* contains anthropomorphic (having human characteristics) animals that react to the types of food they eat. Since *Time to Eat* is considered a nonfiction book, it's important to dispel any student misconceptions about this level of reasoning behavior by the animals. Some guiding questions include:
  —*On the fifth spread of* Time to Eat, *bold text says: "I can't believe I ate the whole thing?" Do you think a snake really thinks that? Why or why not?*
  —Time to Eat *is a book with true information about what animals eat. What parts of* Time to Eat *do you think couldn't really happen? Why?*
- Gobble It Up! *uses the word* you *a lot. How else is the writing in* Gobble It Up! *different from the writing in* Time to Eat? (*Gobble It Up!* has a lot of repetitive text. It is sillier than *Time to Eat*.)
- *Notice that* Time to Eat *shows just one animal on the cover. Now that you've read the book, do you think that makes sense? Why or why not?* (No, the book includes lots of animals. The cover makes it seem like the book will be all about what pandas eat.)
  —*Why do you think the people who made and sell the book decided to put a panda on the cover?* (Pandas are appealing animals and many people buy a book based on the cover.)
  —*Do you think more people or fewer people would buy the book if a tick was on the cover?* (Probably fewer because ticks are less appealing.)

Lesson K.3: How Animals Depend on Their Environment

Just Ducks! by Nicola Davies **&** *Hip-Pocket Papa* by Sandra Markle

About the Books

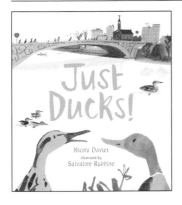

In *Just Ducks*, an enthusiastic young narrator describes the daily activities of the mallard ducks living along a river near her home. Additional bits of information presented in smaller type more fully explain how the ducks interact with their environment. The easy-flowing language along with a subdued palette of mixed-media artwork that offers the spontaneity of a sketchbook combine to create a charming and informative tribute to a bird that is familiar to almost all young readers.

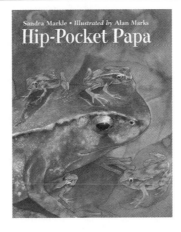

Set in an Australian temperate rain forest, *Hip-Pocket Papa* opens with a pair of tiny hip-pocket frogs guarding their eggs. When the teeny tadpoles emerge, they wriggle up their father's legs and nestle inside hidden pockets on his hip. For the next month, the father depends on his environment to find food, keep his skin moist, and avoid predators while the tadpoles grow and develop. Finally, the youngsters transform into froglets and can survive on their own. Marks's vibrant watercolor, ink, and pencil artwork offer close-up views of the frog and its surroundings.

Wonder Statement: I wonder how animals depend on the places where they live.

Learning Goal In this lesson, students learn how two very different animals, mallard ducks and hip-pocket frogs, get the materials they need to live and grow from their environment.

NGSS Performance Expectation K-ESS3-1. Use a model to represent the relationship between the needs of different plants and animals (including humans) and the places they live.

Prep Steps
1. Post the Wonder Statement, *I wonder how animals depend on the places where they live,* on the wall in the classroom meeting area.
2. To create animal coloring pages, trace the adult frog on the title page of *Hip-Pocket Papa* and the female duck on the title page of

Just Ducks! Make enough frog photocopies for half of your class and enough duck photocopies for the other half.

3. Prepare five What Mallard Ducks Need signs by writing the following phrases on separate pieces of $8\frac{1}{2}$-by-11-inch sheets of paper: *Food, To Attract Mates, A Place to Build Their Nests, A Safe Place for Ducklings, A Place to Sleep.* Post the signs around the room.

4. Prepare five What Hip-Pocket Frogs Need signs by writing the following phrases on separate pieces of $8\frac{1}{2}$-by-11-inch sheets of paper: *Food, A Place to Lay Eggs, A Place to Hide from Enemies, Moist Skin, A Home for Froglets.*

5. Use eleven large sticky notes to write the following words and phrases from the data table titled "How Hip-Pocket Frogs Depend on the Place Where They Live": *crickets, insect eggs, mites, midges, springtails, wood lice, leaf litter (2), log, shadowy nooks, creek bank.*

6. Use index cards to make enough Mallard Duck Cards for one half of your class. Write *Duck* on the blank side of all the cards. Then write one of the following words or phrases on the back of each card: *seeds, small insects, water plants, snails, worms, girl, hidden spots on land, bridges, reeds, river.* List them on chart paper, too.

7. Use index cards to make enough Hip-Pocket Frog Cards for the other half of your class. Write *Frog* on the blank side of all the cards. Then write one of the following words or phrases on the back of each card: *cricket, leaf litter, insect eggs, mites, damp forest floor, midges, log, creek bank.* List them on chart paper, too.

8. Make copies of the Lesson K.3 Wonder Journal Labels in Appendix B for each child in your class and cut them out.

Engaging Students

Begin the lesson by passing out copies of the Lesson K.3 Wonder Journal Label with the Wonder Statement written on it. After reading the Wonder Statement with the class, ask your students to add it to their Wonder Journals.

Take your class outdoors on a warm day and encourage students to find and follow a small animal, such as an ant or a spider. While the children are observing the animal, walk among them and ask: *What do you think the animal is doing? What do you think it will do next?*

After the students have had time to think about these questions, ask them: *How do you think the animal depends on the land, water, and other living things around it? Do you see evidence to support your ideas?*

As the children think about these questions, encourage them to draw a picture of the creature and its surroundings in their Wonder Journals. When they are done, ask the children to circle and label anything in their picture that they think the animal needs to survive.

Before going back inside, invite the students to gather together, and guide a discussion about the physical characteristics of the area where

Teaching Tip

If you can't take your class outdoors, you can divide the students into small groups and invite each group to watch video clips that show animals in their environment. Look for suitable material online or in your school's media center. You may also want to ask your school librarian for assistance.

A student observes insects in a wooded area of his school yard.

the creatures live. This is a great opportunity to introduce the word *environment*. (All the factors—soil, water, and other living things—that affect the life and activities of a creature.) The class should consider some of the following questions: *What kinds of plants grow in the environment? Do the plants seem to be healthy? Is there a source of water in the environment?* Record the students' ideas in a notebook, and transfer them to a piece of chart paper when you return to the classroom. After placing the chart paper below the Wonder Statement, help students make connections between the outside activity and the Wonder Statement.

Exploring with Students

Introduce *Just Ducks!* by reading the title and the name of the author and illustrator. Ask your class to explain the roles of the author and illustrator in creating the book.

Encourage students to take a close look at the book's front cover, and then ask them where they think this story takes place. How do they think the book might help them find information related to the Wonder Statement?

Read up to page ten, and then encourage the students to look closely at the picture. Guide a discussion around the following questions to focus the students' attention on the ways mallard ducks depend on the place where they live:

- *How would you describe the place where the mallard ducks live?*
- *Is there any information that is shown in the art but not mentioned in the text?*
- *Do you think this river environment is a good place for mallard ducks to live? Why or why not?*

- *What other living things are the mallard ducks interacting with in their surroundings?*

You may wish to record the class's ideas on chart paper.

After reading to page thirteen, invite students to Turn and Talk with a partner about how the ducks in the book depend on their surroundings. Then begin a data table like the one that follows to keep track of how the mallard ducks in *Just Ducks!* depend on the place where they live. Work with your students to complete the table as you read the rest of the story.

How Mallard Ducks Depend on the Place Where They Live

What Mallard Ducks Need	What's in Their Environment
Food	Seeds, small insects, water plants, snails in the river Worms on land Girl who feeds them
To attract mates	Drake shows off in the water.
A place to build their nests	Hidden spots on land
A safe place for ducklings	The river
A place to sleep	Bridges, reeds, the river

To review the information in the data table, show students the What Mallard Ducks Need signs that you made earlier. After reading the text and pointing out that it echoes the information in the data table, post the signs around the room. Then divide the class into five groups and ask each group to stand near one of the signs. As you randomly read items from the second column of the data table, members of the corresponding group should carefully and quietly raise their hands and wave them. Members of the four other groups should carefully and quietly point to the matching group.

Introduce *Hip-Pocket Papa* by telling the class that you are going to read a story about an animal dad that depends on his environment as he takes care of his young. Encourage students to predict what role the papa frog might play in caring for his young and how he depends on the place where he lives to do that. Then write the following question on chart paper: *Do you think hip-pocket frogs depend on the place where they live in the same ways as mallard ducks?* After students have provided rationale for their ideas, record their thoughts on chart paper.

Next, tell the class that the title of the book includes an important clue about how the father frog cares for his young. Explain what a hip pocket is and ask the students if they'd like to change their predictions.

Before you begin to read, ask your students to look at their thumbnails. Let them know that an adult hip-pocket frog is about the same

Teaching Tip

Some of the vocabulary in *Hip-Pocket Papa* may be unfamiliar to kindergartners, especially English language learners. When an unfamiliar word or phrase (*drought, brood, leaf litter*) arises, write it on an index card and encourage your students to guide you in creating a sketch to help them remember what it means. Then post the card under the Wonder Statement on the wall.

size. Open the book and point out the image of the frog shown at its actual size on the dust jacket. Let the class know that the hip-pocket papa is a tiny creature with a big job to do.

As you read the book, work with your students to create a data table that lists the ways hip-pocket frogs depend on the place where they live. A sample data table might look like this:

How Hip-Pocket Frogs Depend on the Place Where They Live

What Hip-Pocket Frogs Need	What's in Their Environment
Food	Crickets in leaf litter Insect eggs, mites, midges, springtails, wood lice on damp forest floor Midges in tiny pool in staghorn fern
A safe, moist place to lay eggs	Leaf litter
A place to hide from enemies	Leaf litter, log
A place to keep papa's skin moist, so tadpoles can breathe	Shadowy nooks and spaces
A moist home for the tiny hip-pocket froglets	Creek bank

Teaching Tip

The entries in the sample data tables shown here are fully fleshed out and include all possible answers. You should not expect your class's tables to be as detailed, but they should include enough essential information to fully address the Wonder Statement. Providing students with copies of each data table as soon as possible after the class compiles it will allow each child to keep a record of the investigation in his or her Wonder Journal.

To review the information in the data table, show students the What Hip-Pocket Frogs Need signs that you made earlier. After reading the text on the signs, point out that it echoes the information in the newly created data table. Then post the signs around the room and place a blank piece of $8\frac{1}{2}$-by-11-inch paper below each sign.

Next, pass out the eleven large sticky notes you created earlier to individual students or pairs of students. Using the data table as a guide, students should determine which sign is the best match for the information on their assigned sticky note and then attach the note to the blank piece of paper below that sign. After everyone has finished the activity, carefully collect all the signs and blank pieces of paper with the sticky notes, and bring them to the classroom meeting area. Then work with your students to assemble all the signs and notes into one large data table. Does the final product match the data table you created earlier on chart paper?

Encouraging Students to Draw Conclusions

Give each child the Lesson K.3 Wonder Journal Label that poses the Wonder Statement as a question—*How do animals depend on the places where they live?*—an $8\frac{1}{2}$-by-11-inch piece of drawing paper, and some watercolor paints. Divide the class into two groups: Mallard Ducks and Hip-Pocket Frogs. Invite the Mallard Duck group to paint a river and a riverbank on their papers. The Hip-Pocket Frog group should paint a

forest floor on their papers. If students seem to struggle with this activity, encourage them to look at the art in *Just Ducks!* and *Hip-Pocket Papa*.

While the paintings are drying, pass out the mallard duck and hip-pocket frog coloring pages you created earlier. Students in the Mallard Duck group should receive a duck coloring page, and students in the Hip-Pocket Frog group should get a frog coloring page. Encourage students to color the animals in the style used by the illustrators of *Just Ducks!* and *Hip-Pocket Papa*. Then help the children cut around the images.

After inviting both groups of students to sit on the floor, show the children the chart-paper word lists you prepared earlier and help them review the words and phrases, which represent plants, animals, or environmental features. Next, give each child in the Mallard Duck group a Duck Card and each child in the Hip-pocket Frog group a Frog Card. As you review each term on the chart-paper word lists, point out the same word or phrase in the lesson data tables. Review the role each plant, animal, or environmental feature plays in helping the duck or the frog to grow and stay safe. Then ask students with a matching Duck or Frog card to raise the card and show it to the rest of the class.

When the students' environment paintings are dry, return them to their owners and guide the children in gluing their animal cutouts to their paintings. Then give students permanent markers and invite them to add details to their artwork. The details should show how each child's assigned animal depends on the plant, animal, or environmental feature written on his or her index card to grow or stay safe in its environment. Encourage group members to help one another brainstorm to come up with ideas.

Students proudly show artwork that highlights how mallard ducks (left) and hip-pocket frogs (right) depend on plants, animals, or environmental features.

When the students have completed the activity, ask each child to dictate a sentence that explains what his or her picture represents. Then display the two lesson data tables side by side in the classroom meeting area, and ask the class to gather for a Science Dialogue, with members of the Mallard Duck group sitting on one side of the circle and members of the Hip-Pocket Frog group sitting on the opposite side.

Remind the class of the question you asked when you introduced *Hip-Pocket Papa: Do you think hip-pocket frogs depend on the place where they live in the same ways as mallard ducks?* After reviewing the student ideas that you recorded earlier, draw the class's attention to the Food rows in the two data tables. As you review the information, encourage the students who created paintings with those items to stand up. Ask the students who are seated to look for matches between the Mallard Duck paintings and the Hip-Pocket Frog paintings.

As students share their thoughts and rationale, their classmates should feel free to agree or disagree. They may also ask one another questions. You may facilitate the discussion by helping students stay focused and restating any unclear comments or ideas.

After using a highlighter to mark the similarities your class identifies on the two data tables and adding those items to the list of similarities, repeat the process for the other rows in the data tables.

To bring the lesson to a close, join the artwork from each group to form two murals—the ducks' river bank and the frogs' forest floor. If possible, sequence the paintings in a way that highlights similarities in how the animals depend on the places where they live. For example, the paintings that show both animals eating insects might be first. Paintings that show safe spots for eggs might be next. The rest of the paintings can be assembled in any order. Use a digital camera to take a picture of each mural, and print a copy of the two photos for each child to place in his or her Wonder Journal.

These hip-pocket frog and mallard duck murals are displayed in a way that makes it easy for students to compare them.

In this lesson, students learned that mallard ducks and hip-pocket frogs depend on their environment to meet their needs and used a visual model to represent their new knowledge. With their new insights, the children may now begin to wonder how other kinds of animals depend on the places where they live. They should feel free to record these new questions in their Wonder Journals.

Reinforcing the Concept

- You can extend the lesson by reading the following book pairs and discussing the content with the Wonder Statement in mind:
  —*Eloise's Bird* by Jane Yolen & *What Bluebirds Do* by Pamela F. Kirby
  —*Bat Loves the Night* by Nicola Davies & *Dig, Wait, Listen: A Desert Toad's Tale* by April Pulley Sayre
  —*Ace Lacewing, Bug Detective* by David Biedrzycki & *Monarch and Milkweed* by Helen Frost

- Create Duck and Frog Bingo cards with three rows and three columns. Randomly add nine numbers between one and fifteen to each card. Then create fifteen playing cards with a number written on the front and one of the words or phrases from Duck and Frog Cards you used during the lesson on the back.

  After dividing the class into two teams (Ducks, Frogs), give each child a Bingo card and chips. Shuffle the playing cards, choose one, and read the number and the statement. If mallard ducks depend on the plant, animal, or environmental feature, students on the Duck team should look for that number on their Bingo card. If they see the number, they should place a chip on it. If hip-pocket frogs depend on the plant, animal, or environmental feature, students on the Frog team should follow the same process. Keep reading numbers and statements until a student yells "Bingo" for covering three numbers in a row, column, or diagonal.

- Illustrator Salvatore Rubbino must really like ducks because he had to paint a whole lot of them when he created the artwork for *Just Ducks!* Ask students, *Do you think he drew more ducks on land or in the water?* To find out, assign each student one double-page spread in *Just Ducks!* Don't forget the endpapers and the front and back cover. (If there are more children than spreads in your class, some students can buddy up.). When children have free time, they should borrow the book from the classroom science center and use brown interlocking cubes to represent ducks on land and blue interlocking cubes to represent ducks in the water. When all the children have counted the ducks on their assigned spreads, work with the entire class to find the totals. Arrange the cubes in groups of ten to make counting easier.

ELA Links   By now, students have learned a lot about how two different animals depend on their environment. Two different books—one fiction, one nonfiction—have played important roles in this lesson. The following questions can help students reflect on the aspects of the featured books that aroused their curiosity, generated and maintained their interest, and enhanced their understanding of the natural world.

- *What do the two books have in common?* (They both include information about how animals use the land and water where they live.)
- *How are the two books different?* (*Just Ducks!* is a fictional story in which the main character is a person. She is the story's narrator. The book also includes scattered facts written in smaller type. *Hip-Pocket Papa* is a nonfiction book that explains how a hip-pocket papa cares for his young.)
- *How would you describe the style of the artwork in the two books?* (The art in *Just Ducks!* is loose. It looks like someone was sketching in a notebook. The art in *Hip-Pocket Papa* is more realistic, but it seems soft and a little bit magical.) *Which art do you like better? Why?*
- *A hip-pocket frog is a very small animal. Why do you think illustrator Alan Marks made the frog look so big in Hip-Pocket Papa?* (Because readers get a close-up view of the frog and his world, they feel more connected to the book's main character.)
- *Why do you think author Sandra Markle included an Animal Glossary in* Hip-Pocket Papa? (Because the book includes many unfamiliar animals.) *Why do you think she included the More Information section?* (So readers know where to go if they want to learn more about hip-pocket frogs.)

Lesson K.4: How Animals Can Change an Environment

| *Mole's Hill* by Lois Ehlert | & | *At Home with the Gopher Tortoise* by Madeleine Dunphy |

About the Books

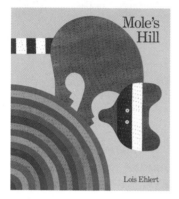

Loosely based on a traditional Seneca tale, *Mole's Hill* will delight young readers with simple text and bold, graphically striking cut-paper collages. Fox, Skunk, and Raccoon tell Mole she must move by autumn because her mound of dirt is blocking their path to the pond. Clever Mole spends the summer expanding her mound into a huge hill. Fox decides that the only solution is for Mole to build a tunnel through her hill, and she happily obliges.

At Home with the Gopher Tortoise features clear, simple text and beautiful, realistic acrylic paintings that highlight the important role the humble gopher tortoise plays in the scrub oak forests of the southeastern United States. At least 360 species, ranging from skunks and birds to frogs and bobcats, depend on the tortoise's burrows for food and shelter for themselves and their young. Rich back matter summarizes the current plight of the endangered gopher tortoise and highlights animals that benefit from the tortoise's network of tunnels.

Wonder Statement: I wonder how animals can change an environment.

Learning Goal In this lesson, students learn that, in an effort to meet their needs, animals may engage in activities and behaviors that change their surroundings.

NGSS Performance Expectation K-ESS2-2. Construct an argument supported by evidence for how plants and animals (including humans) can change the environment to meet their needs.

Prep Steps
1. Post the Wonder Statement, *I wonder how animals can change an environment*, on the wall in the classroom meeting area.
2. Using Google Images, find photos of a mole and a mole hill that you can project on the classroom interactive whiteboard.
3. Copy the text from the Lesson K.4 Building Permit Worksheet (see Appendix B) onto a piece of chart paper. Then make two photocopies of the worksheet for each child in your class.

4. Make copies of the Lesson K.4 Wonder Journal Labels in Appendix B for each child in your class and cut them out.

Engaging Students

Begin the lesson by passing out copies of the Lesson K.4 Wonder Journal Label with the Wonder Statement written on it. After reading the Wonder Statement with the class, ask your students to add it to their Wonder Journals.

Let the class know that today they are going to learn about a fascinating animal that they've probably never heard of. Then, on the classroom interactive whiteboard, project the mole photos you found earlier. Explain that a mole is about the same size as a mouse, but it has a very different lifestyle.

Encourage your class to look closely at the images and list some of its unusual body features. If students have trouble with this activity, ask the following questions:

*   *What do you notice about its eyes and ears?*
*   *What do you notice about its nose?*
*   *How are its front feet different from its back feet?*
*   *Do these body features give you any clues about where it might live?*

Now provide each student with a copy of the Lesson K.4 Wonder Journal Label that says:

This is where I think a mole might live.

After the students have added the label to their Wonder Journals, ask them to use what they have learned about a mole's body to draw and label a picture that shows where they think a mole might live.

Invite a few student volunteers to share their drawings with the class. Then project an image of a mole hill on the classroom interactive whiteboard and explain that moles spend their whole lives tunneling underground. Ask students why they think a mole would live underground. *Would it help them stay safe from enemies? Would it help them get what they need to survive?*

After a brief conversation, ask your students if knowing where a mole lives helps them understand some of its unusual body features. Encourage a few volunteers to share their ideas. Possible ideas include: they don't need to see; large ears might be injured as they moved underground; they use their large front feet to dig.

Now tell the students that you are going to read a book that will tell them how moles change their environment to meet their needs.

Exploring with Students

Introduce *Mole's Hill* by reading the title and the name of the author-illustrator. Ask your class to explain the role of an author and an illustrator in creating the book. Encourage the students to take a close look at the book's cover, and ask them: *Why do you think Mole looks different from the photos we saw of a real mole? What do you think will happen in the story?*

After reading the first page, ask the children: *Where do you think the story takes place now?* (The woods.) Encourage your students to draw a picture of the woods where Mole lives in their Wonder Journals.

As you read the next two double-page spreads, guide students as they make the connection between Mole digging a tunnel and the pile of dirt that results. Ask students to return to their Wonder Journals and create a new drawing that shows (1) Mole creating a pile of dirt as she digs and (2) the reason she is digging.

As students share their drawings and compare them to the one in the book, encourage them to explain why moles dig tunnels. (To find worms and other food.) After reading the page with the note from Fox, Skunk, and Raccoon, ask your students why they think Fox, Skunk, and Raccoon want to meet Mole at the maple tree.

The next page reveals the reason for the meeting—the other animals don't like the pile of dirt Mole had made. The pile will make it hard for them to build a path to the pond. They want Mole to move and start digging somewhere else. At this point, students can answer the question: *How has Mole changed the place where she lives?*

Give each student a copy of the Lesson K.4 Wonder Journal Label that says:

My arrow points to evidence that Mole has changed her environment.
She changed the land because she needed _____.

Two students share the drawings they created to show how Mole has changed the place where she lives.

After reading the label with the class, ask your students to add it to their Wonder Journals near their second drawing. Encourage them to add an arrow to their drawing and then fill in the blank with words or a drawing.

As you read the rest of the book, ask students to look for three more ways that Mole changes her environment. Work with your students to create a data table like the one below, including information about how and why Mole changes the land.

How Mole Changes the Land	Why Mole Changes the Land
She makes a pile of dirt.	She is looking for food underground.
She adds more dirt to the pile until it is the size of a hill.	She doesn't want to move, so she thinks of a plan.
She buries seeds that grow into new plants.	She doesn't want to move, so she makes the hill beautiful.
She digs a tunnel through the hill.	She doesn't want to move, so she digs a path through the hill to the pond for the fox, skunk, and raccoon.

After reviewing the data table with your class, encourage students to record all this information in their Wonder Journals by drawing and labeling new features in their picture of Mole's environment.

Now introduce *At Home with the Gopher Tortoise* by showing your class the front cover and pointing out the names of the author and illustrator. Ask the class: *What do you think the book will be about? What do you think the title means? Do you have any new ideas after seeing the book's back cover? How about the title page?*

Before discussing the students' ideas, pass out copies of the Lesson K.4 Wonder Journal Label that says:

At Home with the Gopher Tortoise

Give students a few minutes to draw a picture in their Wonder Journals that shows (1) where they think a gopher tortoise lives and (2) what they think the title means. Encourage students to keep the Wonder Statement in mind as they create their pictures.

After a few student volunteers have shared their ideas, start reading the book. Skip over the page with the map, and begin with the text that says, "Don't reach down that hole!"

When you have read the entire double-page spread, ask your class: *Do you have any new ideas about where a gopher tortoise lives? What do you think the title means now?*

After reading the page that begins "The gopher tortoise digs burrows to survive . . .", work with your class to complete a data table like the one shown on the next page.

Teaching Tip

Some of the vocabulary in *At Home with the Gopher Tortoise* may be unfamiliar to kindergartners, especially English language learners. When an unfamiliar word or phrase (*prehistoric, patterned, keystone species, haven*) arises, write it on an index card and encourage your students to guide you in creating a sketch to help them remember what it means. Then post the card under the Wonder Statement on the wall.

Teaching Tip

The entries in the sample data tables shown here are fully fleshed out and include all possible answers. You should not expect your class's tables to be as detailed, but they should include enough essential information to fully address the Wonder Statement. Providing students with copies of each data table as soon as possible after the class compiles it will allow each child to keep a record of the investigation in his or her Wonder Journal.

How a Gopher Tortoise Changes the Land	Why a Gopher Tortoise Changes the Land
It digs burrows.	A burrow protects it from: • the heat of summer • the cold of winter • forest fires

Write the following questions on chart paper and introduce them to your class one at a time. After reading each question with your students, encourage them to Turn and Talk with a partner as they think it through. Then invite the entire class to share their ideas before moving on to the next question.

- *How do you think a burrow keeps a gopher tortoise cool on hot days?*
- *How do you think a burrow helps a gopher tortoise stay warm in winter?*
- *How do you think a burrow keeps a gopher tortoise safe during a forest fire?*

Now write one final question on chart paper:

- *How do you think a gopher tortoise's burrowing action may help or hurt other animals that live in its environment?*

Record the students' initial ideas, and let them know that you will add more answers to this question as you continue to read the book. Before you turn the page, be sure to explain the meaning of the term *keystone species* to your class.

Encouraging Students to Draw Conclusions

Give each child the Lesson K.4 Wonder Journal Label that poses the Wonder Statement as a question: *How can animals change an environment?*

After inviting the class to gather for a Science Dialogue, encourage your students to take another look at the last data table and ask: *How did the gopher tortoise change its environment? How did that change help it meet its needs?*

When students have identified the three reasons a gopher tortoise relies on its burrow for shelter, ask them to turn their attention to the How Mole Changes the Land data table. Point out that Mole changed her environment in several ways. Ask the class: *Which of those changes helped Mole meet her needs?* (Only the first one.) *Do you think a real mole does the same thing to meet its needs?* (Yes.)

During the discussion, encourage students to agree or disagree with one another. As children contribute to the conversation, remind them to provide rationale to support their ideas. If the students get off track, gently guide them toward the idea that both Mole and real moles change their environment as they search for food. As the class learned in Lesson K.1, food is one of an animal's basic needs. Mole may *want* to continue living in the same place, but that is not a basic need.

When the class seems to have a solid understanding of how and why both Mole and real moles change an environment, explain that when *people* want to build something new in the area where they live, they have to ask permission by filling out a form called a Building Permit and submitting it to the officials in their town or city. Show students the copy of the Lesson K.4 Building Permit Worksheet that you wrote out on chart paper.

Let the class know that they are going to use drawings and word labels to fill out Building Permits for Mole and the gopher tortoise. After you read through the worksheet text on chart paper with your students and explain the type of information that should go in each blank area, give each child two of the Lesson K.4 Building Permit Worksheets you photocopied earlier. If students seem to struggle with this activity, allow them to work in pairs or small groups.

A student sample of Mole's building permit

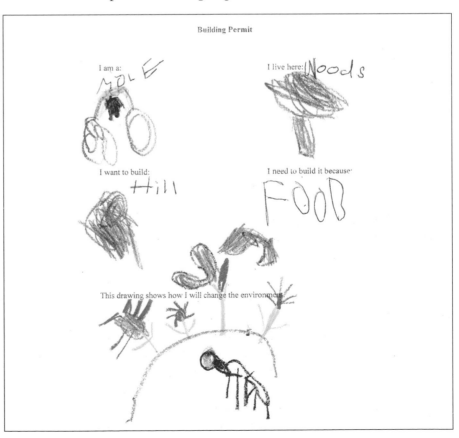

After students have completed the worksheets and added them to their Wonder Journals, invite a few volunteers to share their Building Permits with the class. Then ask: *Do you think the officials in the woods where Mole lives should give her permission to dig tunnels? Why or why not?*

Encourage students to Turn and Talk with a partner before offering ideas to the group. After a brief class discussion, ask: *Do you think the officials in the forest where the gopher tortoise lives should give it permission to dig a burrow?* Before students answer, suggest that they look back at their earlier responses to the question *How do you think a gopher tortoise's burrowing action may help or hurt other animals that live in its environment?* Once again, encourage students to Turn and Talk with a partner before offering ideas to the group.

As the class discusses the question, guide students to the understanding that when a gopher tortoise digs a burrow to meet its own need for shelter, it helps many of its plant and animal neighbors survive. Then ask one final question for the class to discuss: *Do you think the gopher tortoise was happy that it could help other animals?*

To bring the lesson to a close, point out that *Mole's Hill* has a skunk character and *At Home with Gopher Tortoise* includes a page about a skunk that lives in the tortoise's scrub forest environment. Ask the class if they think the skunks are happy or unhappy about the changes in their environments.

To help your students see the changes from the skunks' points of view, work with them to write letters in which the two skunk "cousins"—Woods Skunk from Mole's neighborhood and Forest Skunk from the gopher tortoise's neighborhood—describe how and why their neighbor (Mole/the gopher tortoise) changed the area where each lives. You may wish to use the Lesson K.4 Skunk Cousin Letters in Appendix B

A student's illustration of the class letter from Woods Skunk to his cousin

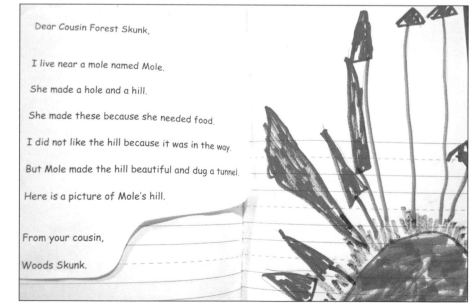

Dear Cousin Forest Skunk,

I live near a mole named Mole.

She made a hole and a hill.

She made these because she needed food.

I did not like the hill because it was in the way.

But Mole made the hill beautiful and dug a tunnel.

Here is a picture of Mole's hill.

From your cousin,

Woods Skunk.

as a model. When the letters are complete, type the text and make copies for your students to add to their Wonder Journals. Then encourage the children to illustrate the letters.

In this lesson, students learned that animals can change an environment as they meet their needs. The changes can either help or harm other creatures living nearby. With these new insights, students may now begin to wonder how other animals can alter their environments. They should feel free to record these new questions in their Wonder Journals.

Reinforcing the Concept

- You can extend the lesson by reading the following book pairs and discussing the content with the Wonder Statement in mind:
  —*Turtle's Race with Beaver* by Joseph and James Bruchac & *Who Lives in an Alligator Hole?* by Anne Rockwell
  —*The Gardener* by Sarah Stewart & *Wiggling Worms at Work* by Wendy Pfeffer
- Encourage your students to create a comparison mural that shows the different ways that Mole and the gopher tortoise changed their environment.
- Provide art materials so students can create a model of a gopher tortoise burrow, showing where each of the animals mentioned in *At Home with the Gopher Tortoise* lived and how they depended on the burrow to help them meet their needs.

ELA Links

By now, students have learned that animals can change an environment as they seek out the food and shelter they need to survive. Two different books—one fiction, one nonfiction—have played important roles in this lesson. The following questions can help students reflect on the aspects of the featured books that aroused their curiosity, generated and maintained their interest, and enhanced their understanding of the natural world.

- *What do the two books have in common?* (They both describe how animals can change an environment.)
- *How are the two books different?* (*Mole's Hill* is fiction and is illustrated with colorful cut-paper collage art. *At Home with the Gopher Tortoise* is a nonfiction description of a keystone species and is illustrated with paintings.)
- *Why do you think Lois Ehlert, the author-illustrator of* Mole's Hill, *used cut-paper collage art illustrations and not photographs?* (Because it is a made-up story, she couldn't find or take photos of animals doing the things she describes.)
- *Why do you think most of the type in* At Home with the Gopher Tortoise *is white?* (Black type would be difficult to read on top of the colorful illustrations.)

Lesson K.5: How People Can Change an Environment

| *On Meadowview Street* by Henry Cole | **&** | *Wangari's Trees of Peace: A True Story from Africa* by Jeanette Winter |

About the Books

In *On Meadowview Street*, economical text and tender, acrylic paintings tell the story of Caroline, a girl whose family has just moved to Meadowview Street. As Caroline wonders why there isn't a meadow in sight, she spots a lone flower and asks her dad to mow around it. Then she uses string and sticks to enclose it in a "wildflower preserve." As other flowers bloom, Caroline enlarges the preserve. Finally, Dad sells the lawn mower and the whole family works to transform their suburban backyard into a teeming ecosystem. Soon the meadow grows as inspired neighbors convert their yards, too.

Using clear, spare prose and richly colored acrylic painting with a warm folk-art influence, *Wangari's Trees of Peace* follows Wangari Maathai, winner of the 2004 Nobel Peace Prize, from the rural Kenyan forests of her childhood to her education in America and then back to a now-barren land. Starting in her own backyard, Maathai plants trees and encourages other women to do the same. More than thirty million trees have been planted by the members of her Green Belt Movement, improving her country's health and economy. An author's note and a quote from Maathai enrich the presentation.

Wonder Statement: I wonder how people can change an environment.

Learning Goal In this lesson, students learn that, in an effort to meet their needs, people can change an environment in both helpful and harmful ways.

NGSS Performance Expectation K-ESS2-2. Construct an argument supported by evidence for how plants and animals (including humans) can change the environment to meet their needs.

Prep Steps 1. Post the Wonder Statement, *I wonder how people can change an environment*, on the wall in the classroom meeting area.

2. Use Google Images to find several photos of a meadow full of wild-flowers (some small trees and shrubs can be growing in or along the edges of the meadow).

3. Cut $8\frac{1}{2}$-by-11-inch sheets of oak tag in half, so that there are two pieces for each child in your class. Set aside half of the sheets for the Engaging Students section of the lesson. On the rest of the sheets, write the following words, one per sheet, butterfly (7), bee (3), dragonfly (1), bird (3), rabbit (2), turtle (2), snake (1), raccoon (1), dragonfly (2 more), bee (1 more), butterfly (4 more), bird (6 more). The class will use the oak-tag sheets to make puppets. You may want to create a tree puppet and a model of a pond with water plants. Obtain craft sticks and enough modeling clay for each student to have a small piece.

4. Prepare the three Lesson K.5 Interactive Whiteboard Slides using the text found in Appendix B. Copy the sentences from Slides 2 and 3 on chart paper. You may wish to cut them into sentence strips.

5. Tape together two 11-by-17-inch pieces of green construction paper to create a 22-by-17-inch "meadow."

6. Make copies of the Lesson K.5 Wonder Journal Labels in Appendix B for each child in your class and cut them out. Then make copies of the Lesson K.5 Concept Map.

Engaging Students   Begin the lesson by passing out copies of the Lesson K.5 Wonder Journal Label with the Wonder Statement written on it. After reading the Wonder Statement with the class, ask your students to add it to their Wonder Journals.

Write the word *meadow* on chart paper, and project the meadow images you found earlier on your interactive whiteboard. Ask your students how they would describe the environment they see in the pictures. After recording their responses, invite students to draw a meadow in their Wonder Journals.

Now pass out the oak-tag half sheets and encourage the children to draw one of the small flowering plants in the meadow. Ask them to cut around the general shape of the plant and glue it to a craft stick to make a plant puppet.

Invite students to find a partner. Then tell the buddies that their plant puppets are going to interview one another using the six questions written on Slide 1, which you prepared earlier.

After reading the first question with the class, give the buddies time to interview one another. When the interview is complete, invite a few groups to share their answers. Then move on to the next question and

This is what the meadow would look like
after people had started living there.

A Wonder Journal entry shows
what a student thinks a meadow
might look like after people
moved in.

repeat the process until the students have considered all six questions. Be sure to record the final question and the class's responses to it on chart paper.

Now pass out copies of the Lesson K.5 Wonder Journal Label that says:

> *This is what the meadow would look like after people had started living there.*

Invite the class to add the label to their Wonder Journals and then draw a picture that shows how they think the meadow would look after people had moved into the environment. As the students finish up, encourage a few volunteers to share their two images of the meadow (prepeople and postpeople) with the class. If students seem to need guidance, suggest that they use the class's responses to the last question on the slide for ideas.

Exploring with Students

After giving each child one of the labeled oak-tag half sheets you prepared earlier, help the students read the labels. Then ask the children to draw a picture to match their label, cut around the general shape of the animal, and glue it to a craft stick.

Next, give each student a small piece of modeling clay and a piece of paper to put underneath it (to avoid messy cleanup). Show the children how to press the base of the sticks into the clay to make their "puppets" stand up on their own.

Now introduce *Wangari's Trees of Peace* and *On Meadowview Street* by reading the titles and the names of the author-illustrators. Ask your class to explain the role of an author-illustrator in creating a book.

Invite the students to look at the covers of the books. What do they think the books will be about? Encourage the class to practice pronouncing the name Wangari [WAHN-gar-ee]. Then ask your students to describe what the person in each front-cover illustration is doing. (One is placing a plant in the soil. The other is roping off a plant.)

Now ask your students: *If the two people could talk to one another, what would they say? What questions do you think they might ask one another?* Record their responses on chart paper. (Questions for *Wangari in Wangari's Trees of Peace* might include: *What are you planting? Why are you planting them?* For Caroline in *On Meadowview Street*, students might suggest asking: *Why are you roping off that plant? What kind of a plant is it?*)

After reading the first page of *On Meadowview Street*, ask the class what they notice about the neighborhood.

- *Do you see a meadow?*
- *Why do you think that the street is named Meadowview Street if there is no meadow there?*
- *Do you think that the area used to be a meadow before people built all the houses?*

When Caroline spots a flower in her yard, show your class the green construction paper "meadow" you created earlier and explain that it represents Caroline's yard. Ask for a volunteer to add his or her flower puppet to the yard.

When Caroline puts a string around the flower, ask the class what they think she has in mind. Then ask: *Why do you think Caroline wants to protect the flower? What other changes do you think Caroline might make to her yard?*

Continue reading until Caroline spots a second flower. Ask for another volunteer to add his or her flower to the yard. Repeat this process as more flowers appear in Caroline's wildflower preserve.

When Caroline notices a butterfly, ask the students: *What happened to Caroline's yard after she protected the flowers?* (The flowers attracted a butterfly.) Invite a student with a butterfly puppet to add it to the yard. At this point, begin making a data table that lists the ways Caroline and her family changed the yard.

Your final table may look like this:

What Caroline (and Her Family) Did	How It Changed the Yard
Protected small flowering plants Planted a tree	Attracted butterflies and other insects
Built a pond with water plants	Attracted birds
	Attracted turtles and dragonflies

As you work your way through the book, students should continue adding their flower and animal puppets to the green construction paper representing Caroline's yard. When the family plants a tree, add one of the tree puppets you made in advance and ask the class to predict how the family's action will change the environment—Caroline's yard. Then read the next couple of pages to see what happens. When the family builds a pond and adds water plants, add the pond model that you made in advance and ask the class to predict how the family's action will change the environment—Caroline's yard.

Teaching Tip

The entries in the sample data tables shown here are fully fleshed out and include all possible answers. You should not expect your class's tables to be as detailed, but they should include enough essential information to fully address the Wonder Statement. Providing students with copies of each data table as soon as possible after the class compiles it will allow each child to keep a record of the investigation in his or her Wonder Journal.

Students used their puppets to build this model of the meadow Caroline's family created in their yard.

When you reach the page with Caroline and her friends having a picnic, place the book beneath a document projector. Have your students look carefully for all the animals and add their puppets to the green paper meadow. Can the class spot six birds, two turtles, a snake, two rabbits, and a raccoon? How many insects do the students see? (Seven—two bees, two dragonflies, and three butterflies.)

After you finish reading the story, review the class data table and pass out copies of the Lesson K.5 Wonder Journal Label with the following sentence frames:

When Caroline let flowers grow in her yard, a _____ came.

When Caroline's family planted a tree, a _____ came.

When Caroline's family built a pond and added water plants, a _____ came.

After writing the sentence frames on chart paper and reading them together with the class, encourage students to fill in the blank in each sentence on their label with a word or picture.

When the students are done, reintroduce *Wangari's Trees of Peace* by reviewing the class's ideas about what Caroline might ask Wangari. Ask the students: *Based on what you learned in* On Meadowview Street, *how do you think Wangari might answer Caroline's questions?*

Read *Wangari's Trees of Peace* to the point where Wangari returns to Kenya and asks, "What has happened? Where are the trees?" At this point, begin a data table that lists ways Wangari's village has changed since people in Kenya (Kenyans) cut down all the trees. Leave space to add a second column to the table later.

A sample data table may look like this:

After Kenyans Cut Down the Trees	
Women have bent backs from hauling firewood.	
No crops grow on the barren land.	
Birds disappear.	
The land seems like a desert.	

After reading the next double-page spread, ask students: *How do you think planting the trees will change the environment where Wangari lives?* Write their predictions on chart paper.

Next, add the title "When Kenyans Planted More Trees" to the second column of the data table. As you read the rest of the book, work with your class to fill in the table.

Your final data table may look like this:

After Kenyans Cut Down the Trees	When Kenyans Planted More Trees
Women have bent backs from hauling firewood.	Women can find firewood nearby.
No crops grow on the barren land.	The soil becomes richer and crops can grow.
Birds disappear.	Birds return.
The land seems like a desert.	A green belt stretches over the land.

When the data table is complete, give each child a copy of the Lesson K.5 Concept Map you photocopied earlier. Read the question in the middle of the concept map, and encourage students to draw three pictures that would help people understand how the trees Wangari and other women planted changed the Kenyan environment. They may use the data table to help them generate ideas. When the children have finished this activity, encourage them to add the Concept Map to their Wonder Journals.

Encouraging Students to Draw Conclusions

Remind your class that all animals need food and shelter to survive, and people are no different. To meet our needs, we sometimes change environments. Those changes can be helpful or harmful to the environment and the creatures living there.

Write the following questions on chart paper:

1. *What did the forest in Kenya look like when Wangari was young?*
2. *How did the people in Kenya change the forest while Wangari was in America?*
3. *Why did the people of Kenya change the forest? Did they need something?*

4. *After the trees were cut down, what problems did the people of Kenya have?*
5. *How did Wangari change the environment after she returned?*
6. *How did the new trees meet the needs of the people in Kenya?*

Introduce the questions to your class one at a time. After reading each question with your students and showing them any related illustrations from *Wangari's Trees of Peace*, encourage them to Turn and Talk with a partner as they think it through. Then invite the entire class to share their ideas, citing information from the data table and the illustrations from the book as evidence, before you move on to the next question.

Now show the class the Kenyan Forest Story on Slide 2, which you prepared earlier. Point out that each sentence in the story matches one of the questions that you just discussed. After asking your class how each sentence might be shown visually, set out art materials and divide the class into six groups. Assign each group one of the story statements, and encourage each child in the group to create his or her own drawing or painting to illustrate it.

As the students finish up their art projects, give each child the Lesson K.5 Wonder Journal Label that poses the Wonder Statement as a question: *How can people change an environment?* After the students have added the labels to their Wonder Journals, ask them to stand if their illustrations show how people changed their environment. (Groups 2 and 5 should stand up.) Ask those students to share their paintings, providing evidence from the book and/or the class data table for what they've shown. Then ask students to stand if their illustrations show how a change people made met their needs. (Groups 3 and 6 should stand.) Ask those students to share their paintings, providing evidence from the book and/or the data table for what they've shown. Finally, lead a class discussion about whether each of the changes was helpful or harmful to the people and their environment.

Now follow the same procedure with the following questions based on *On Meadowview Street*:

1. *What did Meadowview Street probably look like before the neighborhood was built?*
2. *How did people change the environment?*
3. *Why did the people change the environment? What did they need?*
4. *When Caroline moved into the neighborhood, what problem did she see?*
5. *How did Caroline and her family change her their yard?*
6. *Did creating the meadow meet one of Caroline's basic needs—food or shelter? Why did Caroline want to change the land?*

Teaching Tip

If you decide that students should use paint for this activity, we suggest that you invite them to draw their picture in pencil, use a black permanent marker to outline, and then apply the paint. This approach tends to produce more detailed artwork.

Show the class the Meadowview Street Meadow Story on Slide 3, which you prepared earlier. After discussing how each sentence might be illustrated, ask students to reform their groups and create a second set of drawings or paintings that illustrate the story statement with the same number you assigned last time.

When everyone has completed their illustrations, invite the class to gather for a Science Dialogue, and draw your students' attention back to the question: *How can people change an environment?* Point out that, once again, students in groups 2 and 5 illustrated how people changed their environment. Similarly, both sets of the illustrations created by groups 3 and 6 show the results of the changes humans made to an environment.

Encourage the class to compare the Kenyan Forest and Meadowview Street Meadow illustrations done by Group 2. Then ask: *How are the illustrations the same? How are they different?*

As students discuss these questions, they should feel free to agree or disagree with one another. They may also ask their classmates questions. You may facilitate the conversation by helping children stay focused and reminding them to provide rationale to support their ideas.

When the discussion winds down, ask students to compare the illustration sets created by groups 2, 5, 3, and 6 and respond to the same questions. If necessary, guide students toward the following ideas:

- The changes shown in both Group 2 illustrations harm the environment.
- The Group 5 illustrations show that both Wangari and Caroline are problem solvers. They both improved their environments by adding plants.
- The Group 3 illustrations show that people in Kenya and in the Meadowview Street area of North America were trying to meet the same basic need. They needed shelter.
- Group 6 illustrations show that Wangari's changes helped to meet the needs of people in Kenya. Caroline's changes did not meet her family's basic needs for food and shelter, but it did make Meadowview Street a nicer place to live. Her changes did help many other animals meet their needs.

To bring this lesson to a close, post the Slide 2 (Kenyan Forest Story) sentence strips you created earlier in the proper order on a bulletin board or blank wall in the classroom and add your students' pictures near the corresponding sentence. Do the same with the sentence strips and artwork from Slide 3 (Meadowview Street Meadow Story). Ask students in groups 3 and 6 to fill in the blanks in their Meadowview Street Meadow Story statements. Take a photo of each display so everyone in the class can add copies to their Wonder Journals.

Kindergarten students created this illustrated sentence strip for the Meadowview Street Meadow Story.

In this lesson students learned that humans can change an environment to meet their needs. Often those changes are harmful to the environment. But people's need for food and desire for beautiful places can motivate them to restore an environment.

Reinforcing the Concept

- You can extend the lesson by reading the following book pair and discussing the content with the Wonder Statement in mind:
  —*The Curious Garden* by Peter Brown & *The Mangrove Tree: Planting Trees to Feed Families* by Susan L. Roth and Cindy Trumbore
- Work with your class to make a helpful change to the environment around your school by planting a wildlife garden. Encourage the students to watch the garden closely to see if it attracts insects, birds, and other animals.
- Ask students to observe a tree in the school yard, around their neighborhood, or at a local park at least three times over a few days. Then ask them to draw two pictures. The first drawing should show at least one way the tree makes life better for one or more animals that live in the same environment. The second drawing should show how the animal(s) would be affected if people cut down the tree.

ELA Links   By now, students have learned a lot about how people can change an environment. Two different books—one fiction, one nonfiction—have played important roles in this lesson. The following questions can help students reflect on the aspects of the featured books that aroused their curiosity, generated and maintained their interest, and enhanced their understanding of the natural world.

- *What do the two books have in common?* (They both have a main character who works to improve her environment. They are both illustrated with art.)
- *How are the two books different?* (*Wangari's Trees of Peace* tells a true story that affected thousands of people. *On Meadowview Street* is fiction. At the end, the neighborhood matches the name of the street and supports more wildlife, but Caroline's effort doesn't affect thousands of human lives.)
- *In* Wangari's Trees of Peace, *the art is colorful and has a simple, primitive style. In* On Meadowview Street, *the art is more realistic but a bit whimsical. Which style do you prefer? Why? If the two styles were swapped, how do you think it would it affect the storytelling?*
- *In* Wangari's Trees of Peace, *why do you think the author italicized some of the text? Look for italicized text in* On Meadowview Street. *Do you think it is italicized for the same reason? Why or why not?*
- On Meadowview Street *includes words like* Hmph *and* Aha. *Do you think words like these would make sense in* Wangari's Trees of Peace? *Why or why not?*
- *In* Wangari's Trees of Peace, *there is one illustration on each page. In* On Meadowview Street, *some illustrations cross two pages. Other pages feature several small illustrations. Why do you think Jeanette Winter and Henry Cole made these decisions?*

Lesson K.6: How to Reduce Our Impact on Creatures in Land Environments

| *Where Once There Was a Wood* by Denise Fleming | **&** | *A Place for Butterflies* by Melissa Stewart |

About the Books

The gentle, poetic rhythm of the prose and the lush, textured collage artwork featured throughout *Where Once There Was a Wood* lie in sharp contrast to the colors and style employed on the book's final spread, where readers discover a tragedy. The rich community of wildlife that once thrived in a wooded area has been destroyed and replaced by "houses side by side, twenty houses deep." Children won't miss the message in this brilliantly conceived call to action.

Butterflies fill our world with beauty and grace, but sometimes we do things that harm them. Stunning illustrations and simple, gentle language introduce young readers to some of the ways human action and inaction can affect butterfly populations. Smaller secondary text provides additional details about specific types of butterflies. More than just a book about our favorite insects, *A Place for Butterflies* opens readers' minds to a wide range of environmental issues.

Wonder Statement: I wonder how people can work together to protect living things and the land they call home.

Learning Goal In this lesson, students learn that people sometimes change the natural world in ways that are harmful to other living things and their environments. They also discover that there are simple, effective things we can all do to protect wildlife and natural lands.

NGSS Performance Expectation K-ESS3-3. Communicate solutions that will reduce the impact of humans on the land, water, air, and/or other living things in the local environment.

Prep Steps
1. Post the Wonder Statement, *I wonder how people can work together to protect living things and the land they call home*, on the wall in the classroom meeting area.
2. Use Google Images to find photos of the following: woods, a meadow, a creek, a red fox, a fern, violets in bloom, a woodchuck, a horned owl, owl chicks (brood) in a nest, a great blue heron, a

fish (such as a small bass), a brown snake, a raccoon, red berries (such as mulberries), a cedar waxwing, a pheasant, nuts and seeds (such as acorns). Print out the images so your students can view more than one at a time.

3. Write the name of each plant, animal, or habitat from the images on individual pieces of drawing paper. Write *owl chicks* on three pieces of paper. If you have more than nineteen students in your class, write *ferns, violets in bloom, red berries,* or *cedar waxwings* on additional pieces of drawing paper as needed. List the names of each plant, animal, or habitat on chart paper.

4. On chart paper, create a data table with two columns and eleven rows. Label the columns with the headings "Lives in Wild Places" and "When People Change the Land." Leave room to add six more rows at the bottom of the table. Add a piece of double-sided tape to the cells in the first column.

5. Using the maps on the endpapers of *A Place for Butterflies* as a guide, search Google Images to find photos of three to five butterflies that live in your area.

6. Make copies of the Lesson K.6 Wonder Journal Labels in Appendix B for each child in your class and cut them out. Then make copies of the Lesson K.6 Readers Theater Script and the Lesson K.6 Butterfly Outline (also in Appendix B).

Engaging Students

Begin the lesson by passing out copies of the Lesson K.6 Wonder Journal Label with the Wonder Statement written on it. After reading the Wonder Statement with the class, ask your students to add it to their Wonder Journals.

After drawing your students' attention to the list of plant, animal, and habitat names that you prepared earlier on chart paper, read each word and hold up the corresponding image from the photo collection you prepared in advance. Next, pass out the labeled sheets of drawing paper and explain that the word or phrase on each paper matches one of the plant, animal, or habitat names on the chart paper. As students help one another read the words on their papers, scatter the images around the classroom.

Now read through the list with the students a second time, inviting the children to hold up their papers as the class reads the plant, animal, or habitat name they've been assigned. Then encourage students to move around the classroom, hunting for the image that matches the word or phrase on their paper.

Ask your students to turn their papers over and draw a picture that matches the plant, animal, or habitat name on the back side. As the children work on their drawings, explain that they will use their pictures as they practice and perform a fun readers theater. Then pass out copies of the Lesson K.6 Readers Theater Script, highlighting the appropriate words for each child. As the class practices reading through the script,

This readers theater script has been highlighted for the child taking on the role of the snake (left). Kindergarten students practice their readers theater roles (right).

clarify any unfamiliar words, such as *dew, brood, rambled, rummaged,* and *roosted.* Then invite the students to stand at the front of the classroom and practice again. As the children read their parts, they should step forward and hold up their drawings. (The words you wrote on the back of their papers will help them remember their lines.) When the class is ready, they can perform the readers theater for another class.

Exploring with Students

Introduce *Where Once There Was a Wood* by reading the title and the name of the author-illustrator. Ask students what Denise Fleming's role was in creating the book.

After inviting your students to look at the book's front and back cover, ask them what they think the book will be about. Then encourage the class to listen carefully as you read. Ask students to raise a hand when they notice words that remind them of something they've already heard. When the class realizes that the book has the same words as the readers theater script, tell them that the script is based on the book. Since *Where Once There Was a Wood* is a short book, start again at the beginning and invite students to raise their hands when they hear the part of the book that corresponds to their role in the readers theater.

Do they notice anything in the pictures that is not mentioned in the text? Why do they think author-illustrator Denise Fleming decided to include those visual elements?

When you are done reading, show the class the data table you created earlier and pass out the plant and animal photos students used as models earlier in the lesson. (Do not pass out the "fish" or "nuts and seeds" images) As you read through the book a second time, invite students to add their photos to the first column and then work together to fill in the second column. If time permits, you may wish to add more rows to the table and fill in the animals that are shown in the picture but not mentioned in words at the beginning of the book.

Teaching Tip

The entries in the sample data tables shown here are fully fleshed out and include all possible answers. You should not expect your class's tables to be as detailed, but they should include enough essential information to fully address the Wonder Statement. Providing students with copies of each data table as soon as possible after the class compiles it will allow each child to keep a record of the investigation in his or her Wonder Journal.

Lives in Wild Places	When People Change the Land
[Red fox photo]	No place to sleep
[Fern photo]	No place to grow
[Violets photo]	No place to grow
[Woodchuck photo]	No morning dew
[Horned owl & chick photos]	Can't find food
[Heron photo]	Can't find food
[Brown snake photo]	No place to hide
[Raccoon photo]	No place to search for food
[Berries photo]	No place for plants to grow
[Cedar waxwing photo]	No food
[Pheasant photo]	No place to roost, no nuts or seeds to eat
Deer	No plants to eat, no place to sleep
Squirrels	No trees for food or shelter
Bees	No flowers to feed on
Butterflies	No flowers to feed on
Rabbits	No place to hide from enemies, no plants to eat
Kingfisher	No fish to catch

At this point, you may want to guide students in revising the readers theater script so that the new text describes the plight of the plants and animals after people destroyed the natural habitat. For example, the updated script might begin:

Everyone: Now . . .

Child 1: there is no wood

Child 2: no meadow

Child 3: no creek

Everyone: Now . . .

Child 4: a red fox

Teaching Tip

Some of the vocabulary in *A Place for Butterflies* may be unfamiliar to kindergartners, especially English language learners. When an unfamiliar word (*native, swamp, chemicals*) arises, write it on an index card and encourage your students to guide you in creating a sketch to help them remember what the word means. Then post the card under the Wonder Statement on the wall.

After assuring the class that there are plenty of ways people can protect living things and the places where they live, introduce *A Place for Butterflies* by reading the title and the names of the author and illustrator. Invite students to look at the book's front and back cover. What do they think the book will be about? Now show the children the book's title page. Do they have any new ideas? Using the book's endpapers as a guide, point out the images of the butterflies that live in your area.

Show the students that *A Place for Butterflies* has two kinds of text—large, main text and more detailed sidebars. Tell them that you are going to focus on the main text for now. As you read, ask the class to think about the connection between the words they are hearing and the illustrations they are seeing. When you finish, ask students if they heard or saw anything that surprised them.

Using information in *A Place for Butterflies* and the butterfly photos you collected earlier, create a data table focusing on butterflies that live in your area. If you live in New England, your data table might look like the one below. If you live in other areas of North America, please consult the Lesson K.6 Butterfly Data Table found in Appendix B to see sample information for all the butterflies included in *A Place for Butterflies*.

Butterfly	What It Needs	What People Do
[Eastern tiger swallowtail photo]	Flower nectar	Plant gardens
[Mourning cloak photo]	Sugary tree sap	Protect forests
[Hessel's hairstreak photo]	Plants that grow in wet places	Protect swamps and marshes
[Monarch photo]	Caterpillars need plants that make cattle and sheep sick	Let the plants that monarchs eat grow in other fields
[Harris's checkerspot photo]	Natural homes in open fields	Create new grassy areas

When the data table is complete, let the class know that you are going to read the sidebars on the double-page spreads that focus on the butterflies that live in your area. As you read, students should think about the question: *What happens to butterflies when their environment is harmed or destroyed?* Write this question on chart paper so students will have a visual reminder. After reading each spread, discuss the question and record students' ideas.

Encouraging Students to Draw Conclusions

Give each child the Lesson K.6 Wonder Journal Label that poses the Wonder Statement as a question: *How can people work together to protect living things and the land they call home?*

Explain that in *Where Once There Was a Wood*, the author-illustrator, Denise Fleming, focuses on how building human homes can destroy the places where other creatures, including butterflies, live. But in *A Place for Butterflies*, the author, Melissa Stewart, wants to show readers how people can help protect butterflies and their environments.

Invite the class to look closely at the two butterflies shown on the second double-page spread of *Where Once There Was a Wood*. One is orange, and the other is yellow. Now work with the class to try to identify those butterflies using the names and images in *A Place for Butterflies*. (The orange butterfly is probably a monarch, and the yellow butterfly is probably an eastern tiger swallowtail. Both of these butterflies are very common in many parts of the United States.)

This student drawing shows that people can help the Hessel's hairstreak butterfly by protecting the marsh where it lives.

Encourage the class to review the two related pages in *A Place for Butterflies* to answer the question: *If the events in* Where Once There Was a Wood *were happening in our town (city), what could we do to help the eastern tiger swallowtail and monarch butterflies that would lose their homes?* Record their responses on chart paper.

Next, provide each child with a copy of the Lesson K.6 Butterfly Outline that you photocopied earlier. Encourage students to select one of the butterflies in the classroom data table and color the outline to match. After the children have cut out their butterflies, pass out 11-by-17-inch pieces of paper and invite students to glue their butterfly to the large paper. Then encourage them to Turn and Talk with a buddy about how to add a scene that shows ways people can help the butterfly live and grow. If students are having trouble generating ideas, initiate a whole-class discussion and revisit relevant pages of *A Place for Butterflies*. When the class seems ready, encourage each student to create his or her own scene on the 11-by-17-inch sheet of paper.

As the buddies are finishing up, photograph the drawings with a digital camera. You can print out copies for the students later so that they can add the images to their Wonder Journal as a response to the question *How can people work together to protect living things and the land they call home?* Then help the class hang their pictures around the school.

To bring this lesson to a close, remind your class that mourning cloak butterflies live in woodlands just like most of the creatures in *Where Once There Was a Wood*. Ask students: *How can people stop destroying places where butterflies and other animals live if they need places to build homes?* This may be a difficult question for young children to consider. If your students seem apprehensive, invite them to Turn and Talk so that they can discuss their thoughts with a buddy before addressing the whole class.

As the buddies talk, circulate around the room and jot down some of their ideas. When the class seems ready, encourage students to gather for a Science Dialogue. As group members present ideas to the class, encourage them to provide rationale for their suggestions. Then invite other students to respond by questioning the presenters or expanding upon their ideas.

In this lesson students learned that people can harm plants, animals, and other living things by damaging or destroying natural lands. They also discovered that people can work together to protect wildlife and preserve their habitats. With these new insights, students may now begin to wonder if local environments have been damaged or destroyed and what might have happened to the creatures that lived in those places. They should feel free to record these new insights in their Wonder Journals.

Reinforcing the Concept

- You can extend the lesson by reading the following book pairs and discussing the content with the Wonder Statement in mind:
  —*The Great Kapok Tree* by Lynne Cherry & *No Monkeys, No Chocolate* by Melissa Stewart
  —*Dumpster Diver* by Janet S. Wong & *Finding Home* by Sandra Markle
- Young children can often see and evaluate the actions of others, but they may have trouble understanding the impact of their own behaviors. And yet, they need that awareness before they can get involved in meaningful conservation. To help students develop their thinking in this direction, encourage them to discuss how they might be harming the environment without even realizing it. They can use some examples from *A Place for Butterflies* as thought starters. Then encourage the children to suggest ways they might change their behavior to help protect animals and preserve natural environments in your community.
- Invite students to pretend they are butterflies. Ask them to describe what it feels like to flit through the air. Then ask what they wish people would do to help them live and grow. Consider recording a few of the children's responses with the video setting on a digital camera. The videos can be replayed later on an interactive whiteboard or other device.

- To help students evaluate and interpret the data in the *Where Once There Was a Wood* table, ask the class: *How many animals lost their homes?* (Fourteen, if extras rows have been filled in.) *How many plants lost their homes?* (Three.) *In this book, did more plants or animals lose their homes?* (Animals.) *When a real woodland is destroyed, do you think more plants or animals suffer?* (Have them explain their answers.)

ELA Links   By now, students have learned a lot about how people harm the natural world and how we can work together to protect land-based creatures. Two different books—one fiction, one nonfiction—have played important roles in this lesson. The following questions can help students reflect on the aspects of the featured books that aroused their curiosity, generated and maintained their interest, and enhanced their understanding of the natural world.

- *What do the two books have in common?* (They are both about how people can help or harm living things and their environment. Both have illustrations.)
- *How are the two books different?* (*Where Once There Was a Wood* is a fictional story told in verse. It makes us think about how destroying natural areas affects other creatures. The art has jagged edges, and it doesn't feel quite real. *A Place for Butterflies* is nonfiction. It explains the needs of butterflies and how people can help them survive. The art is colorful and realistic.)
- *Why do you think the authors of both books use repetition—the same words over and over?* (In *Where Once There Was a Wood*, the repetition accentuates the soft rhythm of the verse. Then the ending really surprises you. In *A Place for Butterflies* the repetition emphasizes the message of conservation.)
- *Back matter is an important nonfiction text feature, but sometimes fiction authors include it, too. Why do you think the author of* Where Once There Was a Wood *includes lots of back matter in her book? What other helpful information does the author of* A Place for Butterflies *include?*

Lesson K.7: How to Reduce Our Impact on Creatures in Water Environments

| *Big Night for Salamanders* by Sarah Marwil Lamstein | & | *Turtle, Turtle, Watch Out!* by April Pulley Sayre |

About the Books

Big Night for Salamanders elegantly blends fiction and nonfiction, alternating between lyrical, italicized descriptions of the salamanders and their movements and a straightforward narrative about Evan—a boy who helps them cross a dangerous road. The use of present tense lends immediacy and suspense to the tale, and luminous gouache illustrations impart a sense of wonder. Rich back matter provides more details about the life cycle of the spotted salamander, Big Night activities, and vernal pools.

From predation by herons and raccoons to shrimp nets and plastic bags, *Turtle, Turtle, Watch Out!* alerts young readers to the many dangers sea turtles face and explains how people are working to minimize these threats. The simple, direct text reads aloud well, drawing readers into the turtle's story without anthropomorphism. Lovely watercolor, gouache, and pastel illustrations accurately depict the sand and shore of the sea turtle's world. Back matter describes the seven endangered species of sea turtles and the ways people, including children, are helping them survive.

Wonder Statement: I wonder how people can work together to protect creatures that depend on water environments.

Learning Goal In this lesson, students learn that people sometimes change the natural world in ways that are harmful to water-dwelling creatures and their environments. They also discover that there are simple, effective things we can all do to protect watery worlds and the living things that call them home.

NGSS Performance Expectation K-ESS3-3. Communicate solutions that will reduce the impact of humans on the land, water, air, and/or other living things in the local environment.

Prep Steps 1. Post the Wonder Statement, *I wonder how people can work together to protect creatures that depend on water environments*, on the wall in the classroom meeting area.

2. Use Google Images to find photos of common turtles that inhabit freshwater habitats (painted turtles, box turtles, snapping turtles, etc.) and sea turtles.
3. Make a copy of the Lesson K.7 *Turtle, Turtle, Watch Out!* Worksheet in Appendix B.
4. Gather two colors of large sticky notes, such as red and blue. On the front of the red notes write *DANGER*. On the back, write a word or two to describe the dangers that will be added to the left-hand side of the *Turtle, Turtle, Watch Out!* data table. Possibilities include *raccoon, other predators, jeep, house lights, plastic bags, shrimp nets*. On the front of the blue notes write *STAY SAFE*. On the back, draw a picture showing the information that will be added to the right-hand side of the data table. Possibilities include pictures of a girl with a flashlight, a wire mesh, a "No Driving on the Beach" sign, a light switch, a child with a plastic bag, a turtle escaping from a shrimp net.
5. Collect the following props and place them in a box: flashlight, toy car, pink plastic wrap, sign that says "GO SLOW Salamander Crossing!", and a photo of a road.
6. Make copies of the Lesson K.7 Wonder Journal Labels in Appendix B for each child in your class and cut them out.

Engaging Students

Begin the lesson by passing out copies of the Lesson K.7 Wonder Journal Label with the Wonder Statement written on it. After reading the Wonder Statement with the class, ask your students to add it to their Wonder Journals.

Project the freshwater turtle photos you found earlier on the interactive whiteboard, and ask your students if they can name the animal. Then ask if any of them have ever seen a turtle. Explain that these turtles live in freshwater, such as ponds and swamps. Can the class think of some of the dangers these turtles might face?

As the students brainstorm in small groups, pass out the Lesson K.7 *Turtle, Turtle, Watch Out!* Worksheet that you photocopied earlier. Encourage students to draw at least one of their ideas on the top half of the worksheet.

Next, let the class know that there is a second group of turtles. They are called sea turtles. After showing the class the sea turtle photos you found earlier, ask students to compare the two kinds of turtles. How are they the same? How are they different?

Encourage the class to reform their small groups and discuss what dangers sea turtles might face. Do they have to watch out for things that freshwater turtles don't? When the students seem ready, ask them to draw some of their ideas on the bottom half of the worksheet.

Exploring with Students

Introduce *Turtle, Turtle, Watch Out!* by reading the title and the names of the author and illustrator. Ask your class to explain the role of the author and illustrator in creating a book.

Invite the students to look at the book's cover, front and back. Ask the class: *Why do you think the illustrator showed half of the fish's body on the front cover and half on the back cover? What do you think the book will be about?* Now show the children the book's title page. Do they have any new ideas? Do they think the turtle in this story lives in a pond or the sea?

Let the class know that they are going to help you read the story. Every time the words *Turtle, Turtle, Watch Out!* appear in the text, students should say the words aloud and hold up their worksheets. If one of their drawings matches the danger being described in the book, they should show it to the class.

As you read through the book, encourage students to identify not only the dangers but also the ways people help the sea turtle in the book. When you have finished reading, look through the pages a second time and work with the class to create a data table like the one below.

Danger (Reason for Danger)	How People Help
A hungry raccoon (It could eat turtle eggs.)	A girl scares away the raccoon with a flashlight before it eats the turtle eggs.
Other predators (They could eat turtle eggs.)	A boy surrounds the nest with wire mesh to keep predators out.
A Jeep (It could crush the eggs.)	A boy puts up a "No Driving on the Beach" sign.
Human lights (They can confuse turtles.)	A child turns off the lights.
Plastic bags (Turtles might think they are jellyfish.)	A child takes the plastic bag out of the water.
Shrimp nets (Turtles can get stuck in them.)	People build escape hatches in the shrimp nets.

After reviewing the information in the data table, invite your class to play a game of Concentration. Begin by showing the students both sides of the colored sticky notes you prepared in advance. Then place the red notes on one piece of chart paper and the blue notes on a second piece of chart paper. Encourage student volunteers to come forward and test their memories by choosing a red DANGER note and then a blue STAY SAFE note. As the children turn over each sticky note, help them read the information on the back and remind the class of its connection to the information in the *Turtle, Turtle, Watch Out!* data table. If students make a match, remove the sticky notes from the chart paper. Otherwise, turn the sticky notes back over so another student can try.

Now introduce *Big Night for Salamanders* by reading the title and the names of the author and illustrator. Encourage the students to take a close look at the book's full (front and back) cover illustration. Guide a

Teaching Tip

Some of the vocabulary in *Big Night for Salamanders* may be unfamiliar to kindergartners, especially English language learners. When an unfamiliar word or phrase (*dwell, emerging, vernal pool*) arises, write it on an index card and encourage your students to guide you in creating a sketch to help them remember what it means. Then post the card under the Wonder Statement on the wall.

Teaching Tip

The entries in the sample data tables shown here are fully fleshed out and include all possible answers. You should not expect your class's tables to be as detailed, but they should include enough essential information to fully address the Wonder Statement. Providing students with copies of each data table as soon as possible after the class compiles it will allow each child to keep a record of the investigation in his or her Wonder Journal.

discussion about the information the illustration provides. Students may note that the front and back cover illustrations both include a salamander but don't seem to be related. Ask students: *What do you think the story will be about? What do you think the title means?*

After recording your class's ideas, begin reading the story. The page where Evan is drinking hot cocoa has clues about "Big Night." After hearing this page, does the class have new ideas about what it is? Does the art provide any additional clues? Can the students guess what this book has in common with *Turtle, Turtle, Watch Out!*? Record their responses on chart paper. Ask these questions again after reading each of the next two spreads, and continue to update the chart paper with the class's ideas.

By the time you reach the spread in which Evan dashes toward the road with his flashlight, the meaning of "Big Night" and the common link between *Big Night for Salamanders* and *Turtle, Turtle, Watch Out!* should be clear to students. Stop reading, and provide each student with a copy of the Lesson K.7 Wonder Journal Label with the following sentence frames:

On Big Night, spotted salamanders move from _____ to _____.

The boy in this story will help the salamanders cross a _____.

Encourage students to fill in the blanks with pictures or words and insert the label into their Wonder Journals.

When children are done, return to the story. The next double-page spread shows Evan on the left and the salamander on the right. Ask your students: *Why do you think the author decided to make this spread different from earlier ones?*

As you read the rest of the story, ask students to look for specific ways that Evan and his family help the salamander. Let them know that the class will list these in a data table later.

When you finish reading the book, return to the beginning. Leaf through slowly and work with your students to create a data table that addresses the Wonder Statement.

A sample data table may look like this:

Danger (Reason for Danger)	How Evan and His Parents Help
Bright lights (They startle salamanders.)	They wrap the end of a flashlight with pink plastic.
Busy road (Crossing is difficult.)	Evan carries salamanders across the road.
People in cars (They don't know it's Big Night.)	They tell people the salamanders are crossing and ask them to go slowly; Evan makes a sign that says "GO SLOW Salamander Crossing."

To review the information in the data table, pull the props you gathered earlier out of the box one at a time and ask the class what role it played on Big Night. Which props represent a danger? Which ones helped the salamanders stay safe?

Encouraging Students to Draw Conclusions

Give each child a preprinted Wonder Journal Label that poses the Wonder Statement as a question: *How can people work together to protect creatures that depend on water environments?*

Let your students know that *Turtle, Turtle, Watch Out!* and *Big Night for Salamanders* have some important things in common. Can they think of any? (Both animals depend on a water environment.) Encourage the class to look for more similarities as you review the data tables together. Ask students: *Are there any dangers that both salamanders and sea turtles face? Do Evan and the people in* Turtle, Turtle, Watch Out! *help water creatures in ways that are similar?* Encourage students to Turn and Talk about these questions.

As the partners talk, circulate around the room and assist your students as needed. Then give each child a copy of the Lesson K.7 Wonder Journal Label that says:

People can help creatures that depend on water environments.
My evidence is:

Encourage students to use the information in the data tables and their Turn and Talk discussions to complete the sentence with words, pictures, or both.

After allowing a few students to share their entries with the class, explain that Evan lived near a vernal pool, so he found a way to help the salamanders that needed to cross the road. The children in *Turtle, Turtle Watch Out!* lived near the ocean, so they helped a local animal—the sea turtle. In both books, people helped creatures that lived in their local environments.

Ask your class to think of a water environment in your community. If they have difficulty with this question, make a few suggestions and show students images of that environment. Then guide them in creating a list of at least three animals that may depend on that local body of water. Ask the children to think of at least one danger that each of the animals might face, and add their ideas to chart paper. (Possibilities include mistaking litter for food, people eating too many of them, chemicals from factories or farmland making them sick, and people catching and accidentally injuring them.)

After working with your class to brainstorm ways they could help the animals that depend on the local water environment stay safe, set out art

This student's collage shows that he can help pond animals by picking up litter.

materials and give each child an 11-by-17-inch piece of paper. Invite students to create visual models that show the local water environment and the animals that live there. When the collages are well underway, pass out smaller sheets of drawing paper. Encourage the children to draw a picture of themselves, cut it out, and add it to their collages.

As you move from student to student, ask each child to dictate one way he or she could help protect the local water environment and the animals that live there. Write that message on a piece of paper, so students can cut out the words to create a dialogue bubble for their collage.

To bring this lesson to a close, photograph the children holding their collages with a digital camera. You can print out copies for the students later so that they can add the images to their Wonder Journals as a permanent record of the investigation. Then work with your students to display the artwork around the school. You could also ask them to suggest other community buildings, such as the library, churches, or the town hall, where the collages could be hung.

In this lesson students learned that people may harm water-dwelling creatures without even realizing it. They also discovered that when caring people work together, they can protect living things that depend on a local water environment. With these new insights, students may now begin to wonder how they can help other living things stay safe. They should feel free to record these new insights in their Wonder Journals.

Reinforcing the Concept

- You can extend the lesson by reading the following book pairs and discussing the content with the Wonder Statement in mind:

—*Subway Story* by Julia Sarcone-Roach & *A Place for Fish* by Melissa Stewart

—*365 Penguins* by Jean-Luc Fromental & *A Warmer World* by Caroline Arnold

- Encourage students to share any actions that they or their families have taken to protect local creatures.

- Even though sea turtles and spotted salamanders depend on water environments, they both depend on land environments, too. Work with your students to design a class bulletin board that compares how sea turtles and spotted salamanders spend their time on land. How are the challenges the animals face on land similar to or different from one another?

- As you look at the information in the back matter of *Turtle, Turtle, Watch Out!* with your students, use mathematics and modeling to make the facts and figures easier for the children to appreciate. For example, a loggerhead turtle weighs 350 pounds. Ask your class: *What item in your house might weigh about 350 pounds?* (A refrigerator full of food.) A leatherback turtle can be six feet long. Show students six feet on a tape measure, and encourage them to look for objects in your classroom or around the school that are about the same size as a leatherback turtle.

ELA Links   By now, students have learned a lot about the challenges water-dwelling creatures face and how people can work together to protect these animals and their watery worlds. Two different books—one fiction, one nonfiction—have played important roles in this lesson. The following questions can help students reflect on the aspects of the featured books that aroused their curiosity, generated and maintained their interest, and enhanced their understanding of the natural world.

- *What do the two books have in common?* (They both show ways that young people are helping animals that depend on water environments. Both are illustrated with paintings.)

- *How are the two books different?* (*Big Night for Salamanders* is a mix of fiction and nonfiction. It tells parallel stories of a boy and a group of salamanders. *Turtle, Turtle, Watch Out!* is all nonfiction. It focuses on the obstacles one sea turtle faces as it grows up.)

- *Sarah Marwil Lamstein, the author of* Big Night for Salamanders, *could have written just Evan's story or just the salamanders' story. Why do you think she decided to combine them both into one book?* (To show both sides of the story.)

- Turtle, Turtle, Watch Out! *includes repetitive text (the same words over and over) written in larger text. Why do you think the author, April Pulley Sayre, made that decision?* (To highlight the many dangers a young sea turtle faces.)

Picture Books for Kindergarten Lessons

Featured Titles

Arnosky, Jim. *Gobble It Up! A Fun Song About Eating!* New York: Scholastic 2008.
HC 978-0-43990-362-2

Cole, Henry. *On Meadowview Street.* New York: Greenwillow, 2007
HC 978-0-06056-481-0

Davies, Nicola. *Just Ducks!* Cambridge, MA: Candlewick, 2012.
HC 978-0-76365-936-3

Dunphy, Madeleine. *At Home with the Gopher Tortoise: The Story of a Keystone Species.* Berkeley, CA: Web of Life Children's Books, 2010.
HC 978-0-97775-396-3; PB 978-0-97775-395-6

Ehlert, Lois. *Mole's Hill.* San Diego: Harcourt, 1998.
HC 978-0-61309-930-1; PB 978-0-15201-890-0

Fleming, Denise. *Where Once There Was a Wood.* New York: Holt, 2000.
PB 978-0-80506-482-7

Jenkins, Steve, and Robin Page. *Time to Eat.* Boston: Houghton Mifflin, 2011.
HC 978-0-54725-032-8

Lamstein, Sarah Marwil. *Big Night for Salamanders.* Honesdale, PA: Boyds Mills, 2009.
HC 978-1-93242-598-7

Markle, Sandra. *Hip-Pocket Papa.* Watertown, MA: Charlesbridge, 2010.
HC 978-1-57091-708-0

Mazer, Anne. *The Salamander Room.* Boston: Houghton Mifflin, 2000.
HC 978-0-78073-945-1; PB 978-0-67986-187-4

Pfeffer, Wendy. *From Seed to Pumpkin.* New York: HarperCollins, 2004.
HC 978-0-75693-238-1; PB 978-0-06445-190-1

Sayre, April Pulley. *Turtle, Turtle, Watch Out!* Watertown, MA: Charlesbridge, 2010.
HC 978-1-58089-148-6; PB 978-1-58089-149-3

Stewart, Melissa. *A Place for Butterflies.* Atlanta: Peachtree, 2006.
HC 978-1-56145-357-3; PB 978-1-56145-571-3

Winter, Jeanette. *Wangari's Trees of Peace: A True Story from Africa.* San Diego: Harcourt, 2008.
HC 978-0-15206-545-4

Supplementary Titles

Arnold, Caroline. *A Warmer World.* Watertown, MA: Charlesbridge, 2007.
HC 978-1-58089-266-7; PB 978-1-58089-267-4

Biedrzycki, David. *Ace Lacewing, Bug Detective.* Watertown, MA: Charlesbridge, 2008.
PB 978-1-57091-684-7

Brown, Peter. *The Curious Garden.* New York: Little, Brown, 2009.
HC 978-0-31601-547-9

Bruchac, Joseph, and James Bruchac. *Turtle's Race with Beaver.* New York: Puffin, 2005.
PB 978-0-14240-466-9

Campbell, Sarah C. *Wolfsnail: A Backyard Predator.* Honesdale, PA: Boyds Mills, 2008.
HC 978-1-59078-554-6

Cannon, Janell. *Pinduli.* San Diego: Harcourt, 2004.
HC 978-0-15204-668-2

Cherry, Lynne. *The Great Kapok Tree.* San Diego: Harcourt, 1990.
HC 978-0-15200-520-7; PB 978-0-15202-614-1

Cole, Henry. *Jack's Garden.* New York: Greenwillow, 1997.
HC 978-0-68813-501-0; PB 978-0-68815-283-3

Davies, Nicola. *Bat Loves the Night.* Cambridge, MA: Candlewick, 2004.
HC 978-0-75696-561-7; PB 978-0-76362-438-5

Fromental, Jean-Luc. *365 Penguins.* New York: Abrams, 2006.
HC 978-0-81094-460-2; PB 978-0-06058-703-1

Frost, Helen. *Monarch and Milkweed.* New York: Atheneum, 2008.
HC 978-1-41690-085-6.

Hauth, Katherine B. *What's for Dinner? Quirky, Squirmy Poems from the Animal World.* Watertown, MA: Charlesbridge, 2011.
HC 978-1-57091-471-3; PB 978-1-57091-472-0

Kirby, Pamela F. *What Bluebirds Do.* Honesdale, PA: Boyds Mills, 2009
HC 978-1-59078-614-7

Markle, Sandra. *Finding Home.* Watertown, MA: Charlesbridge, 2010.
HC 978-1-58089-123-3

Peterson, Cris. *Seed, Soil, Sun.* Honesdale, PA: Boyds Mills, 2010.
HC 978-1-59078-713-7

Pfeffer, Wendy. *Wiggling Worms at Work.* New York: HarperCollins, 2003.
HC 978-0-06028-448-0; PB 978-0-06445-199-4

Rockwell, Anne. *Who Lives in an Alligator Hole?* New York: HarperCollins, 2006.
PB 978-0-06445-200-7

Roth, Susan L., and Cindy Trumbore. *The Mangrove Tree: Planting Trees to Feed Families.* New York: Lee and Low, 2011.
HC 978-1-60060-459-1

Ryder, Joanne. *The Snail's Spell.* New York: Scholastic, 1991.
HC 978-0-81246-361-3; PB 978-0-14050-891-8

Sarcone-Roach, Julia. *Subway Story.* New York: Knopf, 2011.
HC 978-0-37585-859-8

Sayre, April Pulley. *Dig, Wait, Listen: A Desert Toad's Tale.* New York: Greenwillow, 2001.
HC 978-0-68816-614-4

Schaefer, Lola. *Just One Bite*. San Francisco: Chronicle, 2010.
HC 978-0-81186-473-2

Stewart, Melissa. *No Monkeys, No Chocolate*. Watertown, MA:
Charlesbridge, 2013.
HC 978-1-58089-287-2

———. *A Place for Fish*. Atlanta: Peachtree, 2011.
HC 978-1-56145-562-1

Stewart, Sarah. *The Gardener*. New York: Farrar, Straus and Giroux, 1997.
HC 978-0-37432-517-6

Wilson, Karma. *Bear Wants More*. New York: Margaret K. McElderry,
2003.
HC 978-0-68984-509-3

Wong, Janet S. *Dumpster Diver*. Somerville, MA: Candlewick, 2007.
HC 978-0-76362-380-7

Yolen, Jane. *Eloise's Bird*. New York: Philomel, 2010.
HC 978-0-39925-292-1

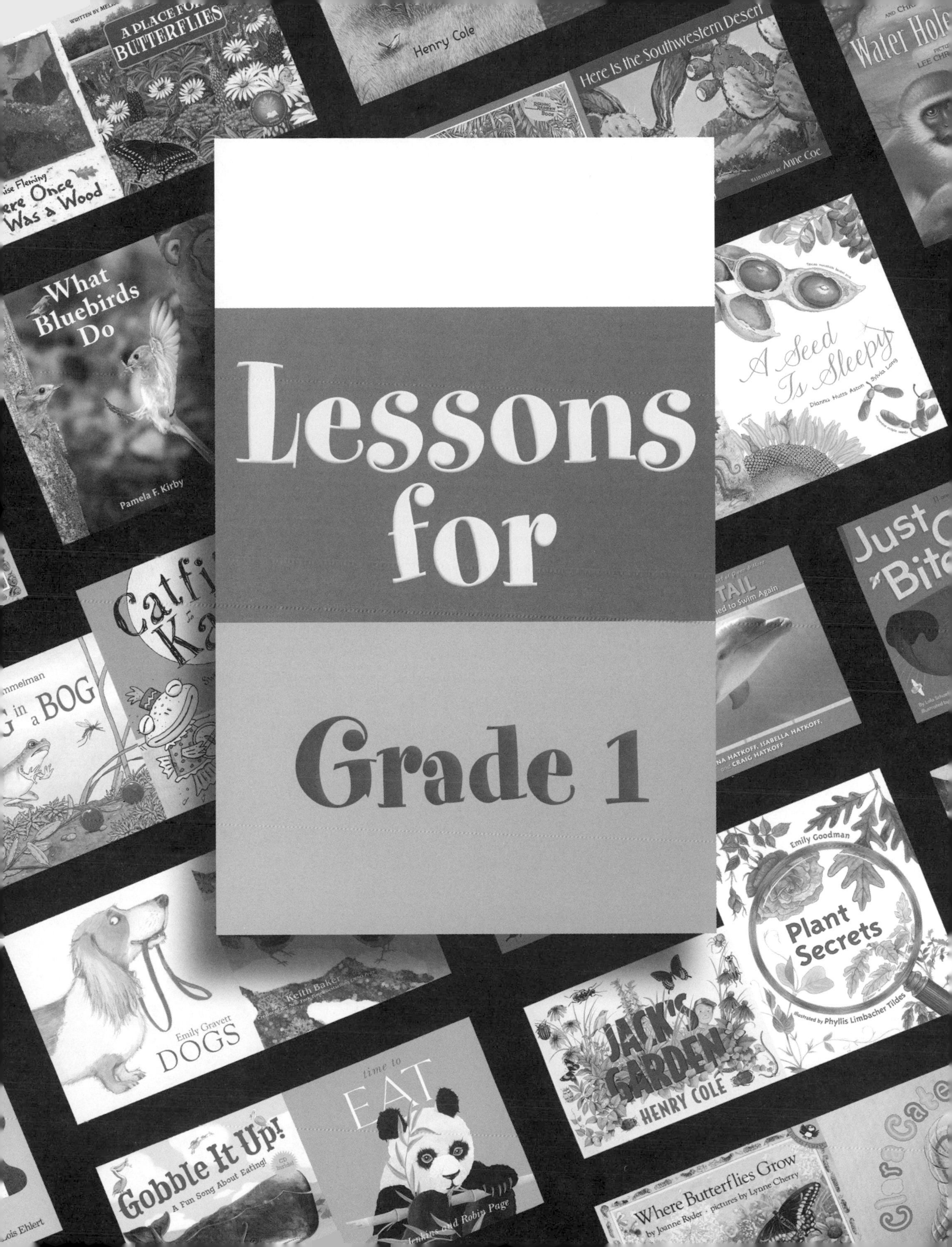

Lessons for Grade 1

Lesson 1.1: How an Animal's Body Parts Help It Survive

| *The Snail's Spell* by Joanne Ryder | **&** | *What Do You Do with a Tail Like This?* by Steve Jenkins |

About the Books

The lovely, lyrical text and soft, detailed watercolors of *The Snail's Spell* invite readers along on an imaginative journey into a snail's world. By experiencing a garden teeming with fresh vegetables and an assortment of wildlife—all from a snail's point of view—children will gain an appreciation for how other creatures go about their daily lives.

As much a game as it is a book, *What Do You Do with a Tail Like This?* explores the many amazing things animals can do with their ears, eyes, mouths, noses, feet, and tails. A nose for digging? Ears for seeing? Eyes that squirt blood? No fact is too bizarre for this Caldecott Honor title. Clear, simple text; vibrant cut-paper collage; and a one-of-a-kind design will entertain as well as inform young readers.

Wonder Statement: I wonder how an animal's body parts help it live and grow.

Learning Goal
Because PE 1-LS1-1 draws upon two content-rich, interconnected Disciplinary Core Ideas (LS1.A Structure and Function and LS1.D Information Processing) as well as a challenging engineering practice, we have written five lessons to fully address it. In this first lesson, students gain a basic understanding of animals' key external body parts and how different animals use them to survive or to make their lives easier. Lesson 1.2 explores specific ways animals use their external body parts to find and catch food, while Lesson 1.3 investigates how animals use their body parts to protect themselves from predators. Lesson 1.4 looks at the structure and function of plant parts. Finally, Lesson 1.5 focuses on the engineering practice by encouraging students to design a solution to a human problem using what they have learned about plants and animals in the previous four lessons.

NGSS Performance Expectation 1-LS1-1. Use materials to design a solution to a human problem by mimicking how plants and/or animals use their external parts to help them survive, grow, and meet their needs.

Prep Steps

1. Post the Wonder Statement, *I wonder how an animal's body parts help it live and grow*, on the wall in the classroom meeting area.
2. Use Google Images to find a variety of photos of common garden snails.
3. Prepare six two-column data tables, each on a separate sheet of chart paper, to highlight information about the animal body parts discussed in *What Do You Do with a Tail Like This?* Give each table a title, using the sample tables in this lesson as a guide. Label the left-hand column of each data table "Animal" and the right-hand column "Use." Then fill in all the cells in the left-hand column with the names of the animals included in the book. Again, use the sample tables as a guide.
4. Make one photocopy of the Lesson 1.1 Animal Cards and four copies of the Lesson 1.1 Body Part Cards found in Appendix B. Then laminate the cards and cut them out.
5. Make copies of the Lesson 1.1 Wonder Journal Labels in Appendix B for each child in your class and cut them out.

Engaging Students

Begin the lesson by passing out copies of the Lesson 1.1 Wonder Journal Label with the Wonder Statement written on it. After reading the Wonder Statement with the class, ask your students to add it to their Wonder Journals.

Divide the class into small groups and let your students know that you are going to list four clues on chart paper. You would like each team to try to guess the identity of a mystery animal that lives in many people's gardens. After you write each clue, read it aloud and give the groups a few minutes to discuss their ideas. Let the teams know that they shouldn't finalize their guesses until they have seen all the clues.

Clue 1: It is small. It has a soft, gray body.

Clue 2: It has two long things sticking out of its head. The "things" move around a lot.

Clue 3: It has no legs.

Clue 4: It has a hard shell.

When the teams are done conferring, ask for one member of each group to announce the team's guess and provide rationale to support the group's thinking. Record the students' responses on chart paper.

Now project on the interactive whiteboard the photo of the garden snail you found earlier. Show your class each of the body structures you described in the clues.

Invite students to draw a picture of a snail below the Wonder Journal Label that they just added to their Wonder Journal. Group members should work together to come up with names for the parts of the snail's

This student drawing includes labels that highlight a snail's antennae, eyes, body, and shell.

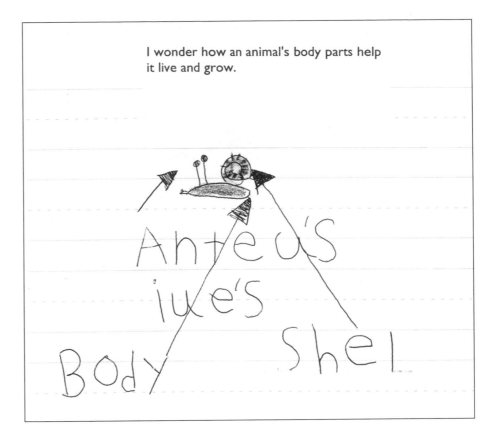

body. After they have added those labels to their drawings, ask a member of each group to share his or her drawing and the names the group chose. Write each set of names on chart paper and have the students vote for the ones they think are most appropriate. Mark those names with a check.

Exploring with Students

Show the students *The Snail's Spell*, and let them know that they are about to learn more about the mystery animal—the snail. Invite the students to look closely at the book's front cover and find the snail. After they have spotted it in the child's hand, ask them: *Why do you think the picture shows a child holding a snail instead of a close-up of the snail? Why do you think the child and snail are in a garden?*

After your students have discussed the questions, ask: *What do you think it would be like to be a snail living in a garden? What kind of adventures do you think you would have? How do you think your external body parts—the parts on the outside of your body—would help you live and grow? Could you survive without them?* Record the class's responses on chart paper.

As you read the first page of *The Snail's Spell*, invite students to pretend they are snails. Encourage them to act out the story as you read it.

When you have finished the book, review the names the class came up with for a snail's outer, or external, body parts and ask: *Did Joanne Ryder, the author of* The Snail's Spell, *use the same names?* Page through the book as needed to help students answer this question. Then ask the class: *Are there any external body parts you would like to add to the class list or the diagrams in your Wonder Journals?* After a short class discussion, allow students time to update their drawings.

Invite a few volunteers to share what they have added to their snail pictures. Then work with your class to write all the external body parts they have learned about in a data table like the one shown below. Look back through the book and fill in the "How the Snail Uses It" column.

Snail Body Parts

External Body Part	How the Snail Uses It
Tiny teeth on its tongue	To eat lettuce and other plants
Short feelers	To avoid hitting things as the snail glides across the ground
Long feelers with eyes	To sense danger
Shell	To stay safe while asleep

Once your class is satisfied with the data table, ask the students to reform their groups and use information from the table to come up with at least one more clue that could be added to the mystery animal game. Then allow time for each group to share its idea with the rest of the class.

Now introduce *What Do You Do with a Tail Like This?* by showing the front cover and asking students what animal they think the tail belongs to. After they make a few guesses, flip the book over to show the back cover. Now that they can identify the animal, ask them how they think the lizard might use its tail. Can they think of any ways the tail might help a lizard find food or stay safe?

After reading the first page, ask the class how the book is similar to the mystery animal game they played at the beginning of the lesson. (It's also a guessing game.) Then ask, *How is it different?* (In addition to guessing the animals, readers also guess how they use a particular external body part.) Let your students know that by playing the game in the book, they will learn how many different animals use their external body structures to help them survive.

As you work through the book with your class, stop after reading each double-page spread with a question about an animal body part. Encourage students to guess which animal each part belongs to. Then turn the page and read how the animals use that external body part. Be sure to spend extra time explaining unique uses of body parts, such as the lizard's ability to lose its tail and the archerfish's ability to knock prey into the water by spitting water at it. To keep track of how animals use

Teaching Tip

The entries in the sample data tables shown here are fully fleshed out and include all possible answers. You should not expect your class's tables to be as detailed, but they should include enough essential information to fully address the Wonder Statement. Providing students with copies of each data table as soon as possible after the class compiles it will allow each child to keep a record of the investigation in his or her Wonder Journal.

Teaching Tip

In some cases, the main text of *What Do You Do with a Tail Like This?* doesn't provide all the information first graders will need to understand the concept, but you can turn to the longer descriptions in the book's back matter for clarification. These entries are indicated by parentheses in the sample data tables. In other cases, the book lacks critical information. When you see an asterisk (*), ask students if they have ideas about how to complete the data table based on their prior knowledge. You may need to fill in some details for them.

their external body parts, work with your students to complete the data tables you prepared earlier. Your final data tables should be similar to the samples below.

How Some Animals Use Their Nose

Animal	Use
Platypus	To dig in the mud (for food)
Hyena	To find food
Elephant	To take a bath
Mole	To avoid getting lost (and to find food)
Alligator	To breathe (by lifting just its nose above the water's surface)

How Some Animals Use Their Ears

Animal	Use
Jackrabbit	To keep cool
Bat	To get a picture of the world (by listening to sounds echoing off nearby objects)
Hippopotamus*	To hear
Cricket	To hear (one another so they can find mates)
Humpback whale	To hear (other whales trying to communicate)

How Some Animals Use Their Tail

Animal	Use
Giraffe	To brush away flies
Skunk	To warn enemies that they are about to get sprayed
Lizard	To escape from enemies
Scorpion	To sting (animals it wants to eat)
Monkey	To hang from tree branches (so it can reach food)

How Some Animals Use Their Eyes

Animal	Use
Eagle	To spot animals (that it can catch and eat)
Chameleon	To look two ways at once (so it can spot food and enemies)
Four-eyed fish	To look above and below water (so it can spot food and enemies)
Horned lizard	To squirt blood (at enemies)
Bush baby	To see (so they can find food)

How Some Animals Use Their Feet

Animal	Use
Chimpanzee	To eat food
Blue-footed booby	To dance (to attract a mate)
Water strider	To walk on water (in search of food)
Gecko*	To walk on ceilings to find food and escape from enemies
Mountain goat	To leap (out of the way of falling rocks or snow)

How Some Animals Use Their Mouth

Animal	Use
Pelican	To catch food
Mosquito*	To suck blood (so it can produce healthy eggs)
Egg-eating snake	To eat food
Anteater	To catch food with its tongue
Archerfish	To catch food

When the data tables are complete, divide the class into six groups and assign each group one of the animal body parts discussed in *What Do You Do with a Tail Like This?* Encourage each group to consider whether the animals in the book depend on the external body part to live and grow or if it just makes their lives easier or better. When each group comes to a consensus, one member should write either an *L* (live and grow) or an *E* (makes life easier) next to each entry in the "Use" column of the data table for the group's assigned body part.

Students decide whether various animals use their noses to live and grow or to make their lives easier.

As the group discussions wind down, invite the class to gather for a Science Dialogue to share their ideas. As members of each group present, encourage their classmates to agree or disagree with the presenters and one another. They should also feel free to ask one another questions. As children contribute to the conversation, they should provide rationale to support their ideas.

Encouraging Students to Draw Conclusions

Give each child the Lesson 1.1 Wonder Journal Label that poses the Wonder Statement as a question: *How do an animal's body parts help it live and grow?*

Guide your class in developing a list of three or four general ways the animals in *What Do You Do with a Tail Like This?* depend on their external body parts to live and grow. Possibilities include:

- To stay safe
- To find, catch, or eat food
- To move from place to place
- To sense their surroundings

After creating a three-column data table template for each idea on your list, as shown below, pass out the Lesson 1.1 Animal Cards you prepared earlier, giving one or more to each student.

Animals Use These External Body Parts to _____

Animal	External Body Part	How It Is Used

Let the class know that all the animals on their cards are from *What Do You Do with a Tail Like This?* Encourage students to Turn and Talk with a buddy about which of the new data tables their animal belongs in. If students can't recall which of their animal's body parts was discussed in the book or how it was used, suggest that they review the data tables you created earlier in the lesson. While students are busy with this task, scatter around the room the Lesson 1.1 Body Part Cards you cut out and laminated earlier. Then, when the children seem ready, invite them to use double-sided tape to post their Animal Cards in the left-hand column of the correct data table.

Next, divide the class into three or four groups, assign each group one of the new data tables, and invite students to move around the room hunting for the Body Part Cards that belong in the center column of their data table. When the members of each team have attached their cards to the table with double-sided tape, encourage them to complete the right-hand column by adding a few words that explain how the animal in the left-hand column uses the body part in the center column for the purpose indicated in the data table's title. A completed Animals Use These External Body Parts to Stay Safe data table might look like this:

Animals Use These External Body Parts to Stay Safe

Animal	External Body Part	How It Is Used
Skunk	Tail	Warn
Lizard	Tail	Escape
Chameleon	Eyes	Look two ways for enemies
Horned Lizard	Eyes	Squirt blood
Mountain goat	Feet	Leap from danger

Now invite the class to gather for a Science Dialogue. After working with your students to verify the accuracy of the information in the new data tables, review the information in the *The Snail's Spell* data table. Then ask: *Can a snail be included in any of our new data tables?* As the class discusses this question, encourage them to explain the rationale for their ideas as they agree or disagree with their classmates. They should also feel free to ask one another questions. To facilitate the discussion, help the students stay focused and restate any unclear comments or ideas.

As the class comes to realize that the snail has body parts that can fit into several of the new data tables, add that information to the appropriate tables.

To bring this lesson to a close, guide students to the idea that different animals may use a particular body part in different ways (to perform different jobs). Similarly, different animals may use different parts for the same purpose. Then provide each student with a copy of the Lesson 1.1 Wonder Journal Labels that say:

A _____ (animal 1) uses its tail to _____ (job 1).
But a _____ (animal 2) uses its tail to _____ (job 2).

A _____ (animal 1) uses its _____ (body part 1) to find, catch, or eat food.
But a _____ (animal 2) uses its _____ (body part 2) to find, catch, or eat food.

Encourage the children to add the labels to their Wonder Journals one at a time, so they have plenty of room to use words and pictures to complete the sentence frames.

A student's completed Wonder
Journal Labels

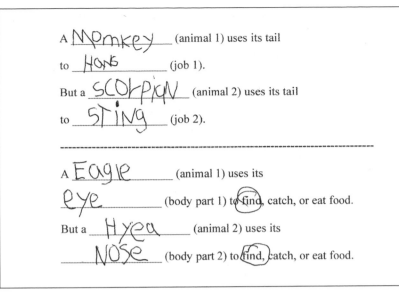

A ___Momkey___ (animal 1) uses its tail

to ___Hons___ (job 1).

But a ___Scorpion___ (animal 2) uses its tail

to ___Sting___ (job 2).

- -

A ___Eagle___ (animal 1) uses its

___eye___ (body part 1) to find, catch, or eat food.

But a ___Hyea___ (animal 2) uses its

___Nose___ (body part 2) to find, catch, or eat food.

In this lesson students learned that animals have body parts that help them live and grow. They also discovered that different animals may use a particular body part in different ways. Similarly, different animals may use different parts for the same purpose. With these new insights, students may now begin to wonder how other kinds of animals use their body parts to survive. They should feel free to record their new questions and ideas in their Wonder Journals.

Reinforcing the Concept

- You can extend the lesson by reading the following book pairs and discussing the content with the Wonder Statement in mind:
  —*No One But You* by Douglas Wood & *My Five Senses* by Aliki
  —*Diary of a Fly* by Doreen Cronin & *Dig, Wait, Listen* by April Pulley Sayre

- Review the information in *What Do You Do with a Tail Like This?* by selecting a body part and asking student volunteers to act out the way it helps a particular animal survive. Remind students that they may use information from the lesson data tables to assist them.

- Invite students to choose a buddy, and give each pair a stick of modeling clay and an $8\frac{1}{2}$ -by-11-inch sheet of oak tag. Working together, the buddies should select one of the animals in *What Do You Do with a Tail Like This?* While one student creates a model of the animal, the other student should fold the oak tag in half and color the bottom so that it represents the ground the model animal is walking on (or swimming in) and the top half so that it represents the habitat where the model animal lives.

Lessons for Grade 1

ELA Links   By now, students have learned a lot about how animals use their body parts to live and grow. Two different books—one fiction, one nonfiction—have played important roles in this lesson. The following questions can help students reflect on the aspects of the featured books that aroused their curiosity, generated and maintained their interest, and enhanced their understanding of the natural world.

- *How are the two books the same?* (They both include information about how animals use their body parts. Both are illustrated.)
- *How are the two books different?* (*The Snail's Spell* is fiction written in a way that makes it easy for the reader to imagine that he or she is a snail. *What Do You Do with a Tail Like This?* is nonfiction with a guessing-game structure.)
- *Look back at the text in* The Snail's Spell. *Who is telling the story?* (The author.) *Who is the main character of the story?* (The reader.) *How does it feel to be the main character of the story you are reading?*
- *Can you find a few words or a sentence in* The Snail's Spell *that you especially like? Why do you like it? Are there words or sentences that make you feel happy, safe, or cozy? What are they?*
- *How does the style of the art in each book seem to match the style of the text?* (The art in *The Snail's Spell* is detailed but soft and realistic. It leaves room for the reader's imagination. The cut-paper collage in *What Do You Do with a Tail Like This?* is realistic and fun. That makes sense because the book is written like a game.)
- *The author-illustrators of* What Do You Do with a Tail Like This? *include information about many different body parts, not just tails. Why do you think they picked the tail to be in the title instead of another animal part? Which part would you have picked for the title? Why?*

Lesson 1.2: How Animals Find and Catch Food

A Frog in the Bog by Karma Wilson	&	*Just One Bite* by Lola Schaefer

About the Books

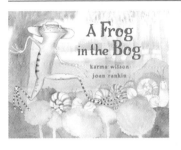

This delightful counting book combines bouncy, rhythmic text and dreamy watercolors to tell the story of a hungry frog chowing down. As his belly grows, we're treated to a hilarious view of the claustrophobic quarters within. But then the frog gets a surprise. The log he's been sitting on develops a pair of yellow eyes and wide jaws. "Gator!" As the frog opens his mouth to scream, all the critters he's eaten scramble out. What happens to the frog? You'll have to read the story to find out.

Using clear, simple text, *Just One Bite* describes what a variety of popular animals—from earthworms and butterflies to elephants and sperm whales—eat in "just one bite." Large, stylized paint-and-crayon artwork shows mouths and mouthparts at life size, giving readers a close-up view of animals and their prey. This fun book includes rich back matter with additional information about the eating habits of the featured creatures.

Lessons for Grade 1

Wonder Statement: I wonder how some animals find and catch food.

Learning Goal Because PE 1-LS1-1 draws upon two content-rich, interconnected Disciplinary Core Ideas (LS1.A Structure and Function and LS1.D Information Processing) as well as a challenging engineering practice, we have written five lessons to fully address it. In Lesson 1.1, students gain a basic understanding of animals' key external body parts and how different animals use them to survive or to make their lives easier. This lesson, 1.2, explores specific ways animals use their external body parts to find and catch food, whereas Lesson 1.3 investigates how animals use their body parts to protect themselves from predators. Lesson 1.4 looks at the structure and function of plant parts. Finally, Lesson 1.5 focuses on the engineering practice by encouraging students to design a solution to a human problem using what they have learned about plants and animals in the previous four lessons.

NGSS Performance Expectation 1-LS1-1. Use materials to design a solution to a human problem by mimicking how plants and/or animals use their external parts to help them survive, grow, and meet their needs.

Prep Steps

1. Post the Wonder Statement, *I wonder how some animals find and catch food*, on the wall in the classroom meeting area.

2. Use Google Images to find a photo of an American bullfrog.

3. Purchase enough party blowers for half the students in your class and a box of $\frac{5}{8}$-inch Velcro Sticky Back coins. Use Google Images to find photos of an ant, a spider, and a fly. Print out the photos and make enough color photocopies of the ant and spider for each child in your class. Make enough copies of the fly for half the students in your class. After cutting out the critters, place two ants and two spiders side by side on strips of lightweight cardboard (such as a flap from a gift box). Place the flies on smaller pieces of cardboard and attach a string to the back.

   Next, laminate all the cardboard strips and attach one side of a Velcro coin next to each critter. Attach the opposite side of the Velcro coins to the tips of the party blowers.

Sample insect and spider strips

Adding a Velcro coin to a party blower

4. Write the name of each of the animals mentioned in *Just One Bite* on separate pieces of white drawing paper. Repeat some of the animal names as needed, so that you have enough papers for every child in the class.

5. Create a data table with four columns and twelve rows and title it How Animals Find and Catch Food. Label the columns with the headings "Animal," "What It Eats," "Finds Food With," and "Catches (Grabs) Food With." Using the sample table in this lesson as a guide, add the names of the animals featured in *Just One Bite* to the cells in the first column. Add a piece of double-sided tape to the cells in the second and fourth columns.

6. Make copies of the Lesson 1.2 What It Eats Cards and Lesson 1.2 Catches (Grabs) Food With Cards found in Appendix B. Then laminate the cards and cut them out.

7. Make copies of the Lesson 1.2 Wonder Journal Labels in Appendix B for each child in your class and cut them out.

Engaging Students

Begin the lesson by passing out copies of the Lesson 1.2 Wonder Journal Label with the Wonder Statement written on it. After reading the Wonder Statement with the class, ask your students to add it to their Wonder Journals.

Project the frog image you found earlier onto the interactive whiteboard in your classroom. After your students have identified the animal, ask them if they know what a frog eats and how it catches food. Let the class know that snatching insects with a sticky tongue is harder than it looks. A frog's eyes and tongue must work together. Tell your students that they are about to play a game that will show them just how tricky it is for a frog to catch its dinner.

After encouraging students to buddy up, give each pair a set of the laminated critter cards and one of the party blowers you prepared earlier. Explain that one buddy will pretend to be a frog and use the party blower with Velcro on the end as a tongue. The other buddy will hold the laminated cards for his or her partner. Because ants scurry across the ground, the ant card should be held horizontally. Spiders climb up walls, so that card should be held vertically. Flies whiz through the air, so students should hold the string and let the fly card dangle in the air.

After the student frogs have had a few minutes to practice using their tongues, call each pair to the front of the classroom one at a time. The

Students model a frog catching a fly with its sticky tongue.

frog will get three chances to catch the ants, three chances to catch the spiders, and three chances to catch the fly. Keep track of each team's success rate on chart paper.

When all the frogs have had a chance to catch their dinner, encourage your class to look at the results you've listed on chart paper. Are they surprised by how hard it was to snag their targets with their party-blower tongues? Why do they think frogs are so much better at it? The students may suggest that frogs get lots of practice using their tongues, but guide them to the idea that a frog's brain helps its eyes and tongue work together. Our brains are better at helping our eyes and hands work together.

Exploring with Students

Introduce *A Frog in the Bog* by showing the front cover and asking: *What do you think this story will be about?* Ask students to support their answers with evidence they see on the cover.

After encouraging the students to look closely at the book's title page, ask them: *What other animals live in the bog with the frog? Do you see any animals that the frog might like to eat?* Record all their responses on chart paper.

Write the following three questions on chart paper and read them with your class:

1. What does the frog eat?
2. What body part does the frog use to find its food?
3. What body part does the frog use to catch its food?

Ask your students to count off by threes, and assign each group one of the questions. If students hear the answer to their assigned question as you read *A Frog in the Bog*, they should raise a hand. Choose one student and ask which question is being addressed and what the answer is. Record the responses on chart paper and then continue reading.

To reinforce what students have learned so far in this lesson, pass out copies of the Lesson 1.2 Wonder Journal Labels with the following sentence frames:

A frog depends on its _____ (body part) to find food.

A frog depends on its _____ (body part) and its _____ (body part) to catch food.

Encourage the children to add the sentence frames to their Wonder Journals one at a time, so they have plenty of room to use words and pictures to fill in the blanks.

This Wonder Journal entry shows that a frog uses its eyes to find food and its tongue (tugh) and eyes to catch food.

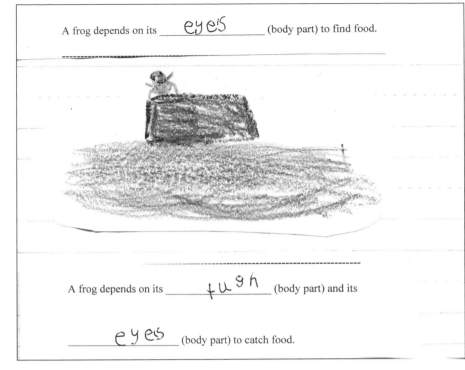

A frog depends on its _____ey e's_____ (body part) to find food.

A frog depends on its _____tu g h_____ (body part) and its

_____e y e's_____ (body part) to catch food.

Now introduce *Just One Bite* by showing the cover and asking your class what they think the book will be about. After recording their ideas on chart paper, begin reading. Be sure to point out what the animals are eating and how much they eat in one scoop, sip, or bite.

When you reach the page with the frog, ask the class: *Is this frog eating the same food as the frog in* A Frog in the Bog? *How is the artwork in this book different from the artwork in* A Frog in the Bog? *Why do you think the illustrators, Joan Rankin and Geoff Waring, decided to use different styles? Which style do you like better?*

When you reach the page with the bear, ask your students if they think the bear eats other foods besides honey. *What else might the bear eat?*

When you finish reading the main text of the book, show your class the How Animals Find and Catch Food data table that you prepared earlier and read the headings and animal names together. After passing out the Lesson 1.2 What It Eats Cards, read the words on the cards with your students. Then look back through the book with your class. When a child spots the illustration that matches the word on his or her card, he or she should come forward and place the card in the proper cell. Next, show your class the back matter and explain that more information about what some animals eat is included in these entries. Read the following sections: Common Octopus, American Black Bear, Reticulated Giraffe, Asian Elephant, Sperm Whale. Encourage students to come forward when they hear the words on their cards.

Teaching Tip

The information about microorganisms in *Just One Bite* is beyond the understanding of most first graders, so you may want to skip it.

Now work with your students to fill in the "Finds Food With" column. *Just One Bite* doesn't provide all the information your students will need. When you see an asterisk (*), ask students for ideas based on their prior knowledge. You may need to guide them to some of the answers.

After passing out the Lesson 1.2 Catches (Grabs) Food With Cards, read the words on the cards with your students. Then look back through the book's main text with the students. When children spot the illustration that matches the body part written on their card, they should come forward and place the card in the proper cell. You will probably have to read the following back matter sections: Common Earthworm, Queen Alexandra Butterfly, Common Octopus, Reticulated Giraffe.

Your final table should look similar to this one:

How Animals Find and Catch Food

Animal	What It Eats	Finds Food With	Catches (Grabs) Food With
Earthworm	Dirt	No need to find food. It is everywhere.	Mouth
Butterfly	Nectar	Antennae*	Proboscis
Frog	Beetles	Eyes	Tongue
Octopus	Crabs, clams, snails	Eyes*	Arms, radula
Parrot	Nuts	Eyes*	Beak
Rabbit	Clover	Nose,* eyes*	Mouth
Komodo dragon	Snake	Nose,* eyes*	Teeth
Bear	Honey, insects, seeds, berries, fish, young deer or elk, garbage	Nose,* eyes*	Tongue, teeth
Giraffe	Leaves, shoots, fruits, seedpods	Eyes*	Upper lip, tongue
Asian elephant	Bamboo, grasses, bark, roots, leaves, herbs, fruit	Eyes*	Trunk
Sperm whale	Giant squid, fish, rays	Sacs in brain sends out click sounds,* teeth and jaws receive echoes and send messages to brain*	Teeth

Now give each student one of the sheets of paper you prepared earlier with the name of an animal from *Just One Bite* printed on it. After each child has drawn his or her assigned animal, read through all the information in the data table with the class. As you mention each animal, students who have drawn that animal should raise a hand. Next, let the class know that you are going to randomly read information from the table. Students should hold their picture high above their heads if they think the information describes their assigned animal.

Encouraging Students to Draw Conclusions

Give each child the Lesson 1.2 Wonder Journal Label that poses the Wonder Statement as a question: *How do some animals find and catch food?*

Encourage your class to focus on the frog entry in the *Just One Bite* data table. Ask them: *Does the frog in* A Frog in the Bog *hunt in the same way as the frog in* Just One Bite? (Yes.) Next, ask: *Why do you think the frogs use their tongues to catch insects? Why don't they chase after their food?*

After students have had a chance to Turn and Talk with a neighbor, invite them to gather for a Science Dialogue. As the students continue the discussion with the larger group, encourage them to provide rationale for their ideas. Then invite other students to respond by questioning the presenters or expanding upon their ideas. To facilitate the discussion, help the students stay focused and restate any unclear comments or ideas.

When the class comes to a consensus, introduce other questions about the body parts animals use to find and catch food. Some possibilities include:

- *Why do you think a giraffe needs a long tongue to grab the leaves of the acacia tree?*
- *Why do you think an octopus has a radula (a tongue with teeth)?*
- *Why do you think a whale uses clicks to find food? Why doesn't it use its eyes?*
- *Why do you think parrots have beaks instead of a mouth with teeth?*
- *How does an elephant use its trunk to get food? How is an elephant's trunk like a giraffe's tongue?*
- *Why do you think a butterfly needs a strawlike proboscis to get nectar from a flower?*

Teaching Tip

Assign each pair of students a different animal-action combination so that the Animal Lunch Quilt features a broad range of interesting animal body parts and behaviors.

To bring the lesson to a close, let your class know that they are going to share what they have learned in this lesson by creating an Animal Lunch Quilt and making it the centerpiece of a fun activity for other students in the school. After students have buddied up, give each child a large, square piece of construction paper and put out a variety of art supplies. Assign each pair of students one of the animals from the data table and one of the food-related actions (finding, catching). Encourage the buddies to work together to create an image that shows how their animal uses its body parts to accomplish the assigned action.

Lessons for Grade 1

An Animal Lunch Quilt

When the students are done, use their drawings to create two similar Animal Lunch Quilts and display them in different areas of the school. Write the following questions above or below the related quilt:

- *Can you find an animal looking for food? What body part is that animal using?*
- *Can you find an animal catching or grasping food? What body part is that animal using?*

Use a digital camera to photograph the quilts, and print copies for your students to add to their Wonder Journals as a permanent record of the investigation.

In this lesson, students learned that animals have body parts that help them find and catch food. With these new insights, students may now begin to wonder how other animals use their own body parts to help them find and catch food. The children should feel free to record these new questions in their Wonder Journals.

Reinforcing the Concept

- You can extend the lesson by reading the following book pairs and discussing the content with the Wonder Statement in mind:
  —*Bear Wants More* by Karma Wilson & *Vulture View* by April Pulley Sayre
  —*Pinduli* by Janell Cannon & *Time to Eat* by Steve Jenkins and Robin Page

- Invite students to select some of the animals they've learned about and make a book of their own with the title *How Animals Find Their Food* or *How Animals Catch Their Food.*
- Create a deck of forty-four cards in which each card includes information from one cell in the How Animals Find and Catch Food data table, and place the deck in your classroom science center. When two or three students have free time, they can use the cards to play a game similar to "Go Fish."

    Using the table in their Wonder Journals as a guide, students remove the Animal Cards from the deck and lay them face up on a table. Then one child deals five cards from the deck to each player.

    Students take turns asking their fellow players for cards that will help them complete a set (three cards from one row in the data table) that describes what one of the eleven animals eats, how it finds food, and how it catches food. If other players do not have the requested card, the student must "go fish." When a player has collected all three cards in one set, he or she should pick up the appropriate Animal Card and place all four cards in a pile. At the end of the game, the student with the most sets of cards wins.

ELA Links   By now, students have learned a lot about how animals find and catch food. Two different books—one fiction, one nonfiction—have played important roles in this lesson. The following questions can help students reflect on the aspects of the featured books that aroused their curiosity, generated and maintained their interest, and enhanced their understanding of the natural world.

- *What do the two books have in common?* (They both include information about what animals eat and how they get their food. Both are illustrated with art.)
- *How are the two books different?* (*A Frog in the Bog* is a fictional story about a frog that eats too much, gets scared, and loses its dinner. *Just One Bite* is nonfiction. It describes what and how much various animals eat.)
- *Look back at the text in* A Frog in the Bog. *Who is telling the story? Who is the main character of the story?*
- *Can you find a few words or sentences in the two books that you especially like? Why do you like them? Do you think the authors of these books chose their words carefully? What is your evidence?*
- *How does the style of the art in each book seem to match the style of the text?* (The art in *A Frog in the Bog* is light and whimsical. It's perfect for the fun, silly text. The large, realistic art in *Just One Bite* has a light-hearted feel to it, which matches the fun approach to the subject matter.)

Lesson 1.3: How Animals Protect Themselves

| *Swimmy* by Leo Lionni | & | *What Do You Do When Something Wants to Eat You?* by Steve Jenkins |

About the Books

In *Swimmy*, a Caldecott Honor Book, delightful art and beautiful, evocative language tell the story of a small fish who devises a clever plan so that he and his fish friends can stay safe while they explore the wonders of their watery world.

The title of *What Do You Do When Something Wants to Eat You?* is a question that we don't have to think about, but most animals do. Using clear, simple text and dynamic, intricate cut-paper collages, Steve Jenkins explores a variety of strange and surprising strategies that animals use to protect themselves from enemies.

Wonder Statement: I wonder how animals protect themselves from predators.

Learning Goal   Because PE 1-LS1-1 draws upon two content-rich, interconnected Disciplinary Core Ideas (LS1.A Structure and Function and LS1.D Information Processing) as well as a challenging engineering practice, we have written five lessons to fully address it. In Lesson 1.1, students gain a basic understanding of animals' key external body parts and how different animals use them to survive or to make their lives easier. Lesson 1.2 explores specific ways animals use their external body parts to find and catch food, while this lesson, 1.3, investigates how animals use their body parts to protect themselves from predators. Lesson 1.4 looks at the structure and function of plant parts. Finally, Lesson 1.5 focuses on the engineering practice by encouraging students to design a solution to a human problem using what they have learned about plants and animals in the previous four lessons.

NGSS Performance Expectation 1-LS1-1. Use materials to design a solution to a human problem by mimicking how plants and/or animals use their external parts to help them survive, grow, and meet their needs.

Prep Steps   1. Post the Wonder Statement, *I wonder how animals protect themselves from predators*, on the wall in the classroom meeting area.

2. Create a data table with two columns and fifteen rows and title it How Animals Protect Themselves. You will add two more columns to this table later, so be sure to leave enough room. In the first row, label one column with the heading "Animal" and the other column with the heading "How Animal Protects Itself." Using the sample table in this lesson as a guide, write *Small fish (Swimmy)* in the first cell in the first column. Then add the names of the animals discussed in *What Do You Do When Something Wants to Eat You?* to the rest of the cells in the first column.

3. Write the name of each of the animals mentioned in *What Do You Do When Something Wants to Eat You?* on separate pieces of white drawing paper. Repeat some of the animal names as needed, so that you have enough papers for every child in the class.

4. Make copies of the Lesson 1.3 Wonder Journal Labels in Appendix B for each child in your class and cut them out. Then make a copy of the 1.3 Wonder Journal Handout, also in Appendix B, for each child.

Engaging Students

Begin the lesson by passing out copies of the Lesson 1.3 Wonder Journal Label with the Wonder Statement written on it. After reading the Wonder Statement with the class, ask your students to add it to their Wonder Journals.

This Wonder Journal entry predicts that a fish uses its mouth to protect itself from predators.

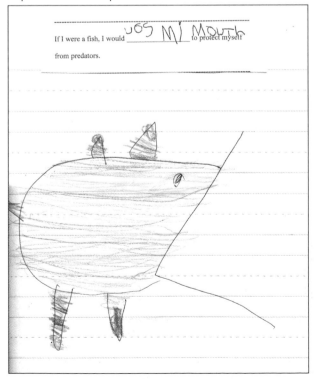

Invite students to pretend they are fish. Will one child volunteer to move like a fish? Will another child describe where he or she lives? Can another student list some of his or her fishy body parts? What do the children think is the greatest danger they might face as a fish?

Invite your class of fish to think about how they might protect themselves from predators. Write their responses on chart paper. Then give each child a copy of the Lesson K.3 Wonder Journal Label with the sentence frame:

If I were a fish, I would _____ to protect myself from predators.

Encourage students to fill in the blank and draw a picture to show how they would protect themselves. They may choose one of the strategies listed on the chart paper or come up with a new idea.

Exploring with Students

Introduce *Swimmy* by asking your class to look at the front cover of the book and locate the fish that looks different from all the others. Tell the children that is Swimmy. Do your students think that looking different from the other fish will help Swimmy stay safe or make him an easier target for predators? Encourage them to Turn and Talk with a buddy to explain why they think Swimmy's appearance will help to protect him or put him in danger. Then record their ideas on a second piece of chart paper.

When this discussion is done, invite the children to look back at their ideas about how they might protect themselves if they were fish. Are there any more ideas they'd like to add to that list? When the class is satisfied, encourage your students to vote for the idea they think Swimmy is mostly likely to use to protect himself. Add the results to the chart paper.

At this point, introduce *What Do You Do When Something Wants to Eat You?* As students examine the front cover of the book, they might notice that a bigger animal is trying to eat a smaller animal, just like in *Swimmy*. The first sentence of the book emphasizes this idea: "Most animals face the constant danger of being eaten by other animals."

The book includes four examples of animals protecting themselves in the ocean: octopus, puffer fish, clown fish, and flying fish. Mark these pages and read them to the class. After reading each page, ask the students: *Could this animal's behavior help Swimmy stay safe? Why or why not?*

Now return to *Swimmy*. After reading the book, invite students to respond to these questions:

- *How did Swimmy protect himself from the big fish that wanted to eat him?*
- *Did looking different from other fish help him stay safe?*
- *Did Swimmy do what you and your Turn and Talk partner predicted before reading the book?*
- *Did Swimmy use any of the ideas we listed on the chart paper?*
- *Do you think a real fish would be more likely to protect itself the way Swimmy did or the way you suggested in your Wonder Journal?*

Next, encourage the class to share ideas and prior knowledge about how other animals protect themselves. The students may be very familiar with some examples, such as skunks and bees. Tell them that they will learn more about how various animals protect themselves from enemies as you read the rest of *What Do You Do When Something Wants to Eat You?*

Because the book is formatted to show an animal being threatened on one page and the animal's defense strategy on the next page, you can make a fun guessing game out of reading the book. Stop after reading each right-hand page and invite a student volunteer to predict how that

Teaching Tip

Some of the vocabulary in *What Do You Do When Something Wants to Eat You?* may be unfamiliar to students in grade one, especially English language learners. When an unfamiliar word (*prey, tentacles, anemone*) arises, write it on an index card and encourage your students to guide you in creating a sketch to help them remember what the word means. Then post the card under the Wonder Statement on the wall.

Teaching Tip

The entries in the sample data table shown on page 115 are fully fleshed out and include all possible answers. You should not expect your class's tables to be as detailed, but they should include enough essential information to fully address the Wonder Statement. Providing students with copies of each data table as soon as possible after the class compiles it will allow each child to keep a record of the investigation in his or her Wonder Journal.

animal will protect itself. Ask the child to explain his or her reasoning by asking: *Why do you think that?*

When you are done reading, show your students the How Animals Protect Themselves data table that you prepared earlier and read the headings and animal names together. As you read through the list a second time, invite students to explain how each animal protects itself, and record their ideas.

A sample data table may look like this:

How Animals Protect Themselves

Animal	How Animal Protects Itself
Small fish (Swimmy)	Travels in schools to look like a bigger fish
Bombardier beetle	Shoots hot chemicals
Puffer fish	Makes itself bigger
Glass snake	Breaks off its tail
Pangolin	Rolls into an armor-plated ball
Basilisk lizard	Runs away on water
Hog-nosed snake	Plays dead
Clown fish	Hides in a sea anemone
Hover fly	Looks like a wasp
Gliding frog	Glides to another tree
Silk moth	Has spots that look like two big eyes
Javanese leaf insect	Looks like a leaf
Flying fish	Leaps out of the water
Blue-tongued skink	Sticks out its large bright-blue tongue

Encouraging Students to Draw Conclusions

Give each child a handout of the class's data table with two additional empty columns, one labeled "Body Part" and the other labeled "Behavior," and the Lesson 1.3 Wonder Journal Label that poses the Wonder Statement as a question: *How do animals protect themselves from predators?*

Ask students to attach the data table to a left-hand page of their Wonder Journal and add the Wonder Journal label with the question on the facing right-hand page. Allow students time to respond to the question individually in their Wonder Journals. Encourage them to use both words and drawings and to choose examples from the data table. They may find it helpful to draw lines from the data table to pictures they drew to show the connections.

Now give each student one of the sheets of paper you prepared earlier with the name of an animal from *What Do You Do When Something Wants to Eat You?* printed on it. Using the How Animals Protect

Two students draw pictures of how their assigned animals protect themselves from enemies.

Themselves data table for reference, the children should draw how their assigned animal protects itself from enemies. Students should feel free to help any classmate who is having difficulty with the task.

When the children have finished their drawings, ask the class to gather for a Science Dialogue. As you add two new columns (one with the heading "Body Part" and the other with the heading "Behavior") to the classroom data table, introduce students to the idea that some animals use an external body part—a part on the outside of the body—to protect themselves from predators. Others use a behavior to stay safe. And some use both a body part and a behavior to avoid being eaten.

Invite students to share their drawings with the class. As each child presents, the rest of the class should think about whether the animal uses a body part, a behavior, or both to stay safe. When the presenter is done, encourage the class to discuss the best way to fill in the new columns of the data table for that animal. Then allow the children a few minutes to make entries in their Wonder Journals as you record the information in the classroom data table.

During this dialogue, students should feel free to ask their classmates questions and agree or disagree with one another. As children contribute to the conversation, they should provide rationale to support their ideas. To facilitate the discussion, help the students stay focused and restate any unclear comments or ideas.

After all the children have presented, ask for a volunteer to complete the table for "Small fish (Swimmy)." Then invite the class to review the entire table. Is there anything they would like to change? Continue the dialogue until everyone is satisfied and the data table is complete.

The final table should look like this:

How Animals Protect Themselves

Animal	How Animal Protects Itself	Body Part	Behavior
Small fish (Swimmy)	Travels in schools to look like a bigger fish		X
Bombardier beetle	Shoots hot chemicals	X	X
Puffer fish	Makes itself bigger		X
Glass snake	Breaks off its tail	X	X
Pangolin	Rolls into an armor-plated ball		X
Basilisk lizard	Runs away on water	X	X
Hog-nosed snake	Plays dead		X
Clown fish	Hides in a sea anemone		X
Hover fly	Looks like a wasp	X	
Gliding frog	Glides to another tree		X
Silk moth	Has spots that look like two big eyes	X	
Javanese leaf insect	Looks like a leaf	X	
Flying fish	Leaps out of the water		X
Blue-tongued skink	Sticks out its large bright-blue tongue	X	X

Lesson 1.3 Wonder Journal Handout

I used to wonder how animals protect themselves from predators.

Now I know that animals have many ways of staying safe.

Some animals use external body parts.

Some animals use behaviors.

Some animals use both.

To bring the lesson to a close, give each student a copy of the Lesson 1.3 Wonder Journal Handout. Encourage the children to model each category on the handout by drawing sample animals under each statement. This is the evidence that supports their claim.

In this lesson, students have learned that animals protect themselves in many different ways. They can use external body parts, behaviors, or a combination of both. With this new insight, students may now begin to wonder how other living things protect themselves. They should feel free to record these new questions in their Wonder Journals.

This Wonder Journal entry shows how animals protect themselves—a puffer fish uses body parts (spines), small fish use a behavior (schooling), and a basilisk lizard uses both (feet, runs across water).

Reinforcing the Concept

- You can extend the lesson by reading the following book pairs and discussing the content with the Wonder Statement in mind:
  —*Monkey: A Trickster Tale from India* by Gerald McDermott & *Never Smile at a Monkey* by Steve Jenkins
  —*Disappearing Desmond* by Anna Alter & *Where in the Wild? Camouflaged Creatures Concealed . . . and Revealed* by David M. Schwartz and Yael Schy
- Invite students to choose one of the animals described in *What Do You Do When Something Wants to Eat You?* and act out its defense strategy. Can other members of the class guess which animal the child is pretending to be?
- Create a bulletin board with the title *How Do Animals Protect Themselves from Predators?* Provide art materials and time for each student to create a representation of how one of the animals they've learned about protects itself from being eaten.

ELA Links

By now, students have learned a lot about how animal body structures and behaviors can help creatures survive. Two different books—one fiction, one nonfiction—have played important roles in this lesson. The following questions can help students reflect on the aspects of the featured books that aroused their curiosity, generated and maintained their interest, and enhanced their understanding of the natural world.

- *What do the two books have in common?* (They include information about ways animals protect themselves.)
- *How are the two books different?* (*Swimmy* is a fictional story in which a fish consciously plans an effective protection strategy. The watercolor paintings are beautiful, but not completely realistic. *What Do You Do When Something Wants to Eat You?* is a fun book that discusses the ways many different animals protect themselves. It features clear, straightforward text with realistic and enticing paper-collage art.)
- *Can fish really plan to form the shape of a bigger fish, with one fish being the eye? Why or why not? Do fish really swim in schools to make the group appear large and scare bigger fish away?*
- *Author Leo Lionni writes that Swimmy saw "an eel whose tail was almost too far away to remember." Is that really true? Why do you think the author used those words?*
- *In* Swimmy, *the watercolor paintings make the ocean seem like a magical place. In* What Do You Do When Something Wants to Eat You? *the paper-collage animals are amazingly detailed and realistic but the backgrounds are just sheets of colored paper. Which art style do you prefer? Why?*
- *The two books have very different endings. Which do you like better? Why?*

Lesson 1.4: How a Plant's Parts Help It Survive

| *Jack's Garden* by Henry Cole | & | *Plant Secrets* by Emily Goodman |

About the Books

With a format echoing the cumulative tale "This Is the House That Jack Built," *Jack's Garden* follows a boy as he plants and tends a backyard garden. Soft colored-pencil artwork highlights the garden's development—seedlings sprout and bud, flowers open, insects and birds visit. Detailed borders feature labeled drawings of tools, insects, birds, eggs, and flowers. The back matter provides instructions for starting a garden.

Plant Secrets features large, bold gouache paintings and a simple text with strong read-aloud potential. Together, text and art describe the life cycles (seed, plant, flower, fruit) of four common plants—pea, oak, tomato, rose.

Additional plants are also shown at each growth stage to emphasize the diversity of the plant world. Rich back matter includes details about each life stage.

Lessons for Grade 1

Wonder Statement: I wonder how a plant's parts help it live, grow, and make more plants.

Learning Goal Because PE 1-LS1-1 draws upon two content-rich, interconnected Disciplinary Core Ideas (LS1.A Structure and Function and LS1.D Information Processing) as well as a challenging engineering practice, we have written five lessons to fully address it. In Lesson 1.1, students gain a basic understanding of animals' key body external parts and how different animals use them to survive or to make their lives easier. Lesson 1.2 explores specific ways animals use their external body parts to find and catch food, while Lesson 1.3 investigates how animals use their body parts to protect themselves from predators. This lesson, 1.4, looks at the structure and function of plant parts. Finally, Lesson 1.5 focuses on the engineering practice by encouraging students to design a solution to a human problem using what they have learned about plants and animals in the previous four lessons.

NGSS Performance Expectation 1-LS1-1. Use materials to design a solution to a human problem by mimicking how plants and/or animals use their external parts to help them survive, grow, and meet their needs.

Prep Steps

1. Post the Wonder Statement, *I wonder how a plant's parts help it live, grow, and make more plants*, on the wall in the classroom meeting area.
2. Buy a packet of lima bean seeds and a small potted plant at a local garden center. Soak the bean seeds overnight before using them in this lesson.
3. Borrow from the school cafeteria enough plastic knives for half of your students.
4. Use Google Images to find photos of rose, oak, pea, and tomato plants as well as their seeds, flowers, and fruits.
5. Make copies of the Lesson 1.4 Wonder Journal Labels in Appendix B for each child in your class and cut them out.

Engaging Students

Begin the lesson by passing out copies of the Lesson 1.4 Wonder Journal Label with the Wonder Statement written on it. After reading the Wonder Statement with the class, ask your students to add it to their Wonder Journals.

Divide the class into pairs and give each pair a lima bean that has been soaked overnight. Tell the children that if they cut the bean in half, they will discover a secret inside. Encourage students to Turn and Talk to their buddies about what they think is hiding inside the seed.

Then pass out copies of the Lesson K.4 Wonder Journal Label that says:

When I cut open a lima bean seed, I think I will find _____.

Encourage students to fill in the blank with words or a picture.

Now give each group a plastic knife, and invite the students to carefully cut the bean in half. (If the children have difficulty cutting the bean, assist them with a sharper knife.) Ask students to observe the inside of the seed closely and draw a picture of what they find inside.

When I cut open a lima bean seed, I think I will

find _____.

A huthr LiYmuBeh

DOt

wet

sluiym

It IS DrIY

DrIY

This Wonder Journal entry shows what a student expects to see inside a lima bean and what she actually observes.

Exploring with Students

Introduce *Plant Secrets* by calling students' attention to the magnifying glass on the cover. Ask them why they think the book's illustrator, Phyllis Limbacher Tildes, included it in her painting. Let the class know that *Plant Secrets* takes an up-close look at all kinds of plants but pays special attention to four familiar ones—rose, oak, pea, and tomato.

On the interactive whiteboard in your classroom, project the plant images you found earlier so students are familiar enough with the seeds, plants, flowers, and fruits to identify them when they appear in the book.

Ask your students if they can think of any secrets these four plants might have. Do they have any questions about these plants? Record their ideas on chart paper.

As you read *Plant Secrets*, encourage the class to look closely at and discuss the artwork. When you reach green text that says, "Next come plants," ask your students: *What plant parts do you see on these pages?* (Leaves, stems.) *How do these parts help plants live and grow?* (Leaves collect sunlight, stems carry water.)

After reading the next double-page spread, ask the class: *Why do you think trees have woody stems?* (To protect and support the tree.) *Why do you think pine trees have needle-like leaves?* (So snow can't rest on top of the leaves and weigh the whole tree down.)

As you read the page that begins, "Plants can grow flowers," point out that flower buds grow out of a plant's stems. Then work with them to identify the four different kinds of flowers shown on the right-hand page. Let them know that many trees have small flowers that they might not even notice, like the ones shown on the oak branch in the picture.

When you reach the page that says, "But all these flowers have a secret," stop reading and invite a few volunteers to guess what the secret might be. Write the children's suggestions on chart paper and ask the class to vote for the one they think is most likely to be correct. Place a check next to that prediction.

Are students surprised by the answer on the next page? Guide them through the text on that page, filling in any additional details they might need to get a basic understanding of pollination. Then work with the class to identify the four different kinds of developing fruits shown on the right-hand page.

One of those four fruits is not shown on the following page. Ask your class: *Which one is missing?* (Rose hip.) You can point out the rose hip on the page that says, "But all these fruits have a secret." Can your students guess what's inside all fruits? If the children struggle to answer this question, encourage them to think about what they see inside apples when they eat them.

After reading the next double-page spread, which says, "Hidden inside fruits are . . . SEEDS!" flip back through the pages of the book and work with your students to create a data table that lists the four plants' secrets mentioned in the book.

Your data table may look like this:

Plant Parts and Secrets

Plant Part	Secret
Seed	Has tiny plant inside
Plant stem	Can grow flowers
Flower	Can make a fruit
Fruit	Has seeds inside

Then encourage the class to think back to the conversation you had while reading the book and ask: *What other plant parts did you discuss?* (Leaves.) *What is a leaf's secret job?* (Collects sunlight.) When students have remembered the answers, add this information to the table.

Next, ask them to look at the second item on the list, "Plant stem." *Does a stem have any other secret jobs that help a plant to live and grow?* (It carries water.) When students have remembered the answer, add this information to the table.

Your final data table may look like this:

Plant Parts and Secrets

Plant Part	Secret
Seed	Has tiny plant inside
Plant stem	Can grow flowers
Flower	Can make a fruit
Fruit	Has seeds inside
Leaf	Collects sunlight

Now introduce *Jack's Garden* by showing the cover and asking: *What do you think Jack will grow in his garden? Do you think it is more likely to have roses or tomatoes? Why? Do you think it is more likely to have pea plants or oak trees? Why?*

As you read the book, encourage students to look closely at the illustrations and notice all the details. When you reach the page that begins, "These are the seedlings," spend some time looking at the plants with the labeled parts. Explain that seed leaves are the first parts of a plant that grow when a seed sprouts.

Next, show the class the potted plant you purchased. Ask the students: *What parts of the plant can you see?* (Stem, leaves, possibly flowers.) *What parts of the plant can you see in the illustration but not by looking at the potted plant?* (Roots.) Pull the plant out of the pot, brush away some of the soil, and show your students the plant's roots.

A student shows her classmates the roots of a plant.

Encourage your students to look back at the *Plant Secrets* data table and review how a plant's leaves and stems (and flowers if the potted plant has them) help it live and grow. Then ask: *Do you see an important plant part that we haven't included in the table yet?* (Yes, the roots.) *How do you think roots help a plant live and grow?*

If your students have difficulty answering this question, guide them to the idea that roots take in water from the soil. Then the water moves into the plant's stems, and the stems deliver the water to the rest of the plant. After you have added this information to the data table, as shown below, continue reading the book.

Plant Parts and Secrets

Plant Part	Secret
Seed	Has tiny plant inside
Plant stem	Can grow flowers
Flower	Can make a fruit
Fruit	Has seeds inside
Leaf	Collects sunlight
Root	Takes in water

After reading the page that begins, "These are the flowers," invite a few volunteers to guess what the text on the next page might be about. Record their ideas on chart paper, and ask the rest of the class to vote for the suggestion they think is most likely to be correct. Place a check next to that idea.

Are students surprised by the answer on the next page? Why do they think the author, Henry Cole, decided to talk about insects instead of fruit?

Now ask your class to predict what the text on the next page might be about. Repeat the process of jotting down a few ideas and asking the class to vote for one of the suggestions.

Are students surprised by the answer on the next page? Ask them: *Why do you think the author is moving the focus of the book away from the plants in the garden?* (Maybe he's trying to show that the insects and birds are also important in a garden.)

When you have finished reading the book, return to the page that begins, "These are the flowers" and read through the text. Then work with your class to rewrite the text on the next three spreads using information in the data table to create an ending that shows how plants make more plants. The final result might look like this:

These are the fruits
that grew from the flowers
that blossomed from the buds
that formed on the plants
that grew from the seedlings
that sprouted with the rain
that wet the seeds
that fell on the soil
that made up the garden
that Jack planted.

These are the seeds
that came from the fruits
that grew from the flowers
that blossomed from the buds
that formed on the plants
that grew from the seedlings
that sprouted with the rain
that wet the seeds
that fell on the soil
that made up the garden
that Jack planted.

And those seeds
grew into even more plants!

Encouraging Students to Draw Conclusions

Give each child the Lesson 1.4 Wonder Journal Label that poses the Wonder Statement as a question: *How do a plant's parts help it live, grow, and make more plants?* Then divide the class into six groups and encourage group members to discuss the question. Let students know that they

Students display their model of a plant's parts.

should consider all six parts listed in the data table—seeds, stems, flowers, fruit, leaves, and roots.

When the students seem ready, invite them to gather for a Science Circle. Assign one of the six plant parts to each group, and ask groups to take turns explaining how their assigned part helps a plant live, grow, and/or make more plants. Because each group discussed all six parts in advance, the entire class should be ready to agree or disagree with the presenters. You should facilitate the discussion by helping children stay focused and reminding them to support their ideas with evidence from the data table.

To bring the lesson to a close, ask the class to reform their small groups. After you set out art materials, each child should create a representation of the group's assigned plant part and a label that specifies how that part helps the plant survive. When the children are done, help them form new groups that include a member from each of the original groups, so that they can assemble a six-part model of a plant on a piece of bulletin-board paper. Then use a digital camera to photograph each group with its plant model. You can print out copies of the photos for the students later so that they can add them to their Wonder Journals as a permanent record of the investigation.

In this lesson, students learned that plants have parts that help them live, grow, and make more plants. With these new insights, students may now begin to wonder why the appearance of a particular part can vary so much from plant to plant. They should feel free to record these new questions in their Wonder Journals.

Reinforcing the Concept

- You can extend the lesson by reading the following book pair and discussing the content with the Wonder Statement in mind:
  —*The Curious Garden* by Peter Brown & *No Monkeys, No Chocolate* by Melissa Stewart
- Invite your students to create visual acrostic poems that describe how a plant's parts help it survive. Here's an example:

  P [picture of a pea flower]
  L [picture of leaf collecting sunlight]
  A [picture of an apple cut in half to show seeds]
  N [picture of nut]
  T [picture of water moving up the trunk of a tall tree]

  When the students are done, you can post their poems on a bulletin board entitled "How a Plant's Parts Help It Live, Grow, and Make More Plants."
- Use Google Images to find an illustration of a plant that has lovely flowers and an extensive root system. Divide the class into two groups. Group A will pretend to be the plant's flowers. Group B will pretend to be the roots. Encourage Group A to act as though they are proud of being so beautiful. Ask them what they think of the roots. Are they as lovely or important? Invite Group B to try to convince the flowers that a plant's roots are just as important as its flowers. As the groups converse with one another, encourage them to back up their statements with evidence from the books they read.

ELA Links

By now, students have learned a lot about how the parts of a plant help it live, grow, and reproduce. Two different books—one fiction, one nonfiction—have played important roles in this lesson. The following questions can help students reflect on the aspects of the featured books that aroused their curiosity, generated and maintained their interest, and enhanced their understanding of the natural world.

- *What do the two books have in common?* (They focus on plants and how they grow. Both books are illustrated with realistic paintings.)
- *How are the two books different?* (*Jack's Garden* is a cumulative poem. It is fiction and has lots of small illustrations around the border of the main illustration. *Plant Secrets* is nonfiction and presents plants as a mysterious life form with lots of secrets. The colorful art is surrounded by a lot of white space.)
- *Look back at the text in* Jack's Garden. *Who is telling the story?* (The author is telling the story. Even though Jack is the main character, we don't really see things from his point of view, and the story has no dialogue.)

- *Both books include back matter. Why do you think the authors felt it was important?*
- *How does the style of the art in each book seem to match the style of the text?* (In *Jack's Garden*, the cumulative poem is playful. The simple, colorful artwork has that same feel to it. *Plant Secrets* is full of interesting facts. The realistic art shows readers exactly what the author is describing.)

Lesson 1.5: Mimicking Plant and Animal Body Parts to Solve Problems

| *Iggy Peck, Architect* by Andrea Beaty | & | *Winter's Tail: How One Little Dolphin Learned to Swim Again* by Juliana Hatkoff, Isabella Hatkoff, and Craig Hatkoff |

About the Books

Since age two, Iggy Peck has had a passion for design, architecture, and engineering, building immense towers from whatever was at hand—fruit, diapers, pancakes. When Iggy enters second grade, his teacher forbids such follies, and Iggy grows bored. But when a rickety footbridge collapses (and so does the teacher) during a class picnic, Iggy saves the day by enlisting his classmates to build a new bridge of shoelaces, tree roots and branches, rulers, and fruit rollups. The rollicking, structured rhymes and crisp, clean pen-and-ink and watercolor illustrations full of humorous details make *Iggy Peck, Architect* a perfect read-aloud for elementary classrooms.

In *Winter's Tail: How One Little Dolphin Learned to Swim Again*, clear, simple text illustrated with copious photos tells the true story of a baby Atlantic bottle-nosed dolphin who lost her tail after becoming entangled in a crab trap. Luckily, Winter was rescued by a fisherman and taken to Clearwater Marine Aquarium, where she learned to swim without her tail. Eventually, she was fitted with a specially-designed artificial tail and learned to use it with the help of her trainers. This heart-warming animal rescue story will appeal to a wide range of young readers.

Wonder Statement: I wonder how people solve problems by designing things that work like plant or animal parts.

Learning Goal   Because PE 1-LS1-1 draws upon two content-rich, interconnected Disciplinary Core Ideas (LS1.A Structure and Function and LS1.D Information Processing) as well as a challenging engineering practice, we have written five lessons to fully address it. In Lesson 1.1, students gain a basic understanding of animals' key external body parts and how different animals use them to survive or to make their lives easier. Lesson 1.2

explores specific ways animals use their external body parts to find and catch food, while Lesson 1.3 investigates how animals use their body parts to protect themselves from predators. Lesson 1.4 looks at the structure and function of plant parts. Finally, this lesson focuses on the engineering practice by encouraging students to design a solution to a human problem using what they have learned about plants and animals in the previous four lessons.

NGSS Performance Expectation 1-LS1-1. Use materials to design a solution to a human problem by mimicking how plants and/or animals use their external parts to help them survive, grow, and meet their needs.

Prep Steps

1. Post the Wonder Statement, *I wonder how people solve problems by designing things that work like plant or animal parts*, on the wall in the classroom meeting area.
2. Bring in a variety of kitchen gadgets or borrow them from your school's lunch workers. Be sure to include the following items: pizza cutter, cheese grater, chopsticks, colander, drinking straw, nut cracker, pepper grinder, potato masher, salad spinner, salad tongs, turkey baster. Make a list of the gadgets' names on a piece of chart paper.
3. Make enough copies of the Lesson 1.5 Body Part Matching Worksheet in Appendix B for all the students in your class.
4. Photocopy and cut out enough of the Lesson 1.5 Steps in the Design Process Cards (see Appendix B) so that each child in your class gets an individual card. Then photocopy the five different Lesson 1.5 Design Task Worksheets (see Appendix B), making enough copies of each one for students on the related design team.
5. Copy the Plant/Animal Part and Use data table in the "Encouraging Students to Draw Conclusions" section of the lesson onto a piece of chart paper. Then use Google Images to find photos of the five plant and animal parts listed in the left-hand column. Print out the photos, so you can add them to the table as you present it to the class.
6. Make copies of the Lesson 1.5 Wonder Journal Labels in Appendix B for each child in your class and cut them out.

Engaging Students

Begin the lesson by passing out copies of the Lesson 1.5 Wonder Journal Label with the Wonder Statement written on it. After reading the Wonder Statement with the class, ask your students to add it to their Wonder Journals.

Show the class the kitchen gadgets you collected earlier. Explain that *gadget* is a fun word that people use to describe a device that solves a problem and makes it easier for people to do a job. Show the class a pizza cutter and a cheese grater. Explain that both of these gadgets were designed to cut up food, so that it's easier to eat.

Some gadgets, like the pizza cutter, have moving parts, but others, like the cheese grater, don't. Some gadgets are electronic, like a battery charger, or have a motor, like a weed whacker. Write the word *gadget* on an index card, and encourage your students to guide you in creating a sketch to help them remember what the word means. Then post the card under the Wonder Statement on the wall.

Let the class know that every gadget has a name. In many cases (but not all), the name consists of two words. For kitchen gadgets, one of the words is often the name of a food. The other word often describes an action that changes the food in a way that makes it easier to cook or eat. Use the pizza cutter and cheese grater as examples.

Divide the class into small groups and give each group one of the kitchen gadgets you collected earlier. (Do not hand out the pizza cutter or cheese grater or any other gadgets with sharp parts.) Invite students to hold and operate each gadget for about ten seconds before passing it to a different group member. When everyone in a group has examined a gadget, the group should exchange gadgets with another group until the entire class has handled all the gadgets.

After returning each gadget to its original group, encourage students to Turn and Talk about what they think the device is called and how it is used. Show the class the list of gadget names that you wrote out earlier on chart paper. Read through the list with your students and let them know that all the devices you've brought to class are on the list. Then work with your students to match the names on the list with each group's device.

Now hold up the pizza cutter again and say: *The sharp edge of a pizza cutter breaks apart food, so it's easier to eat. Can you think of a body part in lions and alligators that does the same job?* (Teeth.) *The pizza cutter's sharp edge works like, or mimics, the sharp teeth of lions, alligators, and other hunters.* Write the word *mimic* on an index card, and add a quick sketch to help your students remember what the word means. Then post the card under the Wonder Statement.

Place the chopsticks, colander, drinking straw, nut cracker, pepper grinder, potato masher, salad spinner, salad tongs, and turkey baster on a table where all students have access to them. Let the class know that each of these gadgets functions like the body part of an animal they learned about in Lessons 1.1 or 1.2.

After giving each child a copy of the Lesson 1.5 Body Part Matching Worksheet that you photocopied earlier, read through the directions as well as the lists of animal parts and kitchen gadgets with your class. Review the meanings of *proboscis, gizzard,* and any other words you think students might not remember from earlier lessons.

Then encourage the children in each group to work together to complete the worksheet.

If students seem to be struggling, remind them of the following:

- A butterfly uses its proboscis to sip nectar.
- A pelican's beak traps food inside and lets water drain out.
- An earthworm doesn't have teeth, so it depends on its gizzard to grind up food.
- An octopus uses its arms to grab food.
- A parrot's hard beak is perfectly designed for cracking nuts.

When the children have finished the activity, review the way each animal uses its body part and the possible matches from the gadget list. Allow students time to "fix" their matches, if they choose, and add the worksheets to their Wonder Journals. Then let the class know that you're going to read two books that describe how people design and build things to solve problems. In the first book, people create a gadget that solves an animal's problem.

Exploring with Students

Introduce *Winter's Tail: How One Little Dolphin Learned to Swim Again* by showing your class the front cover and reading the title. What kind of animal do your students think the people in the book are going to help?

Encourage the children to look closely at the cover photograph. What do they think people in the book are going to design and build to help the dolphin? Next, show the class the title page. Does it provide any additional clues?

Skip the note from the authors in blue type and the page that begins "One cold winter morning . . ." After reading the page that starts with "December 10, 2005," ask your class: *What happened to the dolphin?* (She got tangled in a crab trap.)

Read the next four double-page spreads. When you reach the paragraph that ends, "Winter was a quick and enthusiastic learner," ask the class: *What problem does Winter face?* (Her tail fell off, and she is swimming the wrong way. Swimming like a fish could damage Winter's backbone.)

After reading the page that shows Winter's prosthetic tail, ask students the following questions and record their responses on chart paper:

- Who were some of the members of the team that solved Winter's problem? (Kevin Carroll, vets, dolphin trainers, scientists.)
- Why did the team include so many people? (Each one had special skills that the project required.)
- *What challenges were involved in designing a prosthesis for Winter?* (It had to work in water. It had to withstand the force of thrusting up and down.)

- *What was the team's first step?* (Brainstorming—sharing ideas about how to create the best prosthesis for Winter.)

Now begin a table like the one that follows, focusing on the problems the team faced while designing and building the prosthesis and how they dealt with each challenge. Work with your students to complete the table as you read the next two double-page spreads.

Design Problems and Solutions for Winter's Tail

Problem	Solution
No tail joint for attaching the prosthesis	Made a mold of her tail stub and created a sleeve that fit her body perfectly
Worried about irritating Winter's skin	Developed special silicone gel that made prosthesis comfortable
The prosthesis must mimic real tail movements	After several tries, developed a design with two sleeves
Winter might not like wearing the prosthesis	Trainers worked with Winter

Teaching Tip

The entries in the sample data tables shown here are fully fleshed out and include all possible answers. You should not expect your class's tables to be as detailed, but they should include enough essential information to fully address the Wonder Statement. Providing students with copies of each data table as soon as possible after the class compiles it will allow each child to keep a record of the investigation in his or her Wonder Journal.

After you finish reading the main text, ask your class the following questions and record the answers on a piece of chart paper:

- *How did the people in this book solve Winter's problem?* (They designed a prosthetic tail and trained Winter to use it.)
- *How did Winter's prosthetic tail mimic, or work in the same way as, a real dolphin tail?* (It powered Winter through the water by moving up and down.)

Finally, turn to the back matter section entitled "Kevin Carroll and Hanger Prosthetics & Orthotics." After paraphrasing the information in this section in student-friendly language, ask the following questions:

- *Was Kevin the only person from Hanger Prosthetics & Orthotics involved in solving Winter's problem?*
- *What do you think are the advantages of working as part of a team?*

Introduce *Iggy Peck, Architect* by showing the front cover and asking your students what they think the book will be about. What role do they think the boy on the cover will play in the story? What about the woman? The cat? The birds? Do they have any new ideas after seeing the book's back cover and title page? Do they think the toddler on the title page is related to the boy on the cover? What do they have in common? How are they different?

After reading the first double-page spread of *Iggy Peck, Architect*, ask your students what they notice about the sound of the text as you read the words. (It rhymes and has a structured, singsong rhythm.) Invite a few volunteers to identify their favorite lines of text. Then ask the class what *Ignacious* means and how it's being used. (It's the boy's name, and his nickname is Iggy.) Do the children think Iggy's mother is happy about his interest in building things? What is their evidence?

As the story progresses, ask if the parents seem pleased with Iggy's interest in designing and building towers and other structures? What evidence does the class see to support their ideas?

What does Iggy's second-grade teacher, Miss Lila Greer, think of Iggy's buildings? Why doesn't Miss Greer like tall buildings?

After reading the page that begins "They crossed an old trestle," start a data table like the one below. As you read the next two double-page spreads, work with your students to complete the table. Encourage the children to look for materials in the pictures as well as in the words.

Your final data table may look like this:

Design Problems and Solutions for Iggy's Bridge

Problem	Solution
The class is stranded after the bridge collapses.	Iggy designs a new bridge.
The new bridge must be made from available materials.	The class works together to construct a bridge using shoes/boots, tree branches, tree roots, grass, shoelaces, string, rulers, underwear, fruit rollups.

Encourage your class to look back at the four questions and their answers you recorded on chart paper while reading *Dolphin's Tail*. Then ask the following related questions and record the answers on a second piece of chart paper:

- *In* Iggy Peck, Architect, *who solved the problem?* (Iggy and his classmates.)
- *What challenges did Iggy and his classmates face when designing a new bridge?* (It had to be strong enough to support the weight of the heaviest person—Miss Greer. It had to be made of materials in their immediate environment.)
- *What was the group's first step?* (Iggy shared his design with his classmates.)

Finally, ask the students to consider two more questions:

- *Do Iggy and his classmates use any plant parts to build the bridge?* (Yes.)
- *Do the second graders use the plant parts in ways that mimic the role the plant parts play in helping a plant live and grow?* (No.) *What is the evidence for your answer?*

**Encouraging
Students to Draw
Conclusions**

Give each child the Lesson 1.5 Wonder Journal Label that poses the Wonder Statement as a question: *How do people solve problems by designing things that work like plant or animal parts?*

Write the following steps on a fresh piece of chart paper, and let your class know that they represent the steps scientists and engineers usually follow when designing and building something new:

1. Identify a Problem
2. Identify Challenges
3. Share Ideas
4. Design
5. Build
6. Test

After giving each child one of the Steps in the Design Process Cards that you prepared earlier, encourage the students to add the cards to their Wonder Journals. Then read through the six-step process with your class and point out the connection to the steps you wrote on chart paper.

Now write the following questions on a separate piece of chart paper and introduce them to your class one at a time. After reading each question with your students, encourage them to Turn and Talk with a partner as they think it through. Then invite the entire class to share their ideas before moving on to the next question.

1. *How is the problem in* Iggy Peck, Architect *similar to the problem in* Winter's Tail? (Something needs to be built.)
2. *Look back at the questions you answered after reading each book. How are the challenges each group faced similar?* (The prosthesis and the bridge both had to accomplish specific goals. For example, the prosthesis had to be strong and work in water. The bridge had to be strong and built with limited materials.)
3. a. *Did the groups in the two books share ideas at the same point in the process?* (No. In *Winter's Tail,* the brainstorming came before the tail was designed. In *Iggy Peck, Architect,* Iggy designed the bridge all by himself and then shared the design with his classmates.)
   b. *Why do you think the process described in* Winter's Tail *is more like the process scientists and engineers usually follow?* (Because *Winter's Tail* is nonfiction. It describes a real-world design project.)
4. a. *Do we see the initial design plan in both books?* (We see Iggy's design plan drawn on the ground. We do not see a visual model of the tail's design. We only see the final product.)
   b. *Why do you think we don't see it in* Winter's Tail? (Maybe there was no photo available.)

5. *Who built the new gadget or structure described in each book?* (Iggy and his classmates worked together to collect materials and build the bridge. Kevin Carroll and his coworkers at Hanger Prosthetics & Orthotics built and assembled the parts of the prosthesis.)
6. *Did the groups in the two books test what they built in the same way?* (Yes, they tried it out.)

Now that your students understand the design process, divide them into five design teams and give the members of each team the appropriate Lesson 1.5 Design Task Worksheet, which you photocopied in advance. Ask students to add the worksheet to their Wonder Journals

Next, draw the class's attention to the Plant/Animal Part and Use data table, which you copied onto chart paper in preparation for the lesson, and point out that it's the same as the data table on their Design Task Worksheet.

Plant/Animal Part and Use

Plant/Animal Part	How It Is Used
Tree trunk [photo]	Carries water from the tree's roots to its leaves
Tree roots [photo]	Soak up water
Mole nose [photo]	Has sensors that help a mole avoid getting lost in underground tunnels
Anteater tongue [photo]	Sticks way out to catch food
Gecko feet [photo]	Walk up walls and across ceilings, so a gecko can find food and escape from enemies

As you read through the entries in the classroom data table, add the photos you found and printed in advance. Remind the class that the information in the data table comes from the books they explored during Lessons 1.1 and 1.4.

Explain that each team's Design Task Worksheet has a different design problem. After reading through the design problem text with each team, encourage team members to work together to design a solution to their problem. But here is their challenge: The solution must be a gadget that mimics, or works in the same way as, one of the plant or animal parts in the Plant/Animal Part and Use data table.

Ask students to review the six-step design process one more time. Explain that since they now know the problem (Step 1) and the challenge (Step 2), each team should brainstorm to share ideas on small, handheld whiteboards (Step 3) as they develop a design. Encourage the children to use their imaginations for this activity. Let them know that even though Iggy's classmates and the people in *Winter's Tail* built and tested their designs, the class's final step will be to draw a visual model

Lessons for Grade 1

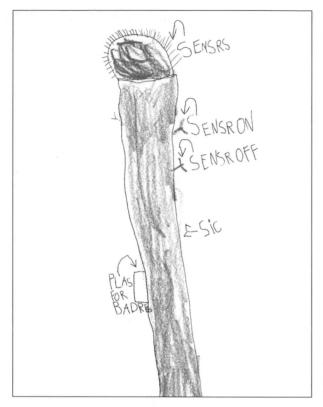

SENSRS

SENSR ON

SENSR OFF

SiC

PLAS FOR BADRE

of their group's design (Step 4) in their Wonder Journals. Students may also enjoy giving their gadgets a name.

To bring the lesson to a close, invite the groups to take turns sharing their visual models with the class. As the children present, encourage them to explain their designs and how they mimic the actions of their chosen plant or animal parts.

In this lesson, students learned that people design and build things to solve problems and make our lives easier. They also designed their own gadget that functions like a plant or animal part to solve a specific problem. With these new insights, students may now begin to wonder about other kinds of gadgets that mimic animal or plant parts. They should feel free to record their new questions and ideas in their Wonder Journals.

This labeled drawing shows a gadget that works like a mole's nose to help a person move safely in a darkened room. Notice the electric sensor and battery box.

Reinforcing the Concept

- You can extend the lesson by reading the following book pairs and discussing the content with the Wonder Statement in mind:
  —*Baby Brains and RoboMom* by Simon James & *How Ben Franklin Stole the Lightning* by Rosalyn Schanzer
  —*Papa's Mechanical Fish* by Candace Fleming & *Neo Leo: The Ageless Ideas of Leonardo da Vinci* by Gene Barretta

- Provide students with art materials and invite each group to create a poster that advertises their new gadgets. As each group shares their poster with the rest of the class, record them with the video setting on a digital camera. Then use an inexpensive video-editing program to create a class commercial for the new products.

- After sharing several product user manuals with your class, invite students to work individually or in pairs to write and illustrate a simple user manual for the gadget they designed. The manual should include a diagram of the gadget with its parts labeled and directions for using it. Encourage students to come up with a name for their gadget that incorporates the plant or animal part that inspired its design.

ELA Links By now, students have learned a lot about the design process employed by scientists and engineers. Two different books—one fiction, one non-fiction—have played important roles in this lesson. The following questions can help students reflect on the aspects of the featured books that aroused their curiosity, generated and maintained their interest, and enhanced their understanding of the natural world.

- *What do the two books have in common?* (They are both about designing and building things.)
- *How are the two books different?* (*Iggy Peck, Architect* is a fictional story told in rhyming couplets. It features humorous artwork. *Winter's Tail* is a nonfiction story that describes how people created a prosthetic tail for a real dolphin. It has clear, straightforward text and photos.)
- *Can you find a few words or sentences in the two books that you especially like? Why do you like them? Which author do you think has more fun playing with language?* (Andrea Beaty.) *Why?*
- Winter's Tail *has three authors. Do you think that made the book easier or more difficult to write?*
- *Do you think the publishing team chose the right style of art for each book?* (Yes, the humorous paintings in *Iggy Peck, Architect* are a perfect match for the book's fun, rhyming writing. Photos make sense in *Winter's Tail* because readers will want to see what Winter and people in the story and the prosthetic tail really look like.)
- *Why do you think the Hatkoffs included so much back matter in* Winter's Tail? (They thought people might have questions after reading the book, so they wanted to add lots of background information to answer those questions.)

Lesson 1.6: How Animal Parents and Young Interact

What Dads Can't Do by Douglas Wood & *Little Lost Bat* by Sandra Markle

About the Books

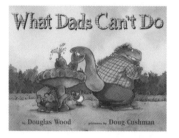

What Dads Can't Do is a delightful, tongue-in-cheek tale that spotlights the rapport between a patient dinosaur dad and his child. The young narrator shares his insights into the things "that regular people can do but dads can't," such as cross the street without holding hands and play hide-and-seek without always getting found. This amusing picture book will tickle youngsters' funny bones and make them smile with recognition. Large, wry watercolor and pen-and-ink art perfectly captures the loving dynamic between parent and child.

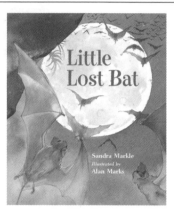

In *Little Lost Bat*, lucid free verse and shadowy watercolors offer a bat's eye view of a Mexican free-tailed bat colony near Austin, Texas, focusing on one female and her newborn pup. Young readers will be fascinated to discover how mama and baby interact and bond, and then heartbroken when the female is killed by a barn owl. The baby bat waits and waits for his mama, nearly starving to death. But then a female who has lost her own pup feeds the baby and takes over the role of caring for him.

Wonder Statement: I wonder how some animal parents help their young grow up.

Learning Goal   In this lesson, students learn that the interactions between young animals and their parents help the offspring survive by focusing on the behaviors of (1) a mother bat and her pup and (2) a humanlike dinosaur dad and his son.

NGSS Performance Expectation 1-LS1-2. Read texts and use media to determine patterns in behavior of parents and offspring that help offspring survive.

Prep Steps
1. Post the Wonder Statement, *I wonder how some animal parents help their young grow up*, on the wall in the classroom meeting area.
2. Use Google Images to find pictures of the following six animals: golden jackal, marmoset monkey, sand grouse, alligator, panda, emperor penguin.

3. Write the six animal names on index cards (one name per card). Then write the following statements on a piece of chart paper in random order:

    •   When this dad returns from hunting, his hungry babies lick his face until he throws up his meal. Then the youngsters gobble up the food.

    •   This dad keeps his twin babies clean, plays with them, and carries them around on his back.

    •   On hot days, this dad cools off by soaking his belly feathers in a water hole. When he returns to his nest, his thirsty chicks peep until he lets them suck his feathers dry.

    •   This mom buries her eggs and then stands guard. When she hears the hatchlings grunt, she digs them up and carries them to water.

    •   This mom licks poop from her baby's bottom after every meal. It keeps their home clean and prevents enemies from sniffing them out.

    •   This mom may travel more than seventy miles to find food. When she hears her little one's hungry peeps, she throws up her last meal and pours the mushy mash into her youngster's mouth.

4. Obtain a copy of *March of the Penguins* or find short video clips that explain the role of both emperor penguin parents and young in guaranteeing the chick's survival.

5. Prepare a set of Yes/No/Maybe cards for each student in your class by cutting sheets of green (Yes), red (No), and yellow (Maybe) construction paper into 4-by-4-inch pieces. If you laminate the cards, you can use them over and over.

6. Make copies of the Lesson 1.6 Wonder Journal Labels in Appendix B for each child in your class and cut them out.

Engaging Students   Begin the lesson by passing out copies of the Lesson 1.6 Wonder Journal Label with the Wonder Statement written on it. After reading the Wonder Statement with the class, ask your students to add it to their Wonder Journals.

As you project the animal images you found earlier on the classroom interactive whiteboard, write the name of each animal on chart paper. Then ask your class what they think all these animals have in common.

Let your class know that many animals never meet their parents. Most insects, fish, frogs, salamanders, lizards, turtles, and snakes hatch from eggs and face life completely alone. But all of the animals you showed them spend a lot of time and energy taking care of their young. They develop a relationship with their little ones, and the parents and young learn to respond to one another in a way that keeps the offspring safe and healthy.

A student places his group's animal card next to the matching description.

Divide the class into six groups, and give each group one of the index cards you prepared earlier. After reading through the statements you wrote on chart paper, explain that each statement describes how one of the six animal parents on the students' index cards responds to its youngsters' actions in a way that helps the offspring survive.

Once group members have had time to discuss which statement matches the animal on their index card, ask one member of each group to come forward and, using double-sided tape, place the group's card next to the statement the group chose. If two groups choose the same statement, encourage the students to discuss their reasoning and then move their index cards as they see fit.

Show each animal image again, and identify the statement that matches each creature. Correct the placement of animal names on the chart as necessary.

Exploring with Students

Introduce *What Dads Can't Do* by showing the front cover. Ask your class the following questions:

- *What kind of animal is shown on the cover?*
- *What does it look like the dad is doing?*
- *What do you think this book will be about?*
- *Do you think it will be funny or serious?*
- *Do you think it will be fiction or nonfiction? Why?*

Teaching Tip

To reduce the time students have to wait while you add information to the data table, consider preparing sentence strips with statements from the first column ahead of time. You can reuse the sentence strips for the review activity that follows.

Guide your students to the idea that children's book creators often use animal characters to stand in for humans. One indication that this will be the case in *What Dads Can't Do* is that the characters are wearing clothes. Can the class think of other stories in which animal characters are used instead of people?

As you read the book, ask your students who is narrating the story. Do your students agree with his statements? Why do they think the narrator has this point of view? If your students struggle to answer these questions, help them to see that the dad is pretending so that his child will feel more grown up and capable. Why do they think the author, Douglas Wood, decided to write the book in this way?

When you have finished reading *What Dads Can't Do*, work with your students to create a data table that lists how the dad's behaviors help his son learn important skills, stay safe and healthy, and have fun.

Your final data table may look like this:

What Dad Does to Help His Son

Dinosaur Dad . . .	So His Son . . .
Holds hands when crossing the street	Stays safe
Pushes the swing, but doesn't swing himself	Has fun
Pitches and hits a baseball softly	Has fun
Gets found in hide-and-seek, but can't find his son	Has fun
Wrestles gently	Stays safe
Lets son win games	Has fun
Lets son comb his hair and watch him shave	Knows how to stay healthy
Goes camping and fishing with son	Has fun
Needs help cooking	Knows how to stay healthy
Has fun	Has fun
Needs help organizing	Learns that skill
Drives slowly	Stays safe
Spends money easily	Has everything he needs
Doesn't notice his son hiding lima beans	Has fun
Eats lots of dessert	Has fun
Gives his son a bath	Knows how to stay healthy
Reads to son	Has fun
Kisses son good night	Feels happy and safe
Leaves night-light on, checks for monsters	Feels safe

To review the information in the data table, write the three headings "Stay Safe/Feel Safe," "Stay Healthy," and "Just for Fun" on a piece of chart paper. Invite your students to hunt for items in the data table that fit into each of these three categories. As they call out ideas, quickly jot them down to create three lists like the ones shown on the next page.

Stay Safe/Feel Safe

Holds hands crossing street
Wrestles gently
Drives slowly
Spends money
Kisses son good night
Leaves night-light on, checks
    for monsters
Kisses son good night

Stay Healthy

Lets son comb hair and watch
    him shave
Lets son help cook
Gives bath
Spends money

Just for Fun

Pushes swing
Plays baseball, hide-and-seek
Lets son win games
Goes camping and fishing
Spends money
Ignores son hiding lima beans
Eats lots of dessert
Reads to son
Kisses son good night

Teaching Tip

Some of the vocabulary in *Little Lost Bat* may be unfamiliar to first graders, especially English language learners. When an unfamiliar word (*membrane, roost, echo, prey*) arises, write it on an index card and encourage your students to guide you in creating a sketch to help them remember what the word means. Then post the card under the Wonder Statement on the wall.

Teaching Tip

The entries in the sample data tables shown here are fully fleshed out and include all possible answers. You should not expect your class's tables to be as detailed, but they should include enough essential information to fully address the Wonder Statement. Providing students with copies of each data table as soon as possible after the class compiles it will allow each child to keep a record of the investigation in his or her Wonder Journal.

When you've finished the lists, ask the children these questions: *Do any of the examples from the book fit into more than one category?* (Goodnight kisses are fun, and they make children feel safe. Spending money fits into all three categories.) *Are there any examples that don't fit into any of these categories?* (Organizing.) *If so, why don't they fit?*

Can your students think of things their own parents do to help them stay safe, stay healthy, and have fun? Add their ideas to the lists.

Now introduce *Little Lost Bat* by showing the front cover and asking: *What do you think this story will be about?* Ask students to support their answers with evidence they see in the painting. Now show the back cover of the book. Does it give the children any new ideas? Who do they think will be the main character of this nonfiction story?

To give your students a sense of how crowded and chaotic a real bat colony can be, look online for a video clip of bat activity inside a cave. Ask the class to think about how difficult it must be for a mother bat to find her pup in that setting.

Before you begin reading, let your class know that *Little Lost Bat* has a sad middle but a happy ending. Encourage the class to look for ways that the behaviors of the baby bat and its mother help the youngster survive.

When you read the page where the mother bat leaves the cave to go hunting, ask your students how they think the mother bat is going to find her baby in a cave where there are millions of baby bats. Record their suggestions on chart paper.

After you've finished the story, be sure to read the author's note, which explains that some baby bats really do get "adopted" by females who have lost their own pups. Then return to the beginning of the book and guide your class in creating two data tables. In the first table, list examples of how the mama bat behaves to help her pup survive. In the second table, describe what the baby bat does to stay safe and how the way he responds to his real mother and his "adoptive" mother help him survive.

Sample data tables may look like this:

How Mama Bat Helps Her Baby

Mama Bat . . .	So Baby Bat . . .
Makes noises before baby is born	Learns to recognize her
Folds her tail membrane around baby	Won't fall and be eaten by predators
Nudges baby	Crawls up her chest and starts to drink milk
Flies to baby a few times a day	Drinks enough milk to survive
Hunts at night	Gets the food and care he needs
Returns to the cave often	Drinks enough milk to survive
Makes high-pitched calls and then listens	Doesn't get lost
Rubs scent on baby	Doesn't get lost
Cuddles baby	Feels safe

How Baby Bat Helps Himself

Baby Bat . . .	So He . . .
Huddles with other baby bats	Stays safe
Listens for high-pitched calls and then calls back	Can find his mama
Scrambles toward female bats returning to cave	Can get food from his mama
Grabs cave ceiling	Won't fall and be eaten by predators
Cries for mama, searches for her	Can get the food and care he needs
Answers another mama bat's calls	Can get the food and care he needs

When the data tables are complete, choose four examples from each table and write them on separate index cards. Divide the class into eight groups, and give each group one card. Working together, the members of each group should think of a way to act out the example on their index card.

When the groups seem ready, invite them to come forward one at a time and act out the information on their index card. Encourage the rest of the class to match the group's actions with the correct item in the data tables.

Encouraging Students to Draw Conclusions

Give each child the Lesson 1.6 Wonder Journal Label that poses the Wonder Statement as a question: *How do some animal parents help their young grow up?*

After showing your class sections of *March of the Penguins* or the short video clips of emperor penguins you found earlier, work with the students to create two data tables like the ones you completed after reading *Little Lost Bat*. You may have to replay relevant video footage several times as you fill in the information on penguin parents and their young.

Now give each student a set of the Yes/No/Maybe cards you prepared earlier. Read through the information in the data tables from *Little Lost*

Bat, one row at a time. As you go, ask students if each behavior is similar to the penguins' behaviors. If they think the answer is yes, they should hold up their green cards. If they think the answer is *no*, they should hold up their red cards. And if they aren't sure, they should hold up their yellow *maybe* cards. You may wish to occasionally choose student volunteers to explain their thinking.

Next, work with your students to sort the penguin data into the three lists you created after reading *What Dads Can't Do* (Stay Safe/Feel Safe, Stay Healthy, Just for Fun). After reviewing the lists, ask the class: *Do the penguins' behaviors seem more similar to the bats' behaviors or the dino-human behaviors?*

Invite the class to gather for a Science Dialogue, and explain that because human children take much longer to grow up than other animals, they spend a lot more time living with their parents. And that means parents have time to teach their children skills that can help them survive later in life.

Encourage your class to look back at the data table from *What Dads Can't Do*. Ask students whether there are any entries that involve learning skills, and record their responses on chart paper.

Next, ask the students to think carefully about the list of fun activities that the dino-human dad does with his son. Then ask: *Will any of those activities help the son develop skills that he can use later in life?*

As the students discuss this question, they should feel free to agree or disagree with one another. They may also ask their classmates follow-up questions. Facilitate the discussion by helping children on both sides of a debate provide rationale for their ideas. If the students get off track, gently guide them toward the idea that activities such as playing games and reading can help children develop skills that will help them when they are adults.

To bring the lesson to a close, give each child copies of the Lesson 1.6 Wonder Journal Labels with the following prompts:

An animal parent's behaviors can help its young survive in the world.
My evidence is:

A young animal's behaviors can help it survive in the world.
My evidence is:

Encourage the children to add the prompts to their Wonder Journals one at a time, so they have plenty of room to draw a picture and write a sentence as one piece of evidence for each statement.

In this lesson, students learned that animal parents, including humans, help their young grow and stay safe and that the behaviors of the young also help them survive. They also discovered that human parents help their children stay safe while they enjoy fun activities and gain

This Wonder Journal entry shows how a baby bat survives by responding to its mother's behaviors.

A young animal's behaviors can help it survive

in the world. My evidence is:

If iŧz Mommy Getz eŧin
it Crolz to the Frut of the Cave
and Waŧ$ for a noo Msm

skills. With these new insights, students may now begin to wonder how other animal parents and young interact as the youngsters grow up. They should feel free to record these new questions in their Wonder Journals.

Reinforcing the Concept

- You can extend the lesson by reading the following book pairs and discussing the content with the Wonder Statement in mind:
  —*What Moms Can't Do* by Douglas Wood & *A Mother's Journey* by Sandra Markle
  —*Do Kangaroos Wear Seatbelts?* by Jane Kurtz & *What to Expect When You're Expecting Joeys* by Bridget Heos
- Search online for a variety of short video clips that show young mammals, reptiles, fish, or birds interacting with their parents. You could try the following keyword searches: "alligator mother responding to hatchlings," "father penguin feeds its chick," "inside a Mexican free-tailed bat cave." After sharing the videos with your students, ask the following questions:

> —*How do the young animal and parent in the video work together to help the youngster survive?*
>
> —*How is the behavior of the young animal(s) in the video similar to the behavior of a baby Mexican free-tailed bat and/or an emperor penguin chick?*
>
> —*How is the behavior of the parent in the video similar to the behavior of a mother bat or the penguin parents?*

- Divide the class into several groups and assign each group a section of a classroom bulletin board. Allow each group to choose one of the dino-human behaviors included in the lesson data table. Then set out a variety of art materials and invite the children to work together in creating a class mural that shows how humans care for their young.

- Invite students to create a Mother's Day or Father's Day card from a young bat, emperor penguin, golden jackal, marmoset monkey, sand grouse, alligator, or panda to its parent. On the front, students can draw a picture showing one of the ways that a parent helps its young survive. On the inside, the children can write a thank-you message for that action.

ELA Links   By now, students have learned some of the ways animal parents and their young interact to help the offspring survive. Two different books—one fiction, one nonfiction—have played important roles in this lesson. The following questions can help students reflect on the aspects of the featured books that aroused their curiosity, generated and maintained their interest, and enhanced their understanding of the natural world.

- *What do the two books have in common?* (They both describe how a parent helps its young grow up. They are both illustrated with paintings.)

- *How are the two books different?* (*What Dads Can't Do* is a fictional story that is silly and sweet at the same time. The art is simple and there is a lot of white space on the pages. It is a story about a humanlike animal dad. *Little Lost Bat* is nonfiction, but it still tells a story. It describes how two female bats—a real mother and an adoptive mother—take care of and interact with a baby bat. Most of the art consists of shadowy full-bleed paintings, and sometimes we see the bats up close.)

- *Can you find a few words or sentences in the two books that you especially like? Why do you like them? Which author do you think has more fun playing with language?* (Sandra Markle.) *Why?* (Her language is more lyrical.)

- *Why does author Sandra Markle include a Resources section in* Little Lost Bat? (So readers know where to go if they want to learn more about bats.)

Lesson 1.7: How Young Animals Are Like Their Parents

Just Like My Papa by Toni Buzzeo	&	*What Bluebirds Do* by Pamela F. Kirby

About the Books

In *Just Like My Papa*, simple, lyrical prose and warm, friendly acrylic illustrations chronicle a day in the life of an adult male lion and his son. The compelling story perfectly blends a fictional narrative about a cub's charming attempts to follow in his father's footsteps and factual information about a lion pride's habitat and behavior.

In *What Bluebirds Do*, young readers get a front-row seat to witness what goes on in the life of young bluebirds and their parents. Clear, simple text and brilliantly sharp, close-up photos combine to create an enthralling introduction to a common North American bird. Back matter includes information about attracting and supporting bluebirds.

Wonder Statement: I wonder how young animals are like their parents.

Learning Goal Because PE 1-LS3-1 draws on two separate Disciplinary Core Ideas (LS3.A: Inheritance of Traits and LS3.B: Variation of Traits), we have written a lesson to address each one.

In this lesson, students focus on Inheritance of Traits by exploring the similarities and differences between young animals and their parents. In Lesson 1.8, they extend their learning and focus on Variation of Traits by investigating the similarities and differences among adult animals of the same species.

NGSS Performance Expectation 1-LS3-1. Make observations to construct an evidence-based account that young plants and animals are like, but not exactly like, their parents.

Prep Steps
1. Post the Wonder Statement, *I wonder how young animals are like their parents*, on the wall in the classroom meeting area.
2. Use Google Images to find photos of the following animals and make photocopies of each one: lion cub, adult male lion, baby langur

monkey, adult langur monkey, baby red kangaroo, adult red kangaroo, baby mouse, adult mouse, king penguin chick, adult king penguin, alligator hatchling, adult alligator, gray wolf pup, adult gray
wolf, bald eaglet, adult bald eagle, baby mountain gorilla, adult sil-
verback mountain gorilla, baby polar bear, adult polar bear. Scatter
the adult animal photos around the classroom.

3. Make copies of the Lesson 1.7 Wonder Journal Labels in Appendix B
for each child in your class and cut them out. Then make copies of
the Lesson 1.7 Bluebird Similarity Data Tables, also in Appendix B.

Engaging Students

Begin the lesson by passing out copies of the Lesson 1.7 Wonder Journal
Label with the Wonder Statement written on it. After reading the
Wonder Statement with the class, ask your students to add it to their
Wonder Journals.

Divide your class into ten small groups and give each group one of
the baby animal photos you found earlier. When you say, "Go," the
teams should begin moving around the room in search of the matching
adult animal photo. When they find it, group members should discuss
how the young animal and the adult animal are similar to and different
from one another. When the groups seem ready, invite a few volunteers
to share their groups' ideas with the rest of the class.

Exploring with Students

Introduce *Just Like My Papa* by asking the students with the lion cub and
adult lion photos to come to the front of the class so everyone can see
the images. Show your class the front cover of the book and encourage
students to look closely at the two lions there. Ask the children:

- *Do the lions in the illustration look like the real lions?*
- *How are they similar?*
- *How are they different?*
- *Do the lion and the cub on the cover of the book look more similar to
one another than the real lion and cub?* (Yes.)
- *What has the illustrator, Mike Wohnoutka, done to make the lion and
the cub on the cover seem like they have a lot in common?* (Their bod-
ies are posed in the same way and their facial expressions match.)

After reading the entire story, take a picture walk back through the
book and work with your class to create a data table that will help students organize information about how a papa lion is similar to and different from his cub. To reduce the time students have to wait while you
add information to the data table, just add a check mark to the second
column if the feature is the same.

A sample data table may look like this:

How Papa Lion and the Young Lion Are Similar

Papa Lion	Young Lion
Four legs	✓
Golden brown fur	Has white spots on belly
Two eyes	✓
Two ears	✓
Whiskers above mouth	✓
Big	Small
Mane	No mane
Tail with black tip	✓

Now that your class has learned how the lion cub is like his dad, let the students know that you are going to read a book called *What Bluebirds Do* to find out how young bluebirds are similar to their parents. But first you'd like the students to use what they've learned so far to guess what a young bluebird looks like.

Project the adult bluebird image you found earlier on the interactive whiteboard in your classroom, and pass out copies of the Lesson 1.7 Wonder Journal Label that says:

This is what I think a young bluebird looks like:

Encourage students to add the label to their Wonder Journal and draw a picture of what they think a bluebird looks like before it's all grown up.

This Wonder Journal entry shows what a student thinks a young bluebird might look like.

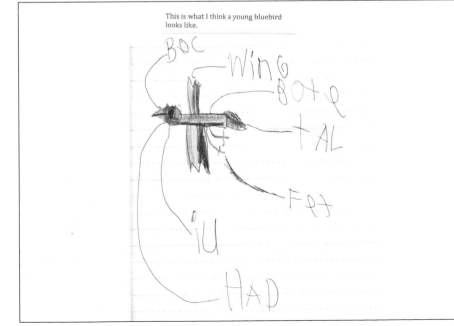

Introduce *What Bluebirds Do* by showing your class the front cover and asking the following questions:

- *What do you think is happening in the photo?*
- *Do you think the two birds are related? If so, describe their relationship.*

Next, show the book's title page and ask the following questions:

- *Do you think there is a connection between this photo and the one on the cover? If so, what is it?*
- *Do you think the bird on the right is a male or a female, a young bird or an adult?*

As the class discusses all four of these questions, encourage students to provide rationale for their ideas. Let the students know that they will find out the answers to these questions as you read the book.

When you reach page 15, ask the class: *What do you think will happen to those five eggs?* Explain that an egg is the first stage in a bird's life, and begin a data table that describes what a bluebird looks like at different stages in its development from egg to adult. (See sample table that follows.)

After reading the text on page 17, point out that the photo here matches the image on the cover. Ask your students: *Now that you have more information about the photo, have your ideas about what the birds are doing changed? If so, how?*

When you reach page 21, which shows a close-up photo of a newly-hatched bluebird chick (hatchling), encourage your students to look back at their Wonder Journal drawings of a young bluebird. Choose a few student volunteers and ask each of them to describe one way his or her drawing is different from the chick in the photo. Ask other volunteers to share ways that their drawings are similar to the real chick.

Now show the class the cover of *Just Like My Papa*. Point out that even though the bluebird chick doesn't look just like its parents, it does look more like an adult bluebird than an adult lion.

After adding information about the bluebird hatchling to the class data table, continue reading the book and filling in the table. Your completed data table should look similar to the one on page 151.

When you reach page 26, flip back to the title page and guide students in noticing that both pages show the same photo. Ask them: *Now that you have more information about the photo, have your ideas about what the birds are doing changed? If so, how?*

When you have finished reading the main text of *What Bluebirds Do* (page 39), give each child a copy of the Lesson 1.7 Bluebird

How a Bluebird's Appearance Changes as It Grows

Life Stage	Appearance
Egg	Pale blue
Hatchling	Pink skin with fuzzy down feathers
	Eyes shut
	Beak
	Two legs and feet with three toes
Chick	Spotted head, back, and chest feathers
	Blue wing and tail feathers
	Eyes open
	Beak
	Two legs and feet with three toes
Adult	Blue head, back, wing, and tail feathers
	Rusty chest feathers
	White belly feathers
	Eyes open
	Beak
	Two legs and feet with three toes

Similarity Data Tables that you photocopied earlier. As you read through the entries with your class, point out that these tables contain the same information as the data table compiled by the class, but in a way that makes it easier to directly compare the body features of the hatchling and the adult (top table) and the chick and the adult (bottom table).

After reviewing the information in the data tables with your class, encourage students to add them to their Wonder Journals. Then ask them: *Which is more like an adult bluebird—a hatchling or a chick?* Encourage students to provide evidence from the Lesson 1.7 Bluebird Similarity Data Tables as they discuss the question.

Encouraging Students to Draw Conclusions

After giving each child the Lesson 1.7 Wonder Journal Label that poses the Wonder Statement as a question, *How are young animals like their parents?*, invite the class to look closely at the data table showing the similarities between the papa lion and his cub. Pass out the Lesson 1.7 Bluebird Similarity Data Tables, and ask students to consider this question: *Which young animal—the bluebird chick or the lion cub—is more like its parent?* As students respond to this question, encourage them to support their ideas with evidence from the tables.

Next, lay out the animal adult-young photo sets the students used at the beginning of the lesson. Invite a few student volunteers to help you rearrange the photo pairs to create two groups—mammals and birds. Then ask: *In general, does one group of young animals looks more like its parents? Are there any exceptions to that general rule? Can you think of any reasons why one group looks more like its parents in these photos?*

As the discussion winds down, invite the class to gather for a Science Dialogue. Encourage students to look at the data tables to find one body feature that both the lion cub and the bluebird chick have but their parents don't.

When the class realizes that both young animals have spots, ask them: *Why do you think the baby animals have spots? Do you think the spots help them survive? If so, in what way?*

As students respond to these questions, encourage them to provide a rationale for their ideas. The children should feel free to agree or disagree with one another. They may also ask their classmates questions.

If students need more guidance, show them the illustration of the lion cub dropping down in the grass to hide from the hyena in *Just Like My Papa*. Ask the class how the lion's spots help it stay safe and why it may not need spots as it gets older. Then show the picture on page twenty-seven of *What Bluebirds Do*. Ask the children how they think the bluebird chick's spots might help it survive. Can the class explain why the bluebird may not need spots as it gets older?

To bring the lesson to a close, give each child copies of the Lesson 1.7 Wonder Journal Labels with the following prompts:

Young animals look like their parents in some ways.
My evidence is:

Young animals look different from their parents in some ways.
My evidence is:

Encourage the children to add the labels to their Wonder Journals one at a time, so they have plenty of room to draw a picture as one piece of evidence for each statement.

In this lesson, students learned that some young animals look similar to, but not exactly like, their parents. However, as the youngsters grow, they become more and more like their parents. With these new insights, students may now begin to wonder how other young animals are similar to or different from their parents. They may also have questions about how a young animal's special body features can help it survive. They should feel free to record these new thoughts in their Wonder Journals.

A student's Wonder Journal drawing shows that both adult animals and their young have similar ears.

Young animals look like their parents in some ways. My evidence is:

the ens or the zaxm

The ens or the zaxm

Reinforcing the Concept

- You can extend the lesson by reading the following book pair and discussing the content with the Wonder Statement in mind:
  —*Stay Close to Mama* by Toni Buzzeo & *Dolphin Baby!* by Nicola Davies

- You can use the use the following book pair, which focuses on plants rather than animals, to support the Performance Expectation in this lesson:
  —*One Red Apple* by Harriet Ziefert & *A Seed Is Sleepy* by Dianna Hutts Aston

- Allow students time to collaborate in pairs or small groups to create a picture story about a young lion with no spots or a young bluebird with no spots and what dangers it might face because of its appearance. After the children have illustrated their stories, add them to the classroom library so classmates can read them.

- Create a set of adult-young animal pair playing cards and place them in the classroom science center. When two students have free time, they can play a game similar to tic-tac-toe. The directions are as follows:

    Draw a tic-tac-toe board on a piece of paper and divide the playing cards into two piles: young animals and adult animals. Place the adult animal cards face down and deal out the young animal cards.

    The first player draws a card from the adult deck. If the player can make a match, he or she lays down the pair and explains one similarity and one difference between the youngster and the adult. Then the player places an *X* or an *O* on the tic-tac-toe board. If the adult animal doesn't match a young animal card in the player's hand, the child must give the card to his or her opponent. Then the second player takes a turn. The game continues until one player gets three *X*s or *O*s in a row on the tic-tac-toe board.

ELA Links   By now, students have learned a lot about ways in which young animals are similar to and different from their parents. Two different books—one fiction, one nonfiction—have played important roles in this lesson. The following questions can help students reflect on the aspects of the featured books that aroused their curiosity, generated and maintained their interest, and enhanced their understanding of the natural world.

- *What do the two books have in common?* (They both include information about how a young animal is similar to its parent(s) in some ways and different in other ways.)
- *How are the two books different?* (*Just Like My Papa* is a fictional story about a young lion who wants to be just like his dad. It is illustrated with paintings. *What Bluebirds Do* is nonfiction. It describes the summertime activities of a bluebird family and is illustrated with photographs.)
- *Why do you think author Pamela F. Kirby included an author's note and back matter in* What Bluebirds Do? (To provide additional information about bluebirds and how and why she created the book.)
- *Look back at the text in* What Bluebirds Do *and* Just Like My Papa. *Who is telling each story?* (The author is telling the story in both books.) *What are some of the differences in the way the two stories are told?* (In *What Bluebirds Do*, we know that the author is right there writing what she sees herself. The story is happening in her yard. On page twenty, she is holding the chick in her hand. In *Just Like My Papa*, the author chooses her words very carefully to bring us into the world of the savanna. Her lyrical language flows beautifully to create a warm, loving mood.)

- *Do you think real lions have thoughts exactly like the ones the author describes in* Just Like My Papa? *Why or why not?*
- *Can you find a few words or sentences in the two books that you especially like? Why do you like them? Which author do you think has more fun playing with language?* (Toni Buzzeo.) *Why?*

Lesson 1.8: How Adult Animals of the Same Species Can Be Different

| *Dogs* by Emily Gravett | & | *No Two Alike* by Keith Baker |

About the Books

Expressive pencil drawings overlaid with soft washes of watercolor on creamy stock and minimal, rhyming text work in tandem to create a delightful introduction to the diversity of dog species with a focus on opposites—big, small, stripy, spotty, tough, and soft. *Dogs* is a wonderfully warmhearted tribute to our four-legged friends.

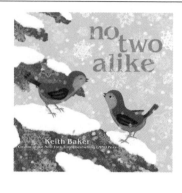

With spare verse and a quiet, winter landscape, *No Two Alike* presents a lovely, joyful ode to uniqueness. While the book focuses on examples from the natural world, children will appreciate the gentle self-esteem boost that comes with the reassurance that they are one of a kind. The lovely, digitally rendered artwork in subdued colors conveys a sense of softness, wonder, and warmth that strengthens the book's quiet message.

Wonder Statement: I wonder how adult animals of the same kind can be different from one another.

Learning Goal

Because PE 1-LS3-1 draws on two separate Disciplinary Core Ideas (LS3.A: Inheritance of Traits and LS3.B: Variation of Traits), we have written a lesson to address each one.

In Lesson 1.7, students focus on Inheritance of Traits by exploring the similarities and differences between young animals and their parents. In this lesson, they extend their learning and focus on Variation of Traits by investigating the similarities and differences among adult animals of the same species.

NGSS Performance Expectation 1-LS3-1. Make observations to construct an evidence-based account that young plants and animals are like, but not exactly like, their parents.

Prep Steps

1. Post the Wonder Statement, *I wonder how adult animals of the same kind can be different from one another*, on the wall in the classroom meeting area.

2. Use Google Images to find two or more photos of adult male cardinals that look noticeably different. Pay close attention to the feather tufts on the birds' heads. They can vary tremendously.

3. Create a data table with three columns and six rows and title it How Adult Animals of the Same Kind Are Similar and Different. Use the first row to label the columns with the headings "Animal," "Similarities," and "Differences." Using the sample table on page 160 as a guide, add the names of the animals featured in *No Two Alike* to the cells in the first column.

4. Prepare index cards with the name of a familiar animal (avoid the animals included in *No Two Alike*) for half the students in your class. No two cards should list the same animal.

5. Create a two-column data table with the headings "Animal" and "How They Are Different," title it How Animals are Different, and add the names of all the animals on the index cards you prepared in Step 4 to the "Animal" column. Leave plenty of room for students to add their observations to the "How They Are Different" column. Make a copy of the data table for each child in your class.

6. Make copies of the Lesson 1.8 Wonder Journal Labels in Appendix B for each child in your class and cut them out. Then make copies of the Lesson 1.8 Venn Diagram Template (also in Appendix B).

Engaging Students   Begin the lesson by passing out copies of the Lesson 1.8 Wonder Journal Label with the Wonder Statement written on it. After reading the Wonder Statement with the class, ask your students to add it to their Wonder Journals.

Next, pass out white drawing paper and invite students to draw a picture that would help someone who has never seen a dog to understand what dogs look like. Ask them to add labels to highlight a dog's most important features.

A student's labeled drawing of a short golden retriever

When the children have finished their drawings, encourage them to Turn and Talk with a neighbor about how their dogs are similar and how they are different. Then invite each pair to share their drawings and ideas with the rest of the class. During the group discussion, record some of the students' ideas on chart paper. When everyone has had a chance to share, ask your students to paste their dog drawings into their Wonder Journals.

Exploring with Students

After introducing *Dogs* by opening the book and showing your class the full cover, encourage students to Turn and Talk about why they think author-illustrator Emily Gravett decided to draw half of the dog's body on the front cover and half on the back cover. Then give students a few minutes to share their thoughts with the whole group.

Encourage the class to listen carefully as you read *Dogs*. When you have finished the book, show the endpapers (the inside front and back covers) and read the name of each breed. Ask your students which two breeds they think look the most different from one another. Help them focus on the rationale for their choices: size, color, amount of fur, and so on.

Explain that even though dogs can look quite different from one another, they are all the same kind, or species, of animal. Tell them: *Scientists say all dogs belong to the same species. If a male and a female animal belong to the same species, they can have babies together. A dog and a cat belong to two different species, so they can't have babies together. Dogs have puppies, and cats have kittens. All horses belong to one species. Sheep belong to a different species. You belong to the same species as all the other people in the world.*

Using the illustrations of the different dogs on the endpapers, work with your class to create a data table that lists what all dogs have in common and the ways that they can differ.

A sample data table may look like this:

How Dogs Are Similar and Different

All Dogs Have	They Can Be
A tail	Short, long; with lots of fur, with very little fur
Two ears	Big, small; stick up, flop down
Two eyes	Big, small
Four legs	Short, tall; thin, fat
Fur	Short, long; brown, black, white; spots, stripes
Paws	Big, small

Now introduce *No Two Alike* by asking students to look closely at the birds on the cover. Ask them: *How are their bodies the same? Do you see any differences in their features?* Suggest that the red birds could be adult male

Teaching Tip

The entries in the sample data tables shown here are fully fleshed out and include all possible answers. You should not expect your class's tables to be as detailed, but they should include enough essential information to fully address the Wonder Statement. Providing students with copies of each data table as soon as possible after the class compiles it will allow each child to keep a record of the investigation in his or her Wonder Journal.

northern cardinals and ask: *Do you think all male cardinals look alike?* After projecting on the classroom interactive whiteboard the male cardinal images you found earlier, ask: *How do these cardinals look the same? How do they look different?*

As you read *No Two Alike*, encourage the students to point out any difference they see between the two red birds. You may also choose to discuss differences they observe in some of the nonliving items shown in the book: nests, animals tracks, branches, leaves (notice that two of the leaves are shaped like snowflakes), trees, fences, roads, and so on. Be sure to distinguish between natural items and human-made objects.

When you have finished the story, turn back to the double-page spread with the text "among you all!" and place it under a document projector. Invite students to find a buddy and choose one of the adult animal pairs in the book (deer, bear, fox, rabbit, squirrel). Each child should turn to a fresh set of facing pages in his or her Wonder Journal and write the name of the animal the buddies have selected at the top of each page.

As the teams discuss how the two individuals in their animal pair are similar to and different from one another, mention that the students may rely on their prior knowledge. For example, they know that all foxes have four legs, even though they aren't all visible in the book.

As the discussions wind down, invite each child to draw the two adult animals of the same kind (one below each name) in their Wonder Journals. Encourage students to add arrows and labels that highlight the animals' similarities and differences. To help students distinguish similarities and differences in their drawing, suggest that they use two different color arrows, one for similarities and one for differences. Then allow time for pairs of students who chose the same animal to compare their drawings and their ideas.

This Wonder Journal entry shows how foxes are similar in some ways and different in others.

Invite the students to share their ideas about how their two adult animals of the same kind are similar to and different from one another. To reduce the amount of sharing time, group students who drew the same animal together. As the students present ideas, record their thoughts in the data table you prepared in advance.

A sample data table may look like this:

How Adult Animals of the Same Kind Are Similar and Different

Animal	Similarities	Differences
Deer	Four legs, brown, two ears and eyes, nose	Size, shade of fur, markings on fur
Foxes	Size, four legs, two ears and eyes, nose	Shade of fur
Squirrels	Size, brown, long tail, two ears and eyes, nose	Markings on fur
Bears	Size, four legs, brown, two ears and eyes, nose	Shade of fur, markings on fur
Rabbits	Brown, two long ears, two eyes, nose	Size, shade of fur, markings on fur and inside ears

Allow students time to revisit their Wonder Journal drawings and make any revisions they think are appropriate.

Encouraging Students to Draw Conclusions

Give each child the Lesson 1.8 Wonder Journal Label that poses the Wonder Statement as a question: *How can adult animals of the same kind be different from one another?*

Ask students to get back together with their buddies, and give each pair one of the animal index cards you prepared earlier. Invite the buddies to discuss how two adult animals of that kind are the same and how they might be different. Encourage students to use the ideas from the two data tables as a guide.

Next, pass out drawing paper and the How Animals Are Different data table you prepared earlier. After students have added the data table to their Wonder Journals, encourage each pair of students to work cooperatively to draw a set of pictures of their assigned animal. The pictures should show the many ways in which the two animals are similar, but include one difference.

After you collect all of the drawings and place them around the classroom, invite the student pairs to circulate clockwise around the room, looking for the difference in each set of drawings and using words and pictures to record their observations on the data table in their Wonder Journals. Allow pairs to spend two or three minutes viewing each set of drawings and recording observations. Then ring a bell to signal that students should move on to the next set of drawings.

Teaching Tip

Some students may have trouble understanding the ways in which animals of the same species can and can't vary. For example, watch for students who draw antlers on a bear or a short deer-like tail on a fox. If this occurs, show students sets of pictures of familiar animals that include possible variations.

At the end of this activity, invite your class to gather for a Science Circle. As the students from each pair hold up their drawings, encourage their classmates to discuss the similarities and differences between the two adult animals by referring to the observations they recorded in their How Animals Are Different data table. During the conversation, students may agree or disagree with one another as they consider whether the difference each set of pictures depicts is feasible.

To bring the lesson to a close, draw the sample diagram below on chart paper to show your class how they can represent the similarities and difference in their drawings using a visual model called a Venn diagram.

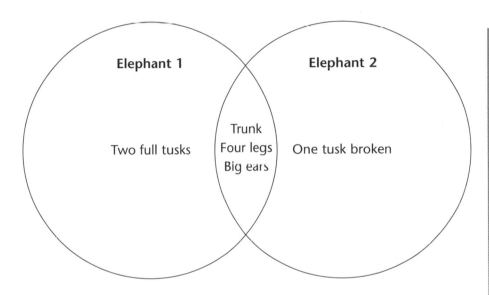

Pass out copies of the Lesson 1.8 Venn Diagram Template that you photocopied earlier, and ask students to add the templates to their Wonder Journals. Encourage the children to use words and pictures to depict the similarities and difference between their animal drawing and the one created by their partner.

In this lesson, students learned that even though adult animals of the same kind (species) are similar in many ways, they are also different in some ways. With these new insights, students may now begin to wonder if and how animals of the same kind tell one another apart or whether twin animals are different in some ways. They should feel free to record these new questions in their Wonder Journals.

Reinforcing the Concept

- You can extend the lesson by reading the following book pair and discussing the content with the Wonder Statement in mind:
  —*Oliver Button Is a Sissy* by Tomie dePaola & *Shades of People* by Shelley Rotner and Sheila M. Kelly

- Give students an outline of a familiar animal to color. When the children are done, encourage them to compare how their colored drawings are the same as and different from those of their classmates.
- Ask students to find a buddy, and give each team two outlines of the same adult animal. Encourage each team to color in the two outlines, making them different in some way. These can be displayed as an interactive bulletin board in which other students try to distinguish how the two animals of the same kind are different from one another.

ELA Links   By now, students have learned a lot about how adult animals of the same species can differ. Two different books—one fiction, one nonfiction—have played important roles in this lesson. The following questions can help students reflect on the aspects of the featured books that aroused their curiosity, generated and maintained their interest, and enhanced their understanding of the natural world.

- *What do the two books have in common?* (They both include descriptions of how adult animals of the same kind can be similar or different. They are both illustrated with simple artwork.)
- *How are the two books different?* (*Dogs* is a fictional story narrated by a cat. It features simple, realistic artwork. *No Two Alike* is a poetic nonfiction exploration of how living things, natural objects, and human-made objects can be similar in some ways and different in other ways. The cut-paper collage art has a whimsical quality.)
- *Look back at the text in* Dogs *and* No Two Alike. *Who is telling each story?* (At the end of *Dogs*, we are surprised to discover that the narrator is a cat. In *No Two Alike*, the author is the narrator.)
- *Can you find a few words or sentences in the two books that you especially like? Why do you like them? Do you think the author-illustrators had fun creating the books and chose their words carefully? What is your evidence?*
- *How does the style of the art in each book seem to match the style of the text?* (The art in *Dogs* is simple and fun. It is just as joyful as the text. The soft, colorful cut-paper collage art in *No Two Alike* feels magical, just like the lovely lyrical text.)

Picture Books for Grade 1 Lessons

Featured Titles

Baker, Keith. *No Two Alike*. San Diego: Beach Lane Books, 2011.
HC 978-1-44241-742-7

Beaty, Andrea. *Iggy Peck, Architect*. New York: Abrams, 2007.
HC 978-0-81091-106-2

Buzzeo, Toni. *Just Like My Papa*. New York: Disney-Hyperion, 2013.
HC 978-1-42314-263-8

Cole, Henry. *Jack's Garden*. New York: Greenwillow, 1997.
HC 978-0-68813-501-0; PB 978-0-68815-283-3

Goodman, Emily. *Plant Secrets*. Watertown, MA: Charlesbridge, 2009.
HC 978-1-58089-204-9; PB 978-1-58089-205-6

Gravett, Emily. *Dogs*. New York: Simon & Schuster, 2010.
HC 978-1-41698-703-1

Hatkoff, Juliana, Isabella Hatkoff, and Craig Hatkoff. *Winter's Tail: How One Little Dolphin Learned to Swim Again*. New York: Scholastic, 2009.
HC 978-0-54512-335-8; PB 978-0-54534-830-0

Jenkins, Steve. *What Do You Do When Something Wants to Eat You?* Boston: Houghton Mifflin, 2001.
HC 978-0-61335-590-2; PB 978-0-61815-243-8

———. *What Do You Do with a Tail Like This?* Boston: Houghton Mifflin, 2003.
HC 978-0-61825-628-0

Kirby, Pamela F. *What Bluebirds Do*. Honesdale, PA: Boyds Mills, 2009.
HC 978-1-59078-614-7

Lionni, Leo. *Swimmy*. New York: Knopf, 1994.
HC 978-0-39481-713-2; PB 978-0-39482-620-2

Markle, Sandra. *Little Lost Bat*. Watertown, MA: Charlesbridge, 2006.
PB 978-1-57091-657-1

Ryder, Joanne. *The Snail's Spell*. New York: Scholastic, 1991.
HC 978-0-81246-361-3; PB 978-0-14050-891-8

Schaefer, Lola. *Just One Bite*. San Francisco: Chronicle, 2010.
HC 978-0-81186-473-2

Wilson, Karma. *A Frog in the Bog*. New York: Margaret K. McElderry, 2007.
HC 978-0-68984-081-4; PB 978-1-41692-727-3

Wood, Douglas. *What Dads Can't Do*. New York: Simon & Schuster, 2000.
HC 978-0-68982-620-7

Supplementary Titles

Aliki. *My Five Senses*. New York: HarperCollins, 1989.
PB 978-0-06445-083-6

Alter, Anna. *Disappearing Desmond*. New York: Knopf, 2010.
HC 978-0-37586-684-5

Aston, Dianna Hutts. *A Seed Is Sleepy*. San Francisco: Chronicle, 2007.
    HC 978-0-81185-520-4

Barretta. Gene. *Neo Leo: The Ageless Ideas of Leonardo da Vinci*. New
    York: Holt, 2009.
    HC 978-0-80508-703-1

Brown, Peter. *The Curious Garden*. New York: Little, Brown, 2009.
    HC 978-0-31601-547-9

Buzzeo, Toni. *Stay Close to Mama*. New York: Disney-Hyperion, 2012.
    HC 978-1-42313-482-4

Cannon, Janell. *Pinduli*. San Diego: Harcourt, 2004.
    HC 978-0-15204-668-2

Cronin, Doreen. *Diary of a Fly*. New York: HarperCollins, 2007.
    HC 978-0-06000-156-8

Davies, Nicola. *Dolphin Baby!* Somerville, MA: Candlewick, 2012.
    HC 978-0-76365-548-8

dePaola, Tomie. *Oliver Button Is a Sissy*. San Diego: Harcourt, 1979.
    HC 978-0-15257-852-7; PB 978-0-15668-140-7

Fleming, Candace. *Papa's Mechanical Fish*. New York: Farrar, Straus and
    Giroux, 2013.
    HC 978-0-37439-908-5

Heos, Bridget. *What to Expect When You're Expecting Joeys: A Guide for
    Marsupial Parents (and Curious Kids)*. Minneapolis, MN: Millbrook,
    2011.
    HC 978-0-76135-858-9

James, Simon. *Baby Brains and RoboMom*. Somerville, MA: Candlewick,
    2008.
    HC 978-0-76363-463-6

Jenkins, Steve. *Never Smile at a Monkey*. Boston: Houghton Mifflin,
    2009.
    HC 978-0-61896-620-2

Jenkins, Steve, and Robin Page. *Time to Eat*. Boston: Houghton Mifflin,
    2011.
    HC 978-0-54725-032-8

Kurtz, Jane. *Do Kangaroos Wear Seatbelts?* New York: Dutton, 2005.
    HC 978-0-52547-358-9

Markle, Sandra. *A Mother's Journey*. Watertown, MA: Charlesbridge,
    2005.
    HC 978-1-57091-621-2; PB 978-1-57091-622-9

McDermott, Gerald. *Monkey: A Trickster Tale from India*. Boston:
    Harcourt, 2011.
    HC 978-0-15216-596-3

Rotner, Shelley, and Sheila M. Kelly. *Shades of People*. New York:
    Holiday House, 2010.
    HC 978-0-82342-191-6; PB 978-0-82342-305-7

Sayre, April Pulley. *Dig, Wait, Listen: A Desert Toad's Tale*. New York: Greenwillow, 2001.
HC 978-0-68816-614-4
———. *Vulture View*. New York: Holt, 2007.
HC 978-0-80507-557-1
Schanzer, Rosalyn. *How Ben Franklin Stole the Lightning*. New York: HarperCollins, 2002.
HC 978-0-68816-993-0
Schwartz, David M., and Yael Schy. *Where in the Wild? Camouflaged Creatures Concealed . . . and Revealed*. San Francisco, CA: Tricycle, 2007.
HC 978-1-58246-207-3; PB 978-1-58246-399-5
Stewart, Melissa. *No Monkeys, No Chocolate*. Watertown, MA: Charlesbridge, 2013.
HC 978-1-58089-287-2
Wilson, Karma. *Bear Wants More*. New York: Margaret K. McElderry, 2003.
HC 978-0-68984-509-3
Wood, Douglas. *No One But You*. Somerville, MA: Candlewick, 2011.
HC 978-0-76363-848-1
———. *What Moms Can't Do*. New York: Simon & Schuster, 2001.
HC 978-0-68983-358-8
Ziefert, Harriet. *One Red Apple*. Maplewood, NJ: Blue Apple Books, 2009.
HC 978-1-93470-667-1

Lessons for Grade 2

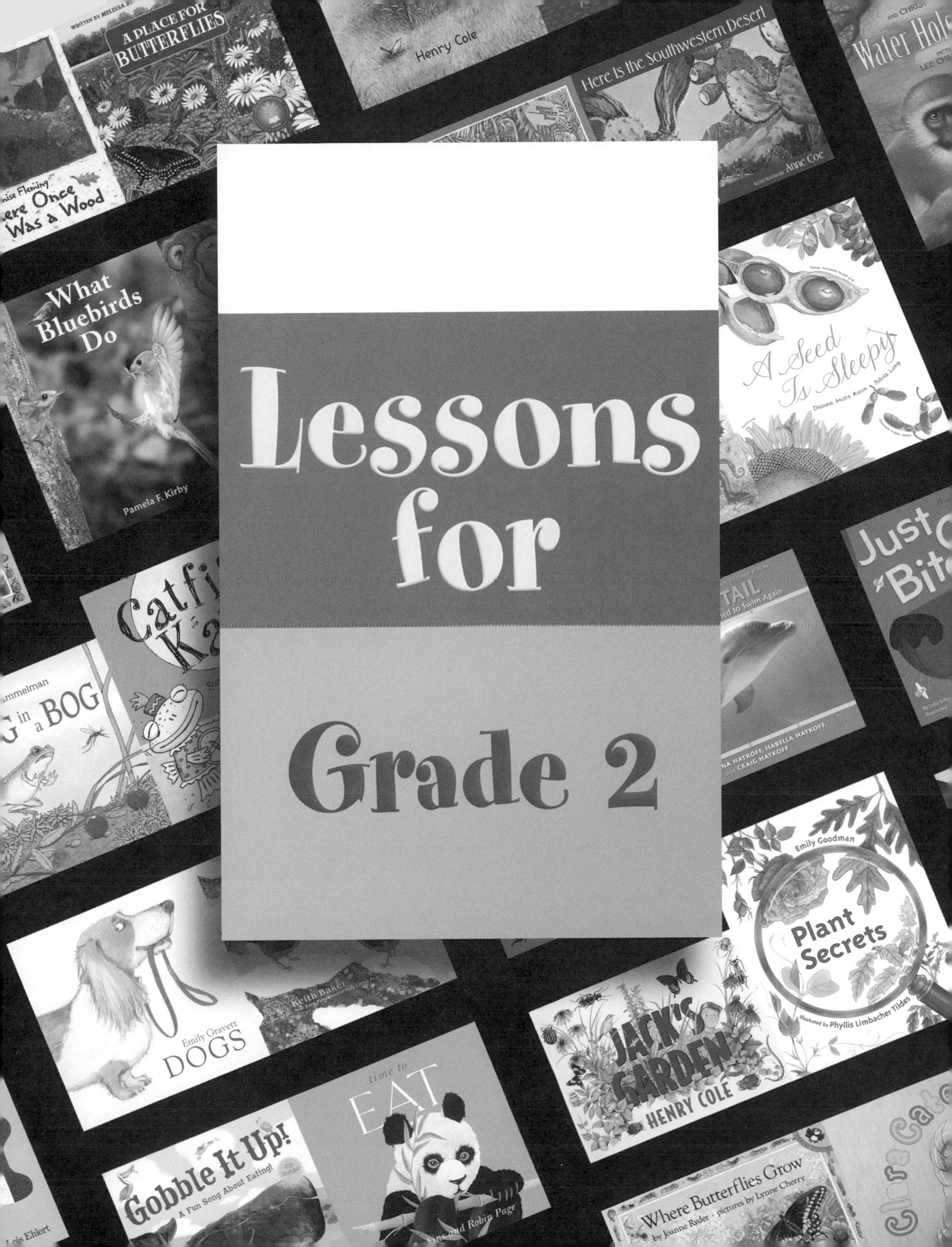

Lesson 2.1: How Wind, Water, and Animals Disperse Seeds

Miss Maple's Seeds by Eliza Wheeler	&	*Planting the Wild Garden* by Kathryn O. Galbraith

About the Books

The whimsical watercolor and pen-and-ink art in *Miss Maple's Seeds* enchants readers, drawing them into a magical tale about a small, fairylike woman who gathers lost seeds, lovingly cares for them through winter, and finally sends them off to find roots of their own in spring. With its positive message about the value of nurturing even the tiniest bit of the natural world, this book is simply wonderful.

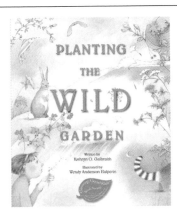

Planting the Wild Garden brings together lyrical language full of fun sound effects and soft, lush pencil-and-watercolor illustrations to share the many ways seeds are spread and planted. From wind and water to birds, squirrels, and even people, we all play a role in the dispersal of seeds throughout our landscape, planting the wild garden together.

Wonder Statement: I wonder how wind, water, and animals help some seeds move to new places.

Learning Goal In this lesson, students learn that (1) wind, water, and animals (including humans) can transport seeds to new places and (2) when a seed sprouts far from its parent plant, it may have a better chance of developing into a healthy plant. Students also create a visual model that highlights the role animals play in dispersing seeds.

NGSS Performance Expectation 2-LS2-2. Develop a simple model that mimics the function of an animal in dispersing seeds or pollinating plants.

Prep Steps
1. Post the Wonder Statement, *I wonder how wind, water, and animals help some seeds move to new places*, on the wall in the classroom meeting area.
2. Gather a dozen hand lenses and some Velcro strips.
3. Use Google Images to find photos of burrs (a type of seed with hooked projections that snag on fur, hair, and clothing).

4. Use Google Images to find photos of the following plants to project on the classroom interactive whiteboard: poppy, wild rice, water lily, impatiens, raspberry, lupine, lentil, buttercup, tomato, honeysuckle.

5. Make copies of the Lesson 2.1 Wonder Journal Labels in Appendix B for each child in your class and cut them out.

Engaging Students

Begin the lesson by passing out copies of the Lesson 2.1 Wonder Journal Label with the Wonder Statement written on it. After reading the Wonder Statement with the class, ask your students to add it to their Wonder Journals.

Next, encourage your students to look at their feet and raise a hand if they are wearing shoes with Velcro straps. Can they think of other clothing or items in their homes that use Velcro? Are there items around the classroom that rely on it?

Let the class know that Velcro was invented by a man named Georges de Mestral. The idea came to him one day after he and his dog had been walking outdoors. Georges noticed that burrs, a kind of plant seed, were sticking to his clothes and his dog's fur.

Project the burr photos you found earlier on the interactive whiteboard, and tell students that when Georges looked closely at the seeds, he saw why they got caught on clothing and fur. Your students can see why, too.

Divide the class into groups of two or three students, and give each group a hand lens and a Velcro strip. Invite group members to take turns looking closely at the Velcro. If students are wearing sneakers with

A student examines Velcro with a hands lens.

Velcro straps, encourage them to look at those straps, too. Students should then draw and label what they see in their Wonder Journals.

After a few students have had a chance to share their drawings, explain that when Georges saw hundreds of tiny hooks on the burrs, he realized that the same kind of little hooks could be used instead of buttons and zippers. Later, someone else realized that Velcro straps could replace shoelaces, so that people wouldn't have to spend a lot of time tying their shoes.

Let the class know that hooking onto clothing and fur isn't the only way that seeds disperse, or move to new places. Write the word *disperse* on an index card and encourage your students to guide you in creating a sketch to help them remember what it means. After posting the card under the Wonder Statement on the wall, ask the class: *How else do you think seeds might be dispersed?* After recording this question and the students' ideas on chart paper, tell them that you are about to read two books that will provide more answers to this question.

Exploring with Students

Introduce *Planting the Wild Garden* by reading the title and asking students what they think the author, Kathryn O. Galbraith, means by "wild garden"? How do they think planting a wild garden might be different from planting a backyard vegetable garden?

Now open up the book and show the full front and back cover. After inviting a few volunteers to describe what they see, ask the class: *Do any of the images give you new ideas about how seeds are planted in wild places?*

As you read *Planting the Wild Garden*, ask students to look closely at the pictures and invite them to join in as you read the sound effects in colored type. While working through the book, periodically ask: *Does the art show what the text says? Do you notice anything in the art that is not mentioned in the text? If so, how do those elements add to the story?*

Be sure to point out the cockleburs on the second page with the fox and rabbit, and explain that they work in the same way as the burrs you learned about earlier in the lesson.

When you reach the end of the book, turn back to the beginning and work with your students to find examples of ways that seeds can be dispersed. Then create a data table like the one on page 172 to organize the information.

After completing the data table, encourage students to look back at their earlier list of ways seeds might be dispersed. Are any of their ideas echoed in the table?

Next, give each child an index card and invite students to pretend that they are seeds. After reviewing the text in the data table, encourage them to draw a picture that shows how they would most like to be

Teaching Tip

Some of the vocabulary in *Planting the Wild Garden* may be unfamiliar to second graders, especially English language learners. When an unfamiliar word (*meadow, shoots*) arises, write it on an index card and encourage your students to guide you in creating a sketch to help them remember what the word means. Then post the card under the Wonder Statement on the wall.

Lessons for Grade 2

How Seeds Are Dispersed in *Planting the Wild Garden*

Who/What Disperses Seeds	How
Wind	Blows seeds to new places
Bird	Shakes seeds loose; eats seeds and then releases them in droppings
Rain	Washes seeds to new places
Stream	Carries seeds to new places
Rabbit	Shakes seeds loose
Fox	Seeds catch on fur and fall off in new places
Raccoon	Carries seeds to new places
Squirrel	Buries seeds
Person	Carries seeds to new places; blows seeds to new places

Teaching Tip

The entries in the sample data tables shown here are fully fleshed out and include all possible answers. You should not expect your class's tables to be as detailed, but they should include enough essential information to fully address the Wonder Statement. Providing students with copies of each data table as soon as possible after the class compiles it will allow each child to keep a record of the investigation in his or her Wonder Journal.

dispersed to a new location. While the class is working, create a graph like the one shown below on a blank wall or bulletin board in your classroom.

When the students are ready, help them add their index cards to complete the bar graph, and then ask: *Which seed dispersal method is most popular among the class? Which is least popular?* Select a few items from the horizontal axis and invite student volunteers to explain why they would (or wouldn't) want to be dispersed in those ways.

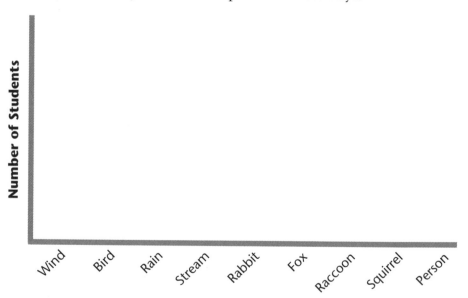

Now introduce *Miss Maple's Seeds* by reading the title and the name of the author-illustrator and asking the class whether they think the book is fiction or nonfiction. What do they think the book will be about?

Open to the title page and ask the class what is unusual about the tree Eliza Wheeler painted. (It looks like someone lives there—perhaps Miss Maple.) Now turn to the dedication page. Ask the students: *What do you think Miss Maple is doing and why? What do you think the birds are doing?*

As you discuss the page of *Miss Maple's Seeds* that shows many different kinds of seeds, avoid focusing on the fern. Ferns reproduce using spores, not seeds.

When you reach the page that shows many different kinds of seeds, let the class know that even though *Miss Maple's Seeds* is fiction, the illustration shows real seeds. On the classroom interactive whiteboard, project the plant images you found earlier, so students can see the plants that will grow from some of the seeds.

After reading the next page, let the class know that rivers really do carry seeds to new places. Then ask: *Based on what we've read, where do the seeds carried by rivers end up?* (In soft, muddy soils.) To help students remember and organize this information and other key science facts embedded in the fictional story, begin a data table with the two headings, "Who/What Disperses Seeds" and "Where Seeds End Up." Be sure to leave room to add a third column on the right-hand side of the table.

As you read the next page, ask the class the following questions:

- *Look back at the table we made while reading* Planting the Wild Garden. *What has the power to blow seeds to new places?* (The wind.)
- *According to* Miss Maple's Seeds, *where can seeds blown by the wind end up?* (Grassy fields and thick forests.)

After writing this new information in the data table, add a third column and label it "So What?" Encourage your students to listen for three reasons why a seed that has moved to a new place might grow better. As you add the three reasons to the new column, explain that if a seed sprouts right next to the plant it came from, the young plant will have to compete with its "parent" for light from the sun and water from the soil. But if a seed sprouts in a new place with just the right conditions (soil, sun, rain), it has a better chance of growing into a healthy plant.

With this idea in mind, invite students to predict how landing in soft, muddy soil might help a seed that is dispersed by river water. After adding their ideas to the "So What?" column of the data table, continue reading.

When you reach the page that begins, "When spring comes," ask your class: *Why does Miss Maple teach the seeds to "dance and burrow into the muddy ground"? How does that description explain what happens to a real seed?* (It's a playful way of describing how a real seed gets planted.)

After you read the page that begins, "They set out on an exciting new journey," encourage students to look closely at the illustration on the left-hand page of the spread. Then ask the following questions:

- *Does the art show exactly what the words say?* (No.)
- *What does it show?* (Squirrels carrying seeds.)
- *Where do you think the squirrels are going? What do you think they will do with the seeds? Do you think the seeds will be better off? Why or why not?* If students struggle to answer these questions, reread the four related pages in *Planting the Wild Garden*.

Use the class's suggestions to complete the data table, and then finish reading the story. Your final data table may look something like this:

How Seeds Are Dispersed in *Miss Maple's Seeds*

Who/What Disperses Seeds	Where Seeds End Up	So What?
River water	Soft, muddy soil	Plants won't have to compete with their parents.
Wind	Grassy fields, thick forests	1. Rich soil keeps plants healthy. 2. Sun and rain helps plants grow. 3. Plants avoid weeds.
Squirrels	Field, forest, backyard	Plants will get just the right amount of sun and rain. They will have plenty of room to grow.

Encouraging Students to Draw Conclusions

Give each child the Lesson 2.1 Wonder Journal Label that poses the Wonder Statement as a question: *How do wind, water, and animals help some seeds move to new places?*

After inviting the class to gather for a Science Circle, draw your students' attention to the data table you created while reading *Miss Maple's Seeds*. Ask the class: *Did Miss Maple teach her seeds about all three of the seed dispersal methods? Why do you think she didn't tell the seeds that squirrels and other animals can move them to new places?*

Next, review the information in the *Planting the Wild Garden* data table with your students. Ask them the following questions one at a time: *How are the seed dispersal methods that Miss Maple teaches her seeds similar to the dispersal methods described in* Planting the Wild Garden? *How are they different?*

As students discuss each question, encourage them to agree or disagree with classmates and to ask one another questions to help clarify ideas. You may facilitate the discussion by reminding students to provide evidence for their ideas and restating any unclear comments or ideas.

As the conversation winds down, encourage the class to look back at the Velcro drawings they made in their Wonder Journals at the beginning of the lesson, and remind them that Velcro mimics, or imitates, burrs—seeds with hooks that snag on animal fur. Ask the students: *How do animals like foxes help burrs to grow into healthy new plants?* If students struggle to answer this question, review the relevant pages of *Planting the Wild Garden*. Then ask: *What do you think would happen to those seeds if foxes and other animals that disperse burrs suddenly disappeared?*

Divide the class into two teams—New Animals and New Machines. Then divide each team into three smaller groups (A, B, and C). Let the students know that each New Animals group will brainstorm to come up with an imaginary animal with unusual or surprising body parts that could spread seeds like the fox (Group A), bird (Group B), or squirrel (Group C) in *Planting the Wild Garden*. The imaginary animal's body parts should make it possible for the creature to disperse more seeds in less time than the real animal it is mimicking. Similarly, each New Machines group will brainstorm to come up with a new machine that could disperse seeds like the fox (Group A), bird (Group B), or squirrel (Group C) in *Planting the Wild Garden*. The invention should disperse seeds more efficiently than the animal it is mimicking. After the brainstorming sessions, each student should create a drawing of their group's new animal or machine.

Student designs for an imaginary animal, the horncorn (top), and a shooting seed machine (bottom)

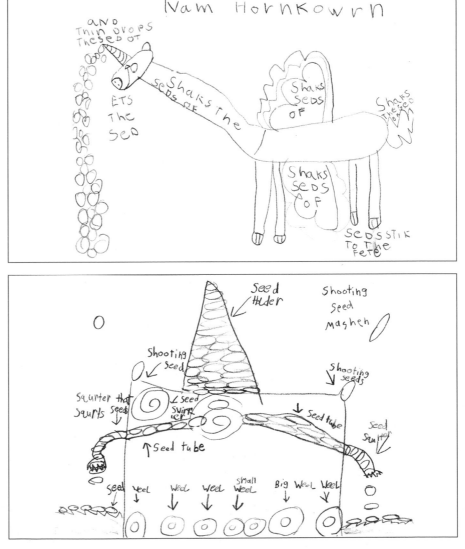

Lessons for Grade 2

To bring the lesson to a close, invite the groups to take turns sharing their visual models with the class. As the children present, encourage them to explain their designs and how they mimic the actions of real animals discussed in *Planting the Wild Garden.*

In this lesson, students learned that wind, water, and animals, including humans, help some seeds grow into healthy plants by carrying them to new places where they won't have to compete with their "parents" for resources. With these new insights, students may now begin to wonder if there are other ways that natural forces or living things help plants grow. They should feel free to record these new questions in their Wonder Journals.

Reinforcing the Concept

- You can extend the lesson by reading the following book pair and discussing the content with the Wonder Statement in mind:
  —*Plant a Little Seed* by Bonnie Christensen & *No Monkeys, No Chocolate* by Melissa Stewart
- Divide the class into two groups, A and B, for a game called Seeds Move. Give each student in Group A an index card with one of the following words: *wind, rain, stream, rabbit, fox, raccoon, squirrel,* and *person.* Students in Group B will be seeds. Have each student in Group B choose a partner from Group A and, using the *Planting the Wild Garden* data table as a guide, work with his or her partner to act out how a seed moves from place to place. When all the seeds have moved, encourage students to exchange cards and repeat the game.
- Gather several kinds of seeds and place them in your classroom science center along with a half dozen hand lenses. When students have free time, encourage them to visit the center, observe the seeds, and predict how they might disperse.

ELA Links

By now, students have learned a lot about how plants depend on wind, water, and animals to move their seeds to new places. Two different books—one fiction, one nonfiction—have played important roles in this lesson. The following questions can help students reflect on the aspects of the featured books that aroused their curiosity, generated and maintained their interest, and enhanced their understanding of the natural world.

- *What do the two books have in common?* (They both include information about seed dispersal. They feature lyrical language and soft, watercolor paintings.)
- *How are the two books different?* (*Planting the Wild Garden* is nonfiction. It includes fun sound effects set in colored type. *Miss Maple's Seeds* is a fictional story with a magical quality.)

- *How would you describe the style of the artwork in the two books?* (Each double-page spread in *Planting the Wild Garden* features a main illustration and many smaller ones, sort of like a comic book. The paintings are realistic. *Miss Maple's Seeds* takes place in the real world, but the creatures and locations seem sweetly fantastical. On some double-page spreads, the illustrator uses silhouetted images and white backgrounds to accentuate key details.) *Which art did you like better?*
- *What do you think is the setting of the two books?* (*Planting the Wild Garden* takes place in a meadow. *Miss Maple's Seeds* takes place in the fields and forest that surround the maple tree where she lives.)
- *Can you find examples of alliteration or repeated phrases in either of the books? How do these language devices contribute to the overall mood of the text?* (They help to establish the author's voice.)

Lesson 2.2: Understanding Habitats

| *A House for Hermit Crab* by Eric Carle | & | *Song of the Water Boatman & Other Pond Poems* by Joyce Sidman |

About the Books

A House for Hermit Crab is two books in one. While the text offers a simply told fable with a gentle message about growing up and moving on, the magnificent, bold collage illustrations take readers on a breathtaking underwater journey where brilliantly colored sea creatures dazzle and delight the eye. Expository text at the beginning and end of the book provides facts about hermit crabs and the six ocean animals the main character encounters in the story.

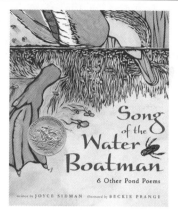

Song of the Water Boatman & Other Pond Poems seamlessly blends vivid poetry and expository paragraphs full of science facts. From peepers to painted turtles, duckweed to diving beetles, this Caldecott Honor title is a celebration of nature that invites readers to take a closer look at ponds and the diverse array of life they support. The striking, hand-colored woodcuts add to the book's uniqueness, leaving readers with a deep sense of the beauty and mystery of wildlife and wild places.

Wonder Statement: I wonder why living things need a habitat.

Learning Goal Because 2-LS4-1 is such a content-rich performance expectation, we have written four lessons to fully address it. In this lesson, 2.2, students learn the meaning of the term *habitat* and that every living thing has its own unique habitat by exploring a hermit crab's habitat in the ocean and a water boatman's habitat in a pond. Lesson 2.3 introduces the term *biome* and compares the features and creatures of forest and desert biomes. Lessons 2.4 and 2.5 focus on the cast of creatures that live in different kinds of wetlands and grasslands, respectively.

NGSS Performance Expectation 2-LS4-1. Make observations of plants and animals to compare the diversity of life in different habitats.

Prep Steps 1. Post the Wonder Statement, *I wonder why living things need a habitat*, on the wall in the classroom meeting area.

2. Use Google Images to find clear photos of a water boatman, a back-swimmer, a hermit crab, several different kinds of sea snails, and a sea urchin in their natural settings. Ideally, the water boatman photo will include vegetation and/or clear indications of water.

3. Create a data table titled Pond Creatures and Their Habitats with four columns and nine rows. Label the columns with the headings "Title of Poem," "Main Character," "Habitat," "Why." Using the sample table on page 181 as a guide, list the titles of the poems from *Song of the Water Boatman & Other Pond Poems* in the first column.

4. Photocopy the Lesson 2.2 Ocean Floor Critter Cards found in Appendix B at the back of this book on white paper. Then cut and laminate each card.

5. Use brown, yellow, and gray construction paper to represent an ocean floor with scattered rocks on a large piece of dark-blue bulletin board paper.

6. Create six Customer Cards by writing each of the following words on an index card: *spring peeper, dragonfly, cattail, lanternfish, seaweed, starfish.*

7. Make copies of the Lesson 2.2 Wonder Journal Labels in Appendix B for each child in your class and cut them out.

Engaging Students

Begin the lesson by passing out copies of the Lesson 2.2 Wonder Journal Label with the Wonder Statement written on it. After reading the Wonder Statement with the class, ask your students to add it to their Wonder Journals.

Let the class know that today they are going to learn about an animal called a water boatman. Encourage your students to use their imaginations to draw what they think a water boatman might look like in their Wonder Journals. Then ask them to show where they think a water boatman might live by adding to their pictures.

Now, on the classroom interactive whiteboard, project the water boatman photo you found earlier. Are the students surprised that a water boatman is an insect? Does the photo include any visual information about where it lives? If the students spot any clues, record them on chart paper.

Exploring with Students

Tell the students that they are going to find out exactly where a water boatman lives—its habitat—by reading a poem in a book called *Song of the Water Boatman & Other Pond Poems*. Show your class the book's full cover (front and back). Can the students identify any of the living things in the illustration? Ask them: *Does the book's cover illustration or title give you any clues about where a water boatman lives?* (A pond.)

Do your students think that an insect as small as a water boatman lives in the whole pond or just one small part of the pond? Let the class know that a habitat is the place *where* a plant, animal, or other creature lives. It can be large, like an entire forest or desert, or it can be a very small area, like the bark of a particular tree or underneath just one rock on the ocean floor.

After writing this *where* part of the definition on an index card, add a quick sketch to help the class remember the meaning. Let the class know that, eventually, you will post the card under the Wonder Statement, but not yet. Tell them: *First, we need to add more information to the definition. There is a reason why every single creature has its very own habitat, a special place where it lives, and we will discover that reason as we work through this lesson.*

Open *Song of the Water Boatman & Other Pond Poems* to the double-page spread with the poem "Song of the Water Boatman and the Backswimmer's Refrain" and show your class the six insects. Explain that three of the insects are water boatmen and three are backswimmers. Backswimmers live in ponds and look similar to water boatmen, but they move through the water on their backs. On the interactive white-board, project the backswimmer photo you found earlier, and ask the class: *How is it similar to the water boatman? How is it different?* Work with your students to identify the three water boatmen and three backswimmers in the book.

Next, point out that in each stanza of the poem, the text about the water boatman comes first. It is followed by italicized text written from the backswimmer's point of view.

As you read the poem and the additional information on the right-hand side of the spread, list phrases that give clues about where in the pond the two insects can usually be found. Your final lists may look like this:

Water Boatman	Backswimmer
Swims down deep	Hangs up top
No fear of plunging deep	Just below the surface of the water
Hides down deep	

When you have completed the lists, ask the class the following questions: *Where is the water boatman's habitat?* (The bottom of the pond.) *Where is the backswimmer's habitat?* (The top of the pond.)

Then ask: *Can you find any clues in the text that explain why the two insects live in different parts of the pond?* If students struggle to answer this question, break it down as follows:

- *What does the text say the water boatman eats?* (Green goo.)
- *According to the text, where is that food found?* (Floating in the water.)
- *What does the text say the backswimmer eats?* (Wee beasties.)

- *According to the text, where is that food found?* (On the water's surface.)
- *Based on the answers to these questions, why do you think water boatmen and backswimmers live in different habitats?* (They eat different foods, and they live in the part of the pond where they can get the food they need to survive.)

Now turn back to the beginning of *Song of the Water Boatman & Other Pond Poems* and show your class the Pond Creatures and Their Habitats data table that you prepared earlier. Explain that after you read each poem, you and your students will work together to add information to the data table. In some cases, the book does not explain why the main character lives in a specific place, so you can leave the cell blank or simply add a question mark. You may want to skip the poem "In the Depths of the Pond Summer" because it doesn't have a main character and includes very little information about the animals' habitats.

The completed data table should look something like this:

Pond Creatures and Their Habitats

Title of Poem	Main Character(s)	Habitat	Why
"Listen for Me"	Spring peeper	Crawls out of water and clings to reeds	Calls for mates
"Spring Splashdown"	Wood duck chicks	Tree cavity, water	?
"Diving Beetle's Food-Sharing Rules"	Diving beetle	"Anywhere" in pond, crawls up smartweed, air above the pond	Finds food
"Fly, Dragonfly"	Green darner dragonfly	Shallows, crawls up reed, flies through air	?
"A Small Green Riddle"	Duckweed	Surface of water	Has long roots to absorb minerals
"Aquatic Fashion"	Caddis fly larvae	Bottom of pond	Stay safe
"Travel Time"	Water bear	Among mosses and lichens, in the water	Stays cool and moist
"The Season's Campaign"	Cattails	Around edge of pond, half in and half out of water	Need moist soil
"Into the Mud"	Painted turtle	Muddy bottom	Body can't function when cold

Next, divide the class into eleven groups. Randomly assign each group the water boatman, the backswimmer, or one of the plants or animals listed in the data table. Then invite the groups to draw and color

Teaching Tip

The entries in the sample data tables shown here are fully fleshed out and include all possible answers. You should not expect your class's tables to be as detailed, but they should include enough essential information to fully address the Wonder Statement. Providing students with copies of each data table as soon as possible after the class compiles it will allow each child to keep a record of the investigation in his or her Wonder Journal.

their assigned creature. If you think it would be helpful, the children may use Google Images to find photo references for unfamiliar creatures.

Encourage students to cut around the general shape of the living things they've drawn. Then, using the data table as a guide, encourage them to arrange the plants and animals in a suitable habitat on a long piece of light-blue bulletin board paper that represents the pond.

As students add labels to identify the creatures, explain that they have created a visual model of a pond and the creatures that live there.

Now introduce *A House for Hermit Crab* by showing the front cover and pointing out that Eric Carle is both the author and the illustrator of this book. Ask the class the following questions:

- *Who do you think is the main character of the story?*
- *Where do you think this story takes place? What clues about the setting do you see on the front cover?* (Wavy blue lines.)
- *Are there any additional clues on the back cover or the title page?*
- *Do you think the story will include any of the plants or animals in* Song of the Water Boatman & Other Pond Poems? *Why or why not?*

The first page of *A House for Hermit Crab* reveals the story's setting—the ocean floor. After reading the page, let the class know that there really is a small ocean animal called a hermit crab. As you project the photo you found earlier on the interactive whiteboard, explain that a hermit crab's habitat is the sandy bottom of shallow seas. Turn back to the page before the title page and read the factual information the author provides about hermit crabs.

As you read the rest of the book, including the factual animal descriptions that follow the story, work with your students to create a data table that lists the living things mentioned in the book and any clues in the words or art about their habitat. Be sure to leave room to add a third column to the right-hand side of the table.

Your initial data table may look like this:

Ocean Creatures and Their Habitats

Living Thing	Habitat
Hermit crab	Shallow ocean water
Green & blue fish	Shallow ocean water
Sea anemone	Ocean floor, shallow ocean
Starfish	Ocean floor, shallow ocean
Coral	Ocean floor, shallow ocean
Sea snail	Ocean floor, shallow ocean
Sea urchin	Ocean floor, shallow ocean
Seaweed	Ocean floor, shallow ocean
Lanternfish	Dark areas of shallow ocean water

Add a third column to the data table with the heading "Why" and tell your class that you are going to work together to fill it in. However, because *A House for Hermit Crab* is a fictional story, not everything in it is true. Explain that:

- There are no real fish that look like the green and blue fish on the first page of the story. Cross out that row of the data table.
- There are snails living in the shallow ocean, but they don't look like the snails shown in the book, and they don't clean hermit crab shells. Project the sea-snail photos you found earlier on the classroom interactive whiteboard.
- Project the sea urchin photo you found earlier, and explain that these ocean animals do not purposely protect other creatures.
- Lantern fish do not live in the same part of the ocean as hermit crabs. As the back matter description points out, lanternfish live in deep, dark areas of the ocean. Change the lanternfish's habitat to "deep ocean." Then reread its back matter description and guide your students in using the information to fill in the "Why" cell in the data table.

Now show your class the seven Ocean Floor Critter Cards that you prepared earlier and let them know that each one contains "Why" information about one of the remaining animals in the data table. Work with the class to match each card with the proper animal and fill in the "Why" column in the data table. (Answers: A. Hermit crab, B. Sea snail, C. Seaweed, D. Sea anemone, E. Starfish, F. Coral, G. Sea urchin.)

Ocean Creatures and Their Habitats

Living Thing	Habitat	Why
Hermit crab	Shallow ocean water	Finds shells to protect its "soft spot"
~~Green & blue fish~~	~~Shallow ocean water~~	
Sea anemone	Ocean floor, shallow ocean	Needs to be anchored to catch food
Starfish	Ocean floor, shallow ocean	Finds food
Coral	Ocean floor, shallow ocean	Needs to be anchored, finds food
Sea snail	Ocean floor, shallow ocean	Finds food
Sea urchin	Ocean floor, shallow ocean	Finds food
Seaweed	Ocean floor, shallow ocean	Needs to be anchored, needs sunlight
Lanternfish	Deep ocean	Finds food

When the data table is complete, divide the class into seven groups. Randomly assign each group one of the shallow-ocean-floor inhabitants listed in the data table, and encourage each child to draw, color, and cut around the general shape of the group's assigned ocean creature. Then guide the children in arranging the ocean life in the proper habitats on

A bulletin-board model of creatures in their habitats on the shallow ocean floor

a long piece of dark-blue bulletin board paper on which you have created an ocean floor with brown or yellow construction paper and scattered rocks with gray construction paper. As students add labels to identify the creatures, explain that they have created a visual model of a shallow ocean seafloor and the creatures that live there.

As you look at the mural with your class, ask the following questions:

- *A hermit crab and a lantern fish both live in the ocean. How are their habitats different?* (A hermit crab lives on the sunny seafloor where it can find empty shells. A lantern fish lives in the deep, dark ocean where it can use its lights to attract food.)
- *A hermit crab and a sea anemone both live on the ocean floor in places where the water is shallow. How are their habitats different?* (A sea anemone's habitat is much smaller because it can't move.)
- *A sea urchin and a sea snail both live on the ocean floor in places where the water is shallow. How are their habitats different?* (A sea snail spends a lot of time on rocks covered with algae. A sea urchin probably avoids rocks as it moves across the ocean floor in search of mussels, sponges, and the other animals it eats.)

Encouraging Students to Draw Conclusions

Give each child the Lesson 2.2 Wonder Journal Label that poses the Wonder Statement as a question: *Why do living things need a habitat?* Then write the following Habitat Real Estate Ads on chart paper:

Cozy habitat at the bottom of a small pond. Features plenty of pebbles, small twigs, and broken bits of snail shells perfect for building a safe home.

Wide-open ocean floor habitat. Includes plenty of rocks covered with algae.

Invite your students to use the information in the data tables to figure out which of the animals they've learned about in *Song of the Water Boatman & Other Pond Poems* and *A House for Hermit Crab* would like to live in these habitats. (Caddis fly larvae and sea snail.)

Let your class know that they are going to pretend that they are real estate agents—people whose job it is to sell places where people or, in this case, a variety of living things will live. Write the names of the following eight living things from *Song of the Water Boatman & Other Pond Poems* and *A House for Hermit Crab* on chart paper in random order: spring peeper, dragonfly, cattail, duckweed, lantern fish, seaweed, starfish, sea anemone.

After reading the list with the class, divide the students into six groups. Give each group a hand-held whiteboard and place one of the Customer Cards you created earlier face down in front of each group. Let the children know that they can look at their card but that they should keep the identity of their customer a secret from the rest of the class.

Members of each group should work together to create a real estate ad for a habitat that would be perfect for their customer. Suggest that students use the information in the data tables and text from the books to generate ideas, and encourage them to use the whiteboards to write and revise their ads until the whole group is satisfied.

When the groups seem ready, ask the class to gather for a Science Circle. After reviewing the names of the eight possible customers that you wrote on chart paper earlier, invite the six groups to come forward one at a time and share their habitat real estate ads. After each group presents, encourage classmates in the audience to guess which customer would prefer to live in the habitat described in the ad.

During each discussion, students should feel free to agree or disagree with one another. They may also ask the group who wrote the ad additional questions. You may facilitate these conversations by helping students stay focused and restating any unclear comments or ideas. You should also encourage students to support their ideas with evidence. As each discussion winds down, have students in the audience vote on which of the eight animals they think the presenters had in mind when they wrote the ad.

Now show students the habitat definition card that you started earlier in the lesson and read the text on the card. Explain that this text describes the *where* part of the definition, but it doesn't explain the reason *why* a creature lives in a particular place. To complete the definition, ask the class to look at the "Why" columns of the two data tables. Work with them to make a list, like the one below, of general "why" reasons:

Reasons Creatures Live in Their Habitats

To find mates
To find food
To stay safe
There is the right amount of water
It is the right temperature

When your class feels the list is complete, ask them: *What do all the reasons in this list have in common?* If students struggle to answer this question, guide them to the idea that living things need mates, food, safety, the right amount of water, and the right temperature to survive. A habitat is a special place because it has everything a plant, animal, or other living thing needs to survive. Add this information to the habitat definition card, and post it under the Wonder Statement.

To bring the lesson to a close, give each child the Lesson 2.2 Wonder Journal Labels with the following sentence frames:

A water boatman lives near the _____ of a _____ because that habitat has everything the insect needs to survive.
My evidence is:

A hermit crab lives on the _____ of a _____ because that habitat has everything the crab needs to survive.
My evidence is:

Encourage the children to add the labels to their Wonder Journals one at a time, so they have plenty of room to draw a picture as one piece of evidence for each statement.

In this lesson, students learned that every living thing has its own unique habitat and that the habitat provides everything the creature needs to survive. With this new insight and knowledge, students may now begin to wonder about the specific habitats of animals that live on land. They should feel free to record these new questions in their Wonder Journals.

Reinforcing the Concept

- You can extend the lesson by reading the following book pairs and discussing the content with the Wonder Statement in mind:
  —*The Raft* by Jim LaMarche & *Trout Are Made of Trees* by April Pulley Sayre
  —*Necks Out for Adventure: The True Story of Edwin Wiggleskin* by Timothy Basil Ering & *Star of the Sea: A Day in the Life of a Starfish* by Janet Halfmann

- Use Google Images to find photos of the ocean creatures mentioned on the final page of *A House for Hermit Crab* (sponges, barnacles, clown fish, sand dollars, electric eels). After sharing the images with your class, encourage students to write a sequel to *A House for Hermit Crab*—a second story in which Hermit Crab travels along the sea floor in his new shell and meets these creatures. How could these new creatures help Hermit Crab?
- Unlike a water boatman, a predacious diving beetle can find food in the air as well as in a pond. Invite your students to write and illustrate an imaginative adventure story in which a predacious diving beetle moves to another habitat. How does it survive in its new home? What does it miss about living in the pond?

ELA Links   By now, students have learned that every living thing has its own unique habitat and that the habitat provides everything the creature needs to live and grow. Two different books—one fiction, one nonfiction—have played important roles in this lesson. The following questions can help students reflect on the aspects of the featured books that aroused their curiosity, generated and maintained their interest, and enhanced their understanding of the natural world.

- *What do the two books have in common?* (They are both about creatures that live in water. They are both illustrated with artwork instead of photos.)
- *How are the two books different?* (*A House for Hermit Crab* is a fictional story that focuses on ocean animals. It is illustrated with cut-paper collages. *Song of the Water Boatman* provides true information about pond creatures in poems and straightforward text blocks. It is illustrated with woodblock prints.)
- *How is the writing style in the two books different?* (*Song of the Water Boatman* includes poetry and straightforward explanations. *A House for Hermit Crab* includes a lot of dialogue.) *Which book is easier to read? Which book is more interesting? Why?*
- *Some people consider* A House for Hermit Crab *to be a fable—a story with animals that has a moral, or lesson. Do you think the book has a lesson? If so, what is it?*
- *Look closely at the words author Joyce Sidman chooses in the poem "Listen for Me" in* Song of the Water Boatman. *Why do you think she repeats the word* night *at the end of the first four lines in the first stanza, but then uses the word* sing *at the end of the last line? Notice how she repeats this pattern throughout the poem. What other patterns do you notice as you examine the poem's structure carefully?*

Lesson 2.3: Understanding Biomes

| *The Great Kapok Tree* by Lynne Cherry | **&** | *Here Is the Southwestern Desert* by Madeleine Dunphy |

About the Books

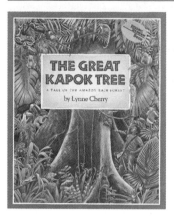

The Great Kapok Tree is a beloved classic in which clear, simple text and lovingly rendered colored-pencil and watercolor art tell the story of a man sent into the Amazon rain forest to chop down a great kapok tree.

Soon, the man grows tired and falls asleep. One by one, forest creatures whisper in his ear about the importance of the tree and how all forest creatures depend on one another. When the man awakes, it's clear that he got the message. He drops his ax and walks out of the forest. Lush endpapers feature a map of tropical rain forests around the world bordered by dozens of fascinating rain forest creatures.

In *Here Is the Southwestern Desert*, lively cumulative verse and luminous acrylic paintings combine to present a variety of Sonoran Desert inhabitants and describe their interactions with one another as well as their environment. The back matter introduces additional desert dwellers and provides more information about North American deserts.

Wonder Statement: I wonder how a rain forest is different from a desert.

Learning Goal Because 2-LS4-1 is such a content-rich performance expectation, we have written four lessons to fully address it. Lesson 2.2 defines the term *habitat* and clarifies that every living thing has its own unique habitat. This lesson, 2.3, introduces the term *biome* and compares the features and creatures of rain forest and desert biomes. Lessons 2.4 and 2.5 focus on the cast of creatures that live in different kinds of wetlands and grasslands, respectively.

NGSS Performance Expectation 2-LS4-1. Make observations of plants and animals to compare the diversity of life in different habitats.

Prep Steps
1. Post the Wonder Statement, *I wonder how a rain forest is different from a desert*, on the wall in the classroom meeting area.
2. Use Google Images to find a wide range of desert photos, including some of the Sonoran Desert, as well as a photo of a collared peccary.
3. Make enough copies of the Lesson 2.3 Concept Map in Appendix B for all the students in your class. Then photocopy the Lesson 2.3 Rain Forest Cards onto a green sheet of paper and the Lesson 2.3 Desert Cards (both are in Appendix B) onto a yellow sheet of paper. Cut out and laminate each card.
4. Make copies of the Lesson 2.3 Wonder Journal Labels in Appendix B for each child in your class and cut them out. Then copy the Lesson 2.3 Sample Poem from Appendix B onto a piece of chart paper.

Engaging Students

Begin the lesson by passing out copies of the Lesson 2.3 Wonder Journal Label with the Wonder Statement written on it. After reading the Wonder Statement with the class, ask your students to add it to their Wonder Journals.

Then give each child a copy of the Lesson 2.3 Wonder Journal Label that says:

This is what I think a desert looks like.

After students have added this second label to their journals, invite them to draw a picture of what they think a desert area looks like. Encourage the children to include plants and animals in their drawings.

Next, give each child an $8\frac{1}{2}$-by-11-inch sheet of paper. Using their Wonder Journal desert pictures as a guide, students should write a word that describes a desert, the name of an animal they think lives in a desert, and the name of a plant they think lives in a desert.

When everyone has written their three words, ask each student to crumple his or her paper into a loose ball and, when you say "Go," gently toss the crumpled paper to a classmate. Students should continue to toss the crumpled balls around the room until you say "Stop." Then each student should pick up the closest paper ball, open it up, and place it on his or her desk.

Write the title "What We Think About Deserts" at the top of a piece of chart paper and add the headings "Desert Descriptions," "Desert Animals," and "Desert Plants" below it. As students share the information on the paper they picked up, record the words under the proper heading. This activity, called Commit and Toss, is adapted from Keeley 2008. It allows students to offer their ideas anonymously and helps you informally assess your students' prior knowledge.

Lessons for Grade 2

Now project the desert photos you found earlier on your classroom interactive whiteboard and ask students to describe what they see (flat land, sandy soil, cactuses and other small plants, no trees). If the class mentions any of the words in the Commit and Toss lists, circle them with a black marker. Then let the children know you are going to read a book about a desert that is in the United States.

Exploring with Students

Introduce *Here Is the Southwestern Desert* by reading the title and showing the cover. Explain that the desert featured in this book is in the southwestern United States and parts of Mexico. Show students the location of the Sonoran Desert on a map. Then point out the state and approximate location of the city or town in which your students live.

Invite the class to look closely at the cover, and ask the following questions one at a time:

- *What animals do you see in the desert painting?*
- *What plants do see in the desert painting?*
- *Can you tell what the weather is like in the desert painting?*

After reading the first page of the book, ask the class the following questions:

- *What animals do you see in the desert painting?*
- *What plants do see in the desert painting?*
- *What land forms do you see in the desert painting? Do you think they are part of the desert?*
- *How would you describe the desert soil?*
- *Can you tell what the weather is like in the desert painting?*

Use your students' answers to begin a set of lists similar to the one you created as part of the Commit and Toss activity. The following sample shows what the lists might look like after your class has examined the first painting:

What We Know About a Southwestern Desert

Desert Descriptions	Desert Animals	Desert Plants
Flat land	Lizard	Many kinds of cactus
Mountains in background	Bird	
Sunny		
Sandy soil		
Some rocks		
Lots of open space		

As you read the rest of the book, work with your students to add information from the text and the paintings to the lists. The main text includes no specific cactus names and only general animal names, but you can update your lists with more specific names as you read the back matter and look at the pen-and-ink drawings. Please note that all of the animals in the back matter are shown in earlier paintings, but some are difficult to spot, even with the assistance of a document projector. Your students may enjoy searching for them.

Your final lists may look something like this:

What We Know About a Southwestern Desert

Desert Descriptions	Desert Animals	Desert Plants
Flat land	Collared lizard	Many kinds of cactus
Mountains in background	Cactus wren	Saguaro cactus
Sunny	Red-tailed hawk	Prickly-pear cactus
Sandy soil	Roadrunner	A couple of trees
Some rocks	Collared peccary	
Lots of open space	Kit fox	
Clear, blue sky	Desert tortoise	
Blazing sun	Bobcat	
High temperatures	Badger	
Not much rain	Round-tailed ground squirrel	
	Coyote	
	Gopher snake	
	Black-tailed jackrabbit	
	Ringtail	
	Chuckwalla	

After reading through the three southwestern desert "What We Know" lists, encourage your students to look back at the Commit and Toss "What We Think" lists and read through those early lists, too. Then invite students to look for descriptions, animals, and plants that appear on both the "think" and "know" lists. Circle any repeated words with a red marker. Are there any words your students would like to remove from the "think" lists? If so, cross them out.

Explain that a desert is one kind of biome and that the second book you will read as part of this lesson takes place in a rain forest, which is another kind of biome. Pass out copies of the Lesson 2.3 Concept Map that you photocopied earlier. As students add it to their Wonder Journals, draw the concept map on a fresh piece of chart paper.

Explain to your students that a biome is a large area of land with special features. *The key features of a desert biome make it different from a rain forest biome. We can find the important features of a desert in the "Desert Descriptions" list we compiled while reading* Here Is the Southwestern Desert. *For example, a desert is usually flat. It has sandy soil with scattered rocks. It has high temperatures and doesn't get much rain.*

As you state each of these features, point to the words on the south-western desert "know" "Desert Descriptions" list and add them to the classroom Concept Map. Invite students to use words or pictures to add the same features to the Lesson 2.3 Concept Maps in their Wonder Journals.

A biome's features determine what kinds of plants and animals can live there. For example, plants that live in a desert must be able to grow in sandy soil. Animals that live in a desert must have body parts or behaviors to help them stay cool and get the water they need.

Ask the class the following questions:

- *Based on what we've learned in the words and pictures of* Here Is the Southwestern Desert, *why do you think cactuses can survive in a desert biome?* (Cactuses don't need as much water as other plants. Their stems store water.)
- *Based on what we've learned in the words and pictures of* Here Is the Southwestern Desert, *why do you think coyotes can survive in a desert biome?* (They know how to find water.)
- *Based on what we've learned in the words and pictures of* Here Is the Southwestern Desert, *why do you think gopher snakes can survive in a desert biome?* (They rest in the shade during the hot day.)

If your students struggle to answer these questions, revisit the related pages in the book and the back matter.

Now introduce *The Great Kapok Tree* by showing the front cover and placing it under a document projector, so students can get a better view. Ask the children to point out the kapok tree and count all the animals in the illustration. Then ask your class the following questions:

- *Can you tell what the soil is like in a rain forest? Why or why not?*
- *Can you tell what the weather is like in this rain forest? Does the name of this biome give you any clues about what the weather might be like?*

Next, turn to the book's endpapers, so students can discover the names of the unfamiliar animals on the cover as well as creatures they might spot as you read the book. As you explain that kapok trees and all the animals shown live in the Amazon rain forest, point out that part of the world on the map. Let the students know that tropical rain forests grow in warm areas all over the world, near the equator. More different kinds of plants and animals live in tropical rain forests than in any other type of environment on Earth.

Take this opportunity to begin a set of rain forest "What We Know" lists similar to the one you created while reading *Here Is the Southwestern Desert*. After working with your students to add the animals shown on the endpapers, write *kapok tree* in the "Rain Forest Plants" list, and ask the children if they can think of any words to add to the "Rain Forest Descriptions" list.

Now draw your class's attention to the book's diagram of rain forest layers. Flip back and forth between the diagram and the explanatory text on the next page. Let your students know that some rain forest animals live only in the canopy, while others live only in the understory or on the forest floor. Explain that the kapok tree is very tall and has branches that stretch up to the top of the canopy, which means many different animals depend on it for food and shelter.

After adding new ideas to the "Rain Forest Descriptions" list, begin reading the story. As you explore each double-page spread, point out all the animals in the illustrations and give students a chance to identify them. Are there new plants or animals that they'd like to add to the "know" lists? Are there new descriptive words?

After reading the page about the troupe of monkeys, ask the class: *The monkeys say that if the rain forest soil is washed away, the forest will become a desert. Do you think they are right? Why or why not?*

Your final lists may look something like this:

What We Know About an Amazon Rain Forest

Rain Forest Descriptions	Rain Forest Animals	Rain Forest Plants
Green, packed with plants	Emerald tree boa	Kapok tree
Layers of life	Scarlet macaw	Lots of different plants
Hot	Toucan	
Canopy is sunny	Frogs	
Understory is shady	Coati	
Steamy, humid	Butterflies	
Noisy	Red-necked tanager	
Heavy rains	Golden tanager	
Tree roots hold soil in place	Parrot	
Fragrant flowers	Monkeys	
	Jaguar	
	Anteater	
	Boa constrictor	
	Silky anteater	
	Iguana	
	Kinkajou	
	Violet-tailed sylph	
	Red-legged honeycreeper	

(continued)

What We Know About an Amazon Rain Forest (*continued*)

Rain Forest Descriptions	Rain Forest Animals	Rain Forest Plants
	Ocelot	
	Parakeet	
	Chestnut-capped puffbird	
	Amazonian katydid	
	Hoazin	
	Giant anteater	
	Tapir	
	Tree porcupine	
	Cock-of-the-rock	
	Three-toed sloth	
	Bees	

When you've finished reading *The Great Kapok Tree*, review the "Rain Forest Descriptions" list. Then ask students: *What are some of the special features of a rain forest biome?* Invite students to Turn and Talk with a classmate as they consider this question. When the buddies agree on three key features of a rain forest biome, they should use words or pictures to add those features to the Lesson 2.3 Concept Maps in their Wonder Journals.

A completed Concept Map showing features of desert and rain forest biomes

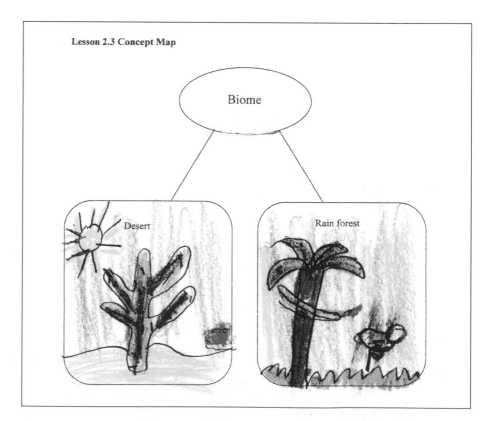

Encouraging Students to Draw Conclusions

Give each child the Lesson 2.3 Wonder Journal Label that poses the Wonder Statement as a question: *How is a rain forest different from a desert?*

Now write the following questions on chart paper and introduce them to your class one at a time. After reading each question with your students, encourage them to Turn and Talk with a partner as they look through the rain forest and desert "know" lists to find similarities and differences between the features of the two biomes and the creatures that live there.

- *What features do a rain forest biome and a desert biome have in common?*
- *How are the two biomes different?*
- *Do you think a kapok tree could grow in a desert? Why or why not?*
- *Do you think a saguaro cactus could grow in a rain forest? Why or why not?*
- *A roadrunner is a desert bird that can fly, but it prefers to run. Why wouldn't a rain forest be a good place for a roadrunner to live?*
- *The macaw, toucan, and cock-of-the-rock are brightly colored birds that eat fruit from rain forest trees. What do you think would happen if they tried to live in a desert?*

When the students seem ready, invite the class to gather for a Science Circle to discuss the questions. As children share their ideas, remind them to provide evidence to support their thoughts. Encourage classmates to agree or disagree, ask questions, and offer their own insights. You may facilitate the discussion by helping students stay on the topic and restating any unclear comments or ideas.

Now project the collared peccary photo you found earlier on the classroom interactive whiteboard. Let your students know that this member of the pig family is unusual because it can live in both rain forest and desert biomes. In the Amazon rain forest, it's active during the day. It spends most of its time eating fallen fruit, small plants, and snails on the shady forest floor. In the southwestern desert, a collared peccary stays cool by only coming out at night. It feeds on cactuses, insects, and sometimes small lizards.

Ask the class the following questions one at a time and guide a class discussion for each:

- *How do you think a rain forest collared peccary would describe its habitat?*
- *How do you think a rain forest collared peccary would describe its plant neighbors?*
- *How do you think a rain forest collared peccary would describe its animal neighbors?*
- *How do you think a desert collared peccary would describe its habitat?*

- *How do you think a desert collared peccary would describe its plant neighbors?*
- *How do you think a desert collared peccary would describe its animal neighbors?*

Let your students know that they are each going to contribute a page to a classroom book called *What a Collared Peccary Sees*. It will compare the plants and animals a rain forest collared peccary and a desert collared peccary see in their different habitats.

After passing out drawing paper to the whole class, give half of your students a Lesson 2.3 Rain Forest Card and the other half a Lesson 2.3 Desert Card. Then guide the children in matching the information on their card to the related entry in the rain forest and desert "know" lists. Eventually, the students should realize that if their card is green, their plant or animal lives in the rain forest. If their card is yellow, their plant or animal lives in the desert. Encourage students with a Rain Forest Card to paint a green wash on their drawing paper and students with a Desert Card to paint a yellow-brown wash on their paper.

While the washes are drying, use a document projector to show students the blue morpho butterfly on the endpapers of *The Great Kapok Tree*. Then draw their attention to the Lesson 2.3 Sample Poem that you copied onto chart paper earlier. After explaining that it describes one creature that the rain forest collared peccary sees in its habitat, let your students know that they are going to create a similar poem for the plant or animal on their rain forest or desert card.

Guide the class in understanding that all their poems will follow a pattern.

Line 1: I see a _____
Line 2: here in the _____ (Amazon rain forest or southwestern desert).
Line 3: It is _____ (words that describe what the plant or animal looks like).
Line 4: It is _____ (words that describe what the plant or animal is doing).
Line 5: (an idea or statement about the plant or animal)
Line 6: (a question or wonder statement about the plant or animal)

Encourage students to write a poem for their plant or animal in their Wonder Journals. They may want to look at the picture of their plant or animal in *Here Is the Southwestern Desert* or *The Great Kapok Tree*, or, if you think it would be helpful, they may use Google Images to find photo references for any creatures that are unfamiliar.

When the washes are dry and the poems have been written, invite students to complete their project by drawing a picture of a collared peccary looking at their assigned plant or animal on top of the color wash. Encourage students to add details from the "Descriptions" lists to their picture.

After students have written their names on the backs of the drawings, collect the artwork and their Wonder Journals. Then invite them to suggest a cover design for the class book.

During a free period, type the poems so that they are easier to read. Attach each child's poem and drawing to a large piece of construction paper to create a single large book page. Then assemble the pages into double-page spreads that pair a rain forest picture and poem with a desert picture and poem in a comparative format. After photographing the pages, so that students can have a copy to add to their Wonder Journals, incorporate the class's ideas into a front cover for the book.

To bring this lesson to a close, allow each child to share his or her picture and poem during a class reading of the book. Then place the book in the classroom library.

In this lesson, students learned that a biome is a large area of land with special features, and those features determine what kinds of plants and animals can live there. They also compared plants and animals that live in a desert biome with those in a rain forest biome. With these new insights and knowledge, students may begin to wonder if there are other kinds of biomes. They should feel free to record these new questions in their Wonder Journals.

Student picture and poem of a bobcat in the desert

I see a bobcat

here in the southwestern desert.

It is striped.

It is catching food.

The bobcat chases animals.

I wonder if the bobcat attacks people.

Reinforcing the Concept

- You can extend the lesson by reading the following book pairs and discussing the content with the Wonder Statement in mind:
  —*Desert Voices* by Byrd Baylor & *Here Is the Tropical Rainforest* by Madeleine Dunphy
  —*The Desert Is Theirs* by Byrd Baylor & *Rain, Rain, Rain Forest* by Brenda Z. Guiberson

- After reviewing the cumulative format of *Here Is the Southwestern Desert*, invite students to create their own cumulative text that features at least three rain forest plants or animals. Here's an example:

  Here is the tropical rainforest.

  Here is the kapok tree
  that grows tall:
  Here is the tropical rainforest.

  Here is the toucan
  who sits in the kapok tree
  that grows tall:
  Here is the tropical rainforest.

  Here is the jaguar
  who hunts the toucan
  who sits in the kapok tree
  that grows tall:
  Here is the tropical rainforest.

  Encourage students to illustrate their cumulative texts.

- When students have some free time, encourage them to read through the poems in the *What a Collared Peccary Sees* classroom book. Ask them to choose one of the questions or wonder statements from the last line of a poem and use it to write a letter from the plant or animal to the collared peccary. The information in the letter does not have to provide a factual answer. It can just be creative.

- Show your class how to make a pyramid diorama by cutting and folding a piece of 12-by-12-inch paper. (Excellent directions can be found online.) After each child has created two pyramids, invite students to turn each pyramid on its side to make a diorama frame. Then provide art materials, so that students can create at least one plant and two animals to add to a desert biome diorama and a rain forest biome diorama. As children finish the project, take a digital photo of each diorama. Then print out the images, so your students can add the pictures to their Wonder Journals.

ELA Links   By now, students have learned what a biome is and compared animals that live in a rain forest biome with those in a desert biome. Two different books—one fiction, one nonfiction—have played important roles in this lesson. The following questions can help students reflect on the aspects of the featured books that aroused their curiosity, generated and maintained their interest, and enhanced their understanding of the natural world.

- *What do the two books have in common?* (They both look at a variety of plants and animals that live in a particular environment and provide extra information at the beginning and end of the book.)
- *How are the two books different?* (*The Great Kapok Tree* is a fictional story that uses animals to explain the important role of the great kapok tree in the Amazon rainforest. *Here Is the Southwestern Desert* is a nonfiction book that introduces a variety of desert plants and animals using a cumulative structure.)
- *In* Here Is the Southwestern Desert, *author Madeleine Dunphy uses cumulative text to introduce readers to the land and creatures that live there. Do you think this is an effective structure? Why or why not?*
- *Some people consider* The Great Kapok Tree *to be a fable—a story with animals that has a moral, or lesson. Do you think the book has a lesson? If so, what is it?*
- *A fiction book usually has a main character. Who or what is the main character of* The Great Kapok Tree?

Reference   Keeley, Page. 2008. *Science Formative Assessment.* Thousand Oaks, CA: Corwin Press, pp. 65–67.

Lesson 2.4: Life in Wetlands

Catfish Kate and the Sweet Swamp Band by Sarah Weeks	&	Frog in a Bog by John Himmelman

About the Books

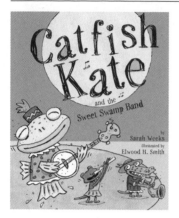

Catfish Kate and the Sweet Swamp Band may be a book about the importance of compromise, but the message of this rhythmic read-aloud is masked by fun, sassy text and colorful cartoon illustrations bursting with lively motion.

As Catfish Kate and her all-girl band battle it out with Skink and his Skunktail Boys, readers are introduced to the cast of characters that make their home in a southern swamp.

In *Frog in a Bog*, simple text and soft, detailed ink-and-watercolor illustrations offer children a close-up look at the natural events that occur on a typical day in a bog. Readers learn the names of common bog plants and animals and come to understand how they interact and that one event can trigger others. The back matter includes a simple field guide to bog life.

Wonder Statement: I wonder what lives in different kinds of wetlands.

Learning Goal Because 2-LS4-1 is such a content-rich performance expectation, we have written four lessons to fully address it. Lesson 2.2 defines the term *habitat* and clarifies that every living thing has its own unique habitat. Lesson 2.3 introduces the term *biome* and compares the features and creatures of rain forest and desert biomes. This lesson, 2.4, compares the cast of creatures living in two different kinds of wetlands, while Lesson 2.5 compares plants and animals that live in two different kinds of grasslands.

NGSS Performance Expectation 2-LS4-1. Make observations of plants and animals to compare the diversity of life in different habitats.

Prep Steps
1. Post the Wonder Statement, *I wonder what lives in different kinds of wetlands*, on the wall in the classroom meeting area.
2. Use Google Images to find a few photos of a wild bog (not an agricultural cranberry bog). Save copies to show later on the classroom interactive whiteboard, and then print out copies of the photos.

3. On chart paper, make two separate lists of the animals (left) and the plants (right) mentioned in the main text of *Frog in a Bog*. Be sure to leave open space on the left-hand side. You will add a title and third list there later in the lesson.

4. Scan and make color printouts of the following pages at the end of *Frog in a Bog*: "insects in the story," "amphibians and reptiles in the story," "birds in the story," "mammals in the story," and "plants in the story." Also, make a color printout of the tamarack tree and royal fern, which are mentioned in the main text. Then cut the printouts into separate labeled images.

5. Write the name of each plant and animal mentioned in *Frog in a Bog* on a separate piece of $8\frac{1}{2}$-by-11-inch drawing paper. Write *mosquito* and *duck* on two pieces of paper. Depending on the number of students in your class, prepare one or more larger pieces of drawing paper that say *bog*.

6. Make a copy of the Lesson 2.4 Readers Theater Script in Appendix B for each student in your class. Then read through the script and decide which part(s) to assign to each student based on his or her reading level.

7. Use Google Images to find a wide range of wetland photos, including some marshes and swamps, to show on the interactive whiteboard. Add the bog photos you found earlier to your collection.

8. Your students may not be familiar with some of the animal characters (catfish, skink) included in *Catfish Kate and the Sweet Swamp Band*. You may wish to use Google Images to find reference photos of these creatures.

9. Use the Lesson 2.4 Sample Slide: Bog Animals Vs. Swamp Animals in Appendix B to create Bog Animal Sticky Notes and Swamp Animal Sticky Notes.

10. Make copies of the Lesson 2.4 Wonder Journal Labels in Appendix B for each child in your class and cut them out. Then make copies of the Lesson 2.4 Concept Map.

Engaging Students   Begin the lesson by passing out copies of the Lesson 2.4 Wonder Journal Label with the Wonder Statement written on it. After reading the Wonder Statement with the class, ask your students to add it to their Wonder Journals.

Project the wild bog images you found earlier on the classroom interactive whiteboard, and explain that a bog is one kind of wetland—an area that is covered with water for at least part of the year. As you read through the *Frog in a Bog* animal and plant lists that you prepared earlier, show your class the matching printouts you made from the book.

Ask students to put their heads down on their desks as you scatter the plant and animal printouts and the bog images around the classroom.

Then give each child the labeled sheet of drawing paper that matches his or her assigned role in the readers theater. Narrators should receive the papers that say *bog*. Invite students to find the image that matches the word(s) on their paper and draw it on the other side.

When the class has finished their drawings, revisit the list of bog plants and animals on chart paper. Slowly read through the names, inviting the children to hold up their papers as the class reads the plant or animal name they've been assigned. Pass out copies of the Lesson 2.4 Readers Theater Script and tell your students that they will use their drawings as they practice and perform a fun readers theater. Help each student find the role that matches his or her drawing. Then guide your class as they practice reading through the script as a group a few times.

Now invite the students to stand at the front of the classroom and practice again. As the children read their parts, they should step forward and hold up their drawings. When the class is ready, they can perform the readers theater for another class.

Exploring with Students

Project the rest of the wetland photos you found earlier on your classroom interactive whiteboard, and ask students to describe what they see (open areas covered with water, a variety of plants, sometimes trees). After writing the class's descriptions on chart paper, let your students know that a wetland is one kind of biome. Tell them: *Just like the rain forest and desert biomes you learned about in Lesson 2.3, a wetland is a large area of land with special features, and those features determine what kinds of plants and animals can live there.*

Let the class know that you are going to read two books about wetlands and the creatures that live there. After introducing *Frog in a Bog* by opening the book and showing your class the full cover, ask the following questions one at a time and guide a class discussion for each:

- *Why do you think author-illustrator John Himmelman decided to create a cover with half of the scene on the front cover and half on the back cover?*
- *Why do you think John Himmelman blocked part of the scene with a white box that shows some animals that live in a bog?*
- *What do you think might be happening behind the white box?*

As students share, encourage them to provide rationale for their ideas.

After reading the first page of *Frog in a Bog*, explain that a bog is a kind of wetland that forms in many parts of the world. The water in a bog comes from rainfall.

The bog described in *Frog in a Bog* is in the northeastern United States. Show students New England and upstate New York on a map.

Then point out the state and approximate location of the city or town in which your students live.

Now show your class the wetland photos for a second time and point out which ones show bogs. Write the word *bog* on an index card, and encourage your students to guide you in creating a sketch to help them remember what the word means. Then post the card under the Wonder Statement on the wall.

Encourage students to listen carefully as you continue reading and to raise a hand when they hear words that remind them of something they've already heard. As soon as the class realizes that the book has a lot in common with the readers theater script, tell them that the script is based on the book. Since *Frog in a Bog* is short, start at the beginning again and invite students to raise their hands when they hear the part of the book that corresponds to their role in the readers theater.

As you read, occasionally stop to have students look carefully at the landscape in the illustrations. Ask them: *How is this painting of a bog similar to the photos we looked at? How is it different?*

When you are done reading the main text, turn back to the beginning of the book and direct your class's attention to the lists of bog animals and plants that you used at the beginning of the lesson. Point out that these lists include all the animals and plants featured in the main text of *Frog in a Bog*. Write the title "What We Know About a Northeastern Bog" above the lists and the heading "Bog Descriptions" in the open space on the left-hand side of the paper. Then work with your class to add information to the "Bog Descriptions" list.

Next, show your class the book's back matter. Do the children recognize the pictures? (They used some of the images to draw the bog animal and plant pictures they held while performing the readers theater.) Point out the other images and let the class know that these creatures are not mentioned in the book's text, but they are shown in the artwork. Work with the children to locate these creatures in the book (using a document projector if necessary), and then add them to your lists. Your completed lists may look like this:

Teaching Tip

The sample lists shown here are fully fleshed out and include all possible answers. You should not expect your class's lists to be as detailed, but they should include enough essential information to fully address the Wonder Statement. Providing students with copies of each list as soon as possible after the class compiles it will allow each child to keep a record of the investigation in his or her Wonder Journal.

What We Know About a Northeastern Bog

Bog Descriptions	Bog Animals	Bog Plants
Flat land	Frog (Spring peeper)	Fern
Wide open space	Mosquitoes	Moss
Soil in some places	Dragonfly	Sundew
Water in some places	Butterfly	Horsetail
Some tall plants	Muskrat	Steeplebush
Some small plants	Mole cricket	Pitcher plant
Blue sky, puffy clouds	Ducks	Leatherleaf

(continued)

What We Know About a Northeastern Bog *(continued)*

Bog Descriptions	Bog Animals	Bog Plants
	Turtle	Tamarack tree
	Fly	Cranberry
	Kingbird	Horned bladderwort
	Hawk	Bog club moss
	Ground cricket	Grass pink
	Water strider	Bulrush
	Katydid	Sensitive fern
	Tree cricket	Nutsedge
	Red-spotted newt	Labrador tea
	Water snake	Marsh fern
	Green frog	
	Yellow warbler	
	Red-winged blackbird	
	Northern waterthrush	

To review the bog word lists, ask students to think about which bog animal they would most like to see up close in real life. Encourage the class to read the bog animal list aloud with you. As you read the list a second time, invite students to vote for their favorite animal by raising a hand when they hear its name. Keep track of student responses to determine the class's overall favorite animal. Then repeat the process to determine the bog plant your class would most like to see up close in real life.

Now introduce *Catfish Kate and the Sweet Swamp Band* by reading the title and opening the book to show the full front and back cover. Then invite students to Turn and Talk about the following questions:

- *What do you think the book will be about?*
- *How do you think it will be different from* Frog in a Bog?
- *What do you think the book's setting will be? Are there any clues about the setting in the book's title?*

When the children seem ready, ask a few volunteers to share their thoughts and the rationale behind them.

Explain that a swamp is a kind of wetland. Like bogs, swamps can form in many parts of the world. But they fill with water when a river, stream, pond, or lake overflows its banks. If a swamp is flooded for only part of the year, some trees and shrubs can grow there. Write the word *swamp* on an index card, and encourage your students to guide you in creating a sketch to help them remember what the word means. Then post the card under the Wonder Statement on the wall.

The swamp described in *Catfish Kate and the Sweet Swamp Band* is in the southeastern United States. Point out this area of the country on a map, and then remind the students where they live.

Revisit just the swamp images you showed the class earlier when they were viewing photos of various wetlands and ask: *How is a swamp similar to a bog? How is it different?* Record your class's ideas on chart paper. Then pass out copies of the Lesson 2.4 Concept Map that you photocopied earlier and ask students to add them to their Wonder Journals. After the children have filled in the Desert and Rain Forest boxes based on the knowledge they gained about those biomes in Lesson 2.3, invite them to use the bog and swamp interactive whiteboard images, the Bog Descriptions list, and the list of similarities and differences you just recorded to add words and pictures to the Bog and Swamp boxes of the concept map in their Wonder Journals.

Invite students to take a second look at the cover of *Catfish Kate and the Sweet Swamp Band.* Ask the students: *How is illustrator Elwood Smith's painting of the swamp similar to the photos we looked at? How is it different?*

A completed Concept Map of a bog and swamp

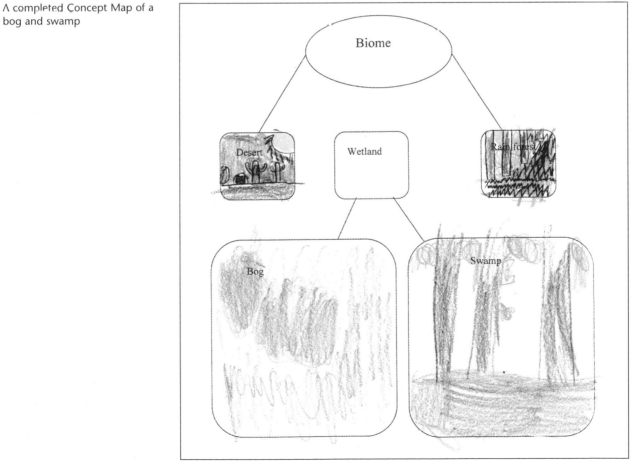

As you read the book, encourage your class to listen carefully to the language that author Sarah Weeks uses. Do they notice anything fun about it? (There is rhyme and strong rhythm.) Why do they think the author wrote the book this way?

You may wish to show your students reference photos of animals that may be unfamiliar to them (catfish, skink). When you reach the page that mentions the "skeeter," assure the class that this is a familiar creature. Encourage students to look at the illustration and guess the animal's identity. If they don't realize that *skeeter* is a slang term for *mosquito*, provide additional hints, such as that the creature is an insect and that it is also found in northeastern bogs.

When you have finished the book, turn back to the beginning and work with your class to create a set of lists titled "What We Know About a Southeastern Swamp." After adding ideas students might already have to the "Swamp Descriptions" list, fill in the animal and plant lists as you revisit the words and pictures. Your completed lists may look like this:

What We Know About a Southeastern Swamp

Swamp Descriptions	Swamp Animals	Swamp Plants
Very green	Catfish	Grassy plants
Some trees and bushes	Newt	Trees
Soil in some places	Bees?	Cattails
Water in some places	Alligator	
Some plants on top of water	Snake	
Sunny in some places	Skeeter	
Shady in some places	Spider	
Spooky	Owl	
	Skink	
	Skunk	
	Worm	

To review the swamp word lists, ask students to think about which swamp animal they would most like to see up close in real life. Encourage the class to read the swamp animal list aloud with you. As you read the list a second time, invite students to vote for their favorite animal by raising a hand when they hear its name. Keep track of student responses to determine the class's overall favorite animal. Then repeat the process to determine the swamp plant your class would most like to see up close in real life.

Next, ask your class to vote on whether they'd rather visit a bog or a swamp. Then invite a few volunteers to explain the rationale behind their decision.

Encouraging Students to Draw Conclusions

During a free period, use a digital camera to take separate photos of your class's "Bog Animals," "Bog Plants," "Swamp Animals," and "Swamp Plants" lists. Use a program like PowerPoint or OneNote to create one interactive whiteboard slide with the animal lists side by side and a second slide with the plant lists side by side. You may wish to use the Lesson 2.4 Sample Slides in Appendix B for guidance.

At the beginning of the class's next science block, give each child the Lesson 2.4 Wonder Journal Label that poses the Wonder Statement as a question: *What lives in different kinds of wetlands?*

After projecting the Bog Animals Vs. Swamp Animals slide, read through the animal names with your students and ask them to buddy up. Give each pair one or two of the Bog Animal Sticky Notes you created earlier.

Hang seven pieces of chart paper around the room and write one of the following animal group names at the top of each paper: Insects, Amphibians, Reptiles, Birds, Mammals, Fish, Other. Below these headings write the subheadings "In a Bog" and "In a Swamp." Spend a few minutes discussing the characteristics of each animal group with your class, and then encourage the buddies to use the back matter of *Frog in a Bog* as a guide as they post their sticky notes under the correct headings. After reviewing the animals under each heading, pass out the Swamp Animal Sticky Notes and repeat the process. The results should look something like this:

Insects

In a Bog	In a Swamp
Mosquitoes	Bees?
Dragonfly	Skeeter
Butterfly	
Mole cricket	
Fly	
Ground cricket	
Water strider	
Katydid	
Tree cricket	

Amphibians

In a Bog	In a Swamp
Frog (Spring peeper)	Newt
Red-spotted newt	
Green frog	

Reptiles

In a Bog	In a Swamp
Turtle	Alligator
Water snake	Snake
	Skink

Birds

In a Bog	In a Swamp
Ducks	Owl
Kingbird	
Hawk	
Yellow warbler	
Red-winged blackbird	
Northern waterthrush	

Mammals

In a Bog	In a Swamp
Muskrat	Skunk

Fish

In a Bog	In a Swamp
	Catfish

Other

In a Bog	In a Swamp
	Spider
	Worm

Invite your students to participate in an Agreement Circle (Keeley 2008). In this activity, the class forms a circle and listens as you read a statement. Students who agree with the statement step inside the circle and turn to face their classmates (who disagree with the statement). Then small groups that include children who agree and disagree should discuss their ideas. When they are done, students may decide to move into or out of the center of the circle.

Here are some statements you might ask students to consider:

- The same kinds of animals live in bogs and swamps.
- Some kinds of animals live in both bogs and swamps.
- There are amphibians living in both swamps and bogs.
- If I were afraid of alligators, I would never visit a bog, but I would visit a swamp.
- If I wanted to go fishing, I should go to a swamp instead of a bog.
- Birdwatchers would have a better time in a bog than a swamp.

- There seems to be more different kinds of insects in a swamp than in a bog.
- There seems to be more different kinds of reptiles in a bog than in a swamp.

When the class has finished the activity, encourage students to take another look at the last two statements. Let the children know that scientists use the word *diversity* when they talk about the number of different kinds of plants or animals that live in an environment. For example, after reading *Frog in a Bog* and *Catfish Kate and the Sweet Swamp Band*, they might say that there seems to be greater diversity of insects in a bog then in a swamp.

Write the word *diversity* on an index card, and encourage your students to guide you in creating a sketch to help them remember what the word means. Then post the card under the Wonder Statement on the wall.

Now project the Bog Plants Vs. Swamp Plants slide, and invite your students to participate in a second Agreement Circle in which they consider the following statements:

- The same kinds of plants live in bogs and swamps.
- A swamp would be a great place to climb trees.
- A bog would be a great place to climb trees.
- If I wanted to take pictures of pretty flowers, I would go to a swamp rather than a bog.
- Cranberry juice is made from a swamp plant.
- Some of the plants that live in a swamp feed on insects.
- There *seems to be* a greater diversity of plants in a bog than in a swamp.

When the class has finished the activity, write the last statement on chart paper. Below it, write a second statement, "There *is* a greater diversity of plants in a bog than in a swamp." Then ask your class the following questions one at a time:

- *What is the difference between these two statements?*
- *Do you think there might be more plants living in a swamp than we saw in the illustrations in* Catfish Kate and the Sweet Swamp Band? *What is your rationale?*
- *Why do you think the author and illustrator of* Catfish Kate and the Sweet Swamp Band *mentioned lots of swamp animals but only a few plants?*

To bring the lesson to a close, give each child copies of the Lesson 2.4 Wonder Journal Labels with the following sentence frames, which are modified from Agreement Circle statements:

Based on the books we've read, there seems to be a greater diversity of insects in a _____ than in a _____.
My evidence is:

Based on the books we've read, there seems to be a greater diversity of reptiles in a _____ than in a _____.
My evidence is:

Based on the books we've read, there seems to be a greater diversity of plants in a _____ than in a _____.
My evidence is:

Encourage the children to add the sentence frames to their Wonder Journals one at a time and use information from the swamp and bog lists and the animal groupings as well as discussions they had during the Agreement Circle activity to fill in the blanks and use words and/or pictures to provide evidence. If students have trouble coming up with evidence, suggest that they list the number of insects, reptiles, and plants in each kind of wetland.

This student uses quantitative data to compare the diversity of creatures living in a bog and a swamp.

Based on the books we've read, there seems to be a greater diversity of insects in a **Bog** than in a **Swamp** My evidence is:

9 Bog   2 swamp

Based on the books we've read, there seems to be a greater diversity of reptiles in a **Swamp** than in a **Bog** . My evidence is:

3 swamp   2 Bog

Based on the books we've read, there seems to be a greater diversity of plants in a **Bog** than in a **Swamp** My evidence is:

lots in a Bog

3 swamp

In this lesson students learned about two different kinds of wetlands and compared the diversity of plants and animals that live in a bog and a swamp. With these new insights and knowledge, students may begin to wonder if there are other kinds of wetlands and, if so, what kinds of creatures live there. They should feel free to record these new questions in their Wonder Journals.

Reinforcing the Concept

- You can extend the lesson by reading the following book pairs and discussing the content with the Wonder Statement in mind:
  —*Frog in the Bog* by Karma Wilson & *Who Lives in an Alligator Hole?* by Anne Rockwell
  —*Big Night for Salamanders* by Sarah Marwil Lamstein & *A Day in the Salt Marsh* by Kevin Kurtz
  —*Deep in the Swamp* by Donna M. Bateman & *The Swamp Where Gator Hides* by Marianne Berkes
- Guide students as they create an interactive bulletin board with the title Where Do These Plants and Animals Live? Ask each student to draw, label, and cut around the edges of two separate pictures—one of a bog plant or animal and one of a swamp plant or animal. Each student must pick different plants and animals, focusing on the examples included in *Frog in a Bog* and *Catfish Kate and the Sweet Swamp Band*. Add one side of a Velcro button to the back of each picture.

  Cover the left side of the bulletin board with light green (top) and blue (bottom) paper and label it bog. Cover the right side with dark green (top) and blue (bottom) paper and label it swamp. Cover a central band of the bulletin board with orange paper and attach seven pockets made from folded sheets of paper and label them: Insects, Amphibians, Reptiles, Birds, Mammals, Fish, Other. After sorting the student artwork into the appropriate pockets, stick the other sides of the Velcro coins to the bog and swamp areas of the bulletin board. When students have free time, they can match the plants and animals pictures to the correct wetland home.
- After reviewing the back matter of *Frog in a Bog*, encourage students to make eight-page booklets, as shown on page 212. Then, using those booklets, create bog or swamp field guides that include a decorative front cover, a blank back cover, and labeled drawings of a plant and one animal from each of the following groups: Insects, Amphibians, Reptiles, Birds, Mammals. When the students are done, they can glue the back covers into their Wonder Journals.

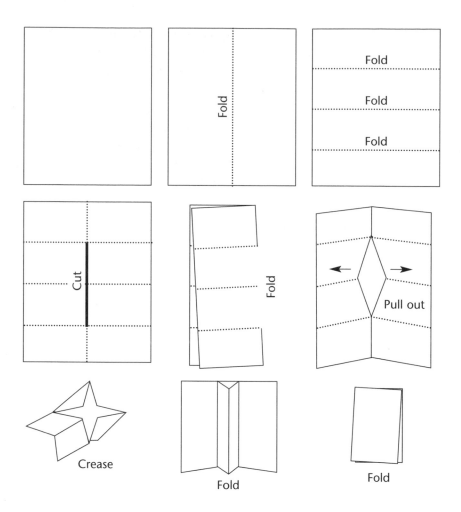

ELA Links   By now, students have learned a lot about the diversity of life in two different kinds of wetlands—a bog and a swamp. Two books—one fiction, one nonfiction—have played important roles in this lesson. The following questions can help students reflect on the aspects of the featured books that aroused their curiosity, generated and maintained their interest, and enhanced their understanding of the natural world.

- *What do the two books have in common?* (They are both set in a wetland and introduce a variety of plants and animals that live there. They are both illustrated with paintings.)
- *How are the two books different?* (*Catfish Kate and the Sweet Swamp Band* is a fun, fictional story about two groups of animals that live in a swamp. *Frog in a Bog* is a nonfiction book that describes how a variety of plants and animals interact in a bog.)
- *How is the writing style in the two books different?* (The text in *Catfish Kate and the Sweet Swamp Band* has a clear rhythm and is full of

rhyme. It sounds like a song. The text in *Frog in a Bog* is simple and straightforward.) *Which book is easier to read? Why? Which book is more fun to read? Why?*

- *How is the style of the artwork in the two books different?* (The art in *Catfish Kate and the Sweet Swamp Band* is colorful and cartoony and silly. The art in *Frog in a Bog* looks almost like photographs. It is easy to identify the plants and animals.)

- *Does the style of the art in each book match the style of the text? Why or why not?*

Reference Keeley, Page. 2008. *Science Formative Assessment*. Thousand Oaks, CA: Corwin Press, pp. 51–53.

Lesson 2.5: Life in Grasslands

| *Water Hole Waiting* by Jane Kurtz and Christopher Kurtz | & | *Out on the Prairie* by Donna M. Bateman |

About the Books

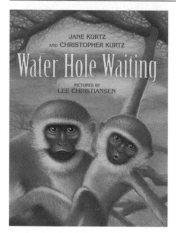

As the sizzling sun beats on an African plain, an impatient young vervet monkey waits for just the right moment to quench his thirst at a busy water hole. Rich, elegant prose and vivid, realistic pastel artwork, often from a monkey's eye view, make *Water Hole Waiting* a wonderful dawn-to-dusk introduction to a savanna habitat and the cast of creatures that call it home.

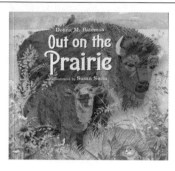

Using the traditional rhyme scheme of "Over in the Meadow," *Out on the Prairie* introduces young readers to a stunning variety of plants and animals that live and grow in the mixed-grass prairie of Badlands National Park in South Dakota. The text's read-aloud potential and the appealing energetic cut-paper, mixed-media collages make the book a delightful introduction to a unique and beautiful ecosystem. An informative illustrated appendix provides further details about American prairies and the creatures that call them home.

Wonder Statement: I wonder what lives in different kinds of grasslands.

Learning Goal   Because 2-LS4-1 is such a content-rich performance expectation, we have written four lessons to fully address it. Lesson 2.2 defines the term *habitat* and clarifies that every living thing has its own unique habitat. Lesson 2.3 introduces the term *biome* and compares the features and creatures of rain forest and desert biomes. Lesson 2.4 compares the cast of creatures living in two different kinds of wetlands, while this lesson, 2.5, compares plants and animals that live in two different kinds of grasslands.

NGSS Performance Expectation 2-LS4-1. Make observations of plants and animals to compare the diversity of life in different habitats.

Prep Steps
1. Post the Wonder Statement, *I wonder what lives in different kinds of grasslands*, on the wall in the classroom meeting area.
2. Use Google Images to find a wide range of grassland photos, including some of African savannas and North American prairies; a world map that highlights the location of savannas in Africa; a

map of North America that highlights the location of prairies; and photos of the following animals: vervet monkey, hippopotamus, zebra, wildebeest, crocodile, lion, elephant, giraffe, bison, pronghorn, prairie dog, coyote, Great Plains toad.

3. Print out the thirteen animal photos and laminate them to create a set of Animal Photo Cards.

4. Using a program like PowerPoint or OneNote, create a slide that shows an African savanna photo and a North American prairie photo side by side.

5. Make enough copies of the Lesson 2.5 Concept Map, Lesson 2.5 Plants on Savannas and Prairies Worksheet, and Lesson 2.5 Animals on Savannas and Prairies Worksheet (all in Appendix B) for all the students in your class.

6. Write each of the following words from the Lesson 2.5 Plants on Savannas and Prairies Worksheet on separate index cards: *prairies, savannas, plants, flowers, grass.* Then do the same for each of the following words from the Lesson 2.5 Animals on Savannas and Prairies Worksheet: *predators, prey, large animals, insects, frog, toad.*

7. Gather a diverse assortment of postcards and bring them to school.

8. Make copies of the Lesson 2.5 Wonder Journal Labels in Appendix B for each child in your class and cut them out. Then make copies of the Lesson 2.5 Sample Bison Postcard for half the students in your class and copies of the Lesson 2.5 Sample Wildebeest Postcard for the other half of the class.

Engaging Students　Begin the lesson by passing out copies of the Lesson 2.5 Wonder Journal Label with the Wonder Statement written on it. After reading the Wonder Statement with the class, ask your students to add it to their Wonder Journals.

As you project the African savanna/North American prairie slide you created earlier on the classroom interactive whiteboard, ask students to buddy up. Give each pair an Animal Photo Card and encourage the children to discuss the following questions with their partner:

- *What kind of animal is it?*
- *Does the animal live on an African savanna or on a North American prairie?*

Next, one member of each pair will act as a Desk Reference, while the other becomes a Desk Roamer. Each Reference will stay at his or her desk. Roamers will move around the room, visiting other desks. Each Reference will try to convince Roamers that the answers his or her team came up with are correct. If Roamers disagree, they should explain why.

When Roamers have finished visiting all the References, allow pairs a final opportunity to exchange ideas while you write the headings "Savanna Animals" and "Prairie Animals" on a piece of chart paper. Then encourage the partners to take turns coming forward to share the name of their animal and, using double-sided tape, attach their Animal Photo Card where they think it belongs. Write the name of each animal next to the image.

Exploring with Students

Project the rest of the grassland photos you found earlier on your classroom interactive whiteboard, and ask students to describe what they see (flat areas of land covered with grass and other small plants; not many trees). After writing the class's ideas on chart paper, let your students know that a grassland is one kind of biome. Tell them: *Just like the rain forest, desert, and wetland biomes you learned about in Lessons 2.3 and 2.4, a grassland is a large area of land with special features, and those features determine what kinds of plants and animals can live there.*

Let the class know that in this lesson, they are going to learn about two different kinds of grasslands—African savannas and North American prairies. Introduce *Water Hole Waiting* by reading the title and showing the front and back covers. Then ask the following questions one at a time:

- *What do you think the book will be about?*
- *What do you think the title means?*
- *What do you think the book's setting will be—an African savanna or a North American prairie?*

As students share ideas, encourage them to explain their rationale.

After reading the first page of the book, take a few minutes to project the African savanna map you found earlier on the interactive whiteboard. Let your class know that in central and southern Africa, there are two seasons instead of four. During the rainy season, it rains almost every day. *Water Hole Waiting* takes place at the beginning of the dry season, when it hardly rains at all and water is getting harder to find.

Now show your class the grassland photos for a second time, and point out which ones show the African savanna. Write the word *savanna* on an index card, and encourage your students to guide you in creating a sketch to help them remember what the word means. Then post the card under the Wonder Statement on the wall.

Hold up the book's first page and ask your class: *How is illustrator Lee Christiansen's painting of the African savanna similar to the photos we looked at? How is it different?*

As you read the next two spreads, ask your class to listen carefully to the language the authors, Jane and Christopher Kurtz, use. Do they

Teaching Tip

Some of the vocabulary in *Water Hole Waiting* may be unfamiliar to second graders, especially English language learners. When an unfamiliar word (*foraging, cartwheels*) arises, write it on an index card and encourage your students to guide you in creating a sketch to help them remember what the word means. Then post the card under the Wonder Statement on the wall.

notice anything fun about it? (There is internal rhyme.) Do they notice any surprising word choices? ("Silence pokes," "sun cartwheels.") Why do your students think the authors use this kind of language?

When you reach the page that begins "Monkey thinks it's time for a drink," explain that a water hole is an important savanna feature. During the dry season, savanna animals depend on water holes to quench their thirst. When small animals, like monkeys, visit a water hole, they have to be careful. Larger animals, like hippos, might not want to be disturbed. And sometimes predators wait at water holes, so they can attack thirsty animals.

After you read the next double-page spread, ask students to look closely at the illustration. Do they see any clues that can help them predict what animals will visit the water hole next? (Zebras.) Encourage them to look for more clues in the art as you continue to read. Also, ask the class to keep paying attention to the book's beautiful language.

When you have finished reading the book, turn back to the beginning and work with your class to create a list of savanna descriptions as well as lists of plants and animals that live in the grassland biome where *Water Hole Waiting* is set. Your completed lists may look like this:

What We Know About an African Savanna

Savanna Descriptions	Savanna Animals	Savanna Plants
Flat land	Frog	Grass
Sunny	Crickets	Acacia tree
Two seasons	Vervet monkeys	
Limited water in dry season	Hippopotamuses	
Lots of open space	Birds	
Sizzling heat	Insects	
	Zebras	
	Wildebeest	
	Crocodile	
	Lion	
	Elephants	
	Giraffe	

> **Teaching Tip**
>
> The sample lists shown here are fully fleshed out and include all possible answers. You should not expect your class's lists to be as detailed, but they should include enough essential information to fully address the Wonder Statement. Providing students with copies of each list as soon as possible after the class compiles it will allow each child to keep a record of the investigation in his or her Wonder Journal.

Encourage students to revisit the chart paper with the Animal Photo Cards and compare the names and images there to the animal names in the "What We Know About an African Savanna" animal list and the animals shown in *Water Hole Waiting*. Ask the class:

- *Are there any Animal Photo Cards in the wrong place?*
- *Were any of the Animal Photo Cards misidentified?*

If the answer to either question is yes, invite student volunteers to correct the mistakes. Then, as a class, read through all the animal names, plant names, and savanna descriptions in the "What We Know About an African Savanna" lists.

Now introduce *Out on the Prairie* by reading the title and showing the front and back cover. Then ask the same three questions you used to begin the class's exploration of *Water Hole Waiting*:

- *What do you think the book will be about?*
- *What do you think the title means?*
- *What do you think the book's setting will be?*

As students share ideas, encourage them to explain their rationale.

Explain that a prairie is a kind of grassland found in the United States and Canada. While projecting the North American prairie map you found earlier, point out Badlands National Park in South Dakota, where *Out on the Prairie* is set, as well as the state and approximate location of the city or town in which your students live.

Revisit the prairie images that you showed the class earlier and ask: *How is a prairie similar to a savanna? How is it different?* Record your class's ideas on chart paper. Then pass out copies of the Lesson 2.5 Concept

A completed Concept Map for savanna and prairie

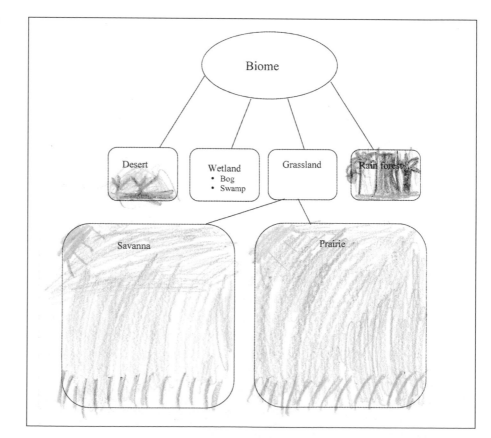

Map that you photocopied earlier, and ask students to add it to their Wonder Journals.

After the children have filled in the Desert and Rain Forest boxes based on the knowledge they gained about those biomes in Lesson 2.3, invite them to use the savanna and prairie interactive whiteboard images, the "Savanna Descriptions" list, and the list of similarities and differences you just recorded to add words and pictures to the Savanna and Prairie boxes of the concept map in their Wonder Journals.

Next, begin a set of prairie "know" lists similar to the ones you created while reading *Water Hole Waiting*. After adding ideas students might already have to the "Prairie Descriptions" list, begin reading the book, filling in the lists as you go. Your completed lists may look like this:

What We Know About a North American Prairie

Prairie Descriptions	Prairie Animals	Prairie Plants
Flat land	Bison	Snakeroot
Wide open space	Pronghorn	Long grasses
Sea of grass	Meadowlark	Various wildflowers
Sunny	Prairie dog	Grama grass
Dusty: dry, loose soil	Grasshopper	Daisies
Blue sky, puffy clouds	Sharp-tailed grouse	Yucca
Constant wind	Beetles	Primrose
	Howdy owl	Clover
	Rattlesnake	
	Coyote	
	Great Plains toad	

As you read through the lists of prairie descriptions, animals, and plants with the class, ask students to raise a hand if they see and hear a word or phrase that they would also use to describe a savanna. When you have completed the lists, ask the class: *How are the plants and animals that live on a North American prairie similar to those living on an African savanna? How are they different?*

Encouraging Students to Draw Conclusions

During a free period, use a digital camera to take separate photos of your class's "Savanna Animals," "Savanna Plants," "Prairie Animals," and "Prairie Plants" lists. Use a program like PowerPoint or OneNote to create one slide with the animal lists side by side and a second slide with the plant lists side by side. You may wish to use the Lesson 2.5 Sample Slides in Appendix B for guidance.

At the beginning of the class's next science block, give each child the Lesson 2.5 Wonder Journal Label that poses the Wonder Statement as a question: *What lives in different kinds of grasslands?* Ask students to place the label in their Wonder Journal on a left-hand page.

Project the Savanna Plants Vs. Prairie Plants slide on the classroom interactive whiteboard. After reading through the plant names with your students, ask the class: *What do you notice about the two lists?* Encourage students to Turn and Talk with a classmate as they consider this question.

Give each student a copy of the Lesson 2.5 Plants on Savannas and Prairies Worksheet, and invite the children to use the words in the boxes at the bottom of the page to complete the sentences. Students may work together to figure out where the words belong, but each child should complete a worksheet and add it to his or her Wonder Journal.

As students work on this activity, copy the four sentences from the worksheet onto a piece of chart paper. When the students seem ready, invite them to grab their Wonder Journals and gather for a Science Circle. Randomly pass out the Plants on Savannas and Prairies index cards you prepared earlier.

As you read each sentence on the chart paper, invite student volunteers to suggest answers that are supported by evidence from the Savanna Plants and Prairie Plants lists. Classmates should feel free to agree or disagree with one another or ask questions. If a discussion develops, you should help students stay focused and restate any unclear comments or ideas. When the class is in agreement, the student with the appropriate index card should tape it to the blank line. (Answer Key: 1. prairies, savannas; 2. plants; 3. flowers; 4. grass.)

When the class has discussed all four sentences, ask students to return to their seats. Encourage the children to circle one sentence on

A student adds an index card to the classroom version of the Lesson 2.5 Plants on Savannas and Prairies Worksheet.

the plants worksheet in their Wonder Journals and use words and pictures to provide evidence for that statement on the journal page.

Now project the Savanna Animals Vs. Prairie Animals slide. After reading through the animal names with your students and giving them time to Turn and Talk as they compare the two lists, give each child a Lesson 2.5 Animals on Savannas and Prairies Worksheet and randomly pass out the six Animals on the Savannas and Prairies index cards that you prepared earlier. Then repeat the activity outlined above. (Answer Key: 1. predators, prey; 2. large animals; 3. insects; 4. frog, toad.)

Invite students to take another look at the wildebeest and bison Animal Photo Cards, and explain that even though these two animals are not closely related, they have a lot in common. They look similar and are both plant eaters with large habitats.

Divide the class into two groups. Tell students in the first group that they are going to pretend to be a herd of wildebeest living on an African savanna. They think their grassland habitat is a very special place. The second group will pretend to be a herd of bison living on a North American prairie. They also think their grassland habitat is a very special place.

As you pass out the copies of the Lesson 2.5 Sample Bison Postcard and Lesson 2.5 Sample Wildebeest Postcard that you prepared earlier, let the class know that each herd is going to send the other one postcards from its members that explain why their home and their neighbors are so special. Show your class some real postcards, and point out that one side has a picture and the other side has writing. On the front of their postcards, the children should draw their assigned animal in its grassland habitat. On the back, they should write several sentences that explain what makes the grassland special. Encourage group members to help one another brainstorm to come up with ideas.

To bring this lesson to a close, allow students to share their postcards with the rest of the class. Then encourage the children to staple their

A drawing on the front of a North American Prairie Postcard (left) and a note on the back (right)

Dear Wildebeest,

I live on a prairie grassland. My habitat is special because it is very sunny and you can eat a lot of food like long grass, but you need to look out for small animals like snaks! There are lots of animals I can huddle up with wene it gets cold.

Your Friend,

_____ Mr. _____ Bison

postcards into their Wonder Journals so that they can view both sides easily. This artwork will serve as a physical record of what they have learned during the lesson.

In this lesson students learned about two different kinds of grasslands and compared the diversity of plants and animals that live on a savanna and a prairie. With these new insights and knowledge, students may begin to wonder if there are other kinds of grasslands and, if so, what kinds of creatures live there. They should feel free to record these new questions in their Wonder Journals.

Reinforcing the Concept

- You can extend the lesson by reading the following book pairs and discussing the content with the Wonder Statement in mind:
  —*The Great Fuzz Frenzy* by Janet Stevens and Susan Stevens Crummel & *African Acrostics* by Avis Harley
  —*Pinduli* by Janell Cannon & *Butterfly Eyes and Other Secrets of the Meadow* by Joyce Sidman
- Haiku poetry has three nonrhyming lines. The first line has five syllables, the second has seven, and the third has five. Invite students to use information from the "know" lists and their own creative ideas to write and illustrate haiku poems about the African savanna and the North American prairie. For example:

  Primrose and daisies
  Bison roam the wide prairie
  Prairie in summer

  Zebras are thirsty
  Less water in dry season
  Sizzling savanna

- Encourage students to use their imaginations to answer the following question in words and pictures: *What would savanna grass and prairie grass whisper to one another if they met?*
- *Diversity* is a word that has special meaning in both Lessons 2.4 and 2.5. Encourage students to draw a picture that shows the diversity of living things (trees, birds, insects, etc.) that inhabit the area around your school.

ELA Links   By now, students have learned a lot about the diversity of life in two different kinds of grasslands—an African savanna and a North American prairie. Two different books—one fiction, one nonfiction—have played important roles in this lesson. The following questions can help students reflect on the aspects of the featured books that aroused their curiosity, generated and maintained their interest, and enhanced their understanding of the natural world.

- *What do the two books have in common?* (They are both set in grass-land environments and introduce a variety of plants and animals that live there.)
- *How are the two books different?* (*Water Hole Waiting* is a fictional story told from a young monkey's point of view. *Out on the Prairie* is a nonfiction counting book that highlights a broad range of creatures that live and interact on a prairie.)
- *How is the writing style in the two books different?* (The text in *Water Hole Waiting* is beautiful, with some surprising word choices. The text in *Out on the Prairie* has a simple, repetitive rhythm and rhyme.) *Which style do you like better? Why?*
- *How is the style of the artwork in the two books different?* (The art in *Water Hole Waiting* is realistic and luminous. The mixed media collages in *Out on the Prairie* are realistic, too, but sometimes include some surprising materials.)
- *In* Water Hole Waiting, *do you see things in the pictures that aren't mentioned in the text? What, if anything, do they add to the story?* (Some animals are shown in the pictures, but not mentioned in the text. Sometimes these animals foreshadow what will be discussed on the next double-page spread.)

Lesson 2.6: How Plants Change as They Grow

Plantzilla by Jerdine Nolen	&	*A Seed Is Sleepy* by Dianna Hutts Aston

About the Books

Through a series of letters and postcards, *Plantzilla* tells the story of a family's summer with a most unusual plant. At the end of the school year, Mortimer Henryson takes home the class plant. As he loves and nurtures Plantzilla, the plant grows wildly, develops an appetite for meat (the family dog disappears), and begins performing all sorts of amazing feats. Mortimer's parents worry, but the boy is delighted with his clever, increasingly humanlike plant. Exuberant watercolor-and-pencil illustrations show Plantzilla's tendrils creeping and crawling from spread to spread, each one doing something different.

Full of rich color and intricate detail, the breath-taking, beautiful ink-and-watercolor art in *A Seed Is Sleepy* is sure to captivate young readers. Short lyrical phrases in large print describe seeds with accessible qualities ("A seed is sleepy." "A seed is adventurous.") that will intrigue children, while more sophisticated secondary text in smaller print expands on each phrase to introduce basic botany concepts. The book includes a wonderful chart depicting the stages of plant growth for five diverse plant species.

Wonder Statement: I wonder how plants change as they grow.

Learning Goal   This lesson focuses on how flowering plants change as they grow, a topic that has traditionally been part of the K–2 life-science curricula but is not included in the NGSS for K–2. Because some states have chosen to adapt rather than adopt the NGSS, we believe that many K–2 educators will continue to teach this concept. In this lesson, students learn that even though seeds come in a variety of shapes and sizes, they all have the potential to develop into plants. They also discover that plants grow and change in predictable ways throughout their lives.

Prep Steps   1. Post the Wonder Statement, *I wonder how plants change as they grow*, on the wall in the classroom meeting area.

2. Using a color copier and the heaviest-weight paper available, make six photocopies of the first and last double-page spreads in *A Seed Is Sleepy*. After cutting out the seed and plant images, choose the

twelve seeds and matching plants that you think will interest your students most and create six decks with twenty-four cards in each deck. Don't worry if the cards vary in shape and size.

3. Use Google Images to find photos of a bean plant with flowers and a rice plant with flowers and fruits.

4. Do an Internet search to find time-lapse videos of plants growing.

5. Make copies of the Lesson 2.6 Wonder Journal Labels in Appendix B for each child in your class and cut them out. Then make copies of the Lesson 2.6 True/False Student Worksheet for each child and one copy of the Lesson 2.6 Plant Growth Statement Cards (see Appendix B). You may wish to laminate the statement cards after cutting them up.

Engaging Students

Begin the lesson by passing out copies of the Lesson 2.6 Wonder Journal Label with the Wonder Statement written on it. After reading the Wonder Statement with the class, ask your students to add it to their Wonder Journals.

Divide the class into six groups, and give each group a deck of the seed-plant cards you prepared earlier. Look at the cards with your students and help them read the labels. After pointing out that the deck contains twelve matching seed-plant pairs and giving the class time to notice how different a seed can look from the plant it becomes, invite the groups to play Concentration with the cards. In this memory game, students randomly place their cards face down in orderly rows. Then each child

Students play the seed-plant Concentration game.

takes a turn flipping over two cards. If the cards do not represent a matching plant-seed pair, the child turns them face down and the next child takes a turn. If the cards do show a matching plant-seed pair, the cards remain face up and the student who made the match gets a point.

When the students have played a few rounds of Concentration, encourage them to look at and compare all their seed cards. Ask the class: *Is there anything all your seeds seem to have in common?* After recording their responses on chart paper, invite the students to look at and compare all their plant cards.

Ask them: *What do all the plants seem to have in common?* After adding their ideas to the chart paper, encourage each group to choose one seed-plant pair and discuss how the seed is different from the plant it will become. Then ask each of the six groups to choose a spokesperson. Use the video setting on a digital camera to record the student spokespeople explaining their groups' thoughts. Later, you can use a simple video editing program to create a class video.

Exploring with Students

Introduce *Plantzilla* by showing the front cover and asking students if they think the book is fiction or nonfiction. Why? How would they describe the character on the cover? How would they describe the plant? Can they point out the plant's leaves? How about the flowers?

Next, ask this question: *What do you think the plant in the book looked like when it was younger?* Encourage students to respond to this question in their Wonder Journals, using a combination of words and pictures. When the class seems ready, invite a few volunteers to share their ideas.

As you read *Plantzilla*, work with your students to begin a data table like the one below. Record any changes the students notice in the plant as the story progresses. (Be sure to leave extra room on the right, so you can add another column later.)

How Plantzilla Changes as He Grows	
He starts eating real food.	
He can move on his own.	
He shows feelings.	
He blooms.	
He writes a letter.	

When you are done reading, ask the students if they think *Plantzilla* describes how a real plant changes as it grows. *Does anything listed in the data table seem unrealistic?*

Now introduce *A Seed Is Sleepy* by asking students to look at the cover and predict whether the book is fiction or nonfiction. Encourage them to explain their rationale.

Lessons for Grade 2

Teaching Tip

Some of the vocabulary in *Plantzilla* and *A Seed Is Sleepy* may be unfamiliar to second graders, especially English language learners. When an unfamiliar word (*symbiotic, Chihuahua, metamorphosis, germinate, dormant*) arises, write it on an index card and encourage your students to guide you in creating a sketch to help them remember what the word means. Then post the card under the Wonder Statement on the wall.

Teaching Tip

The entries in the sample data tables shown here are fully fleshed out and include all possible answers. You should not expect your class's tables to be as detailed, but they should include enough essential information to fully address the Wonder Statement. Providing students with copies of each data table as soon as possible after the class compiles it will allow each child to keep a record of the investigation in his or her Wonder Journal.

Next, ask the class why they think the author, Dianna Hutts Aston, chose the title for the book. After students have had a few minutes to Turn and Talk with a neighbor, invite a few volunteers to share their ideas with the class.

Show the students the book's first double-page spread and ask them if any of the images remind them of something they've seen before. Why do they think the illustrator, Sylvia Long, decided to show so many seeds at the beginning of the book?

After reading the first page of *A Seed Is Sleepy*, ask the students if the author's use of the word *sleepy* makes more sense now. As you continue reading the book, point out unusual descriptive words in the large text and ask students to guess why the author chose those words. Then read the explanatory text in smaller type.

When you reach the page with the words "A seed is inventive," draw the class's attention to the three things a plant needs to live and grow: sunlight, soil, and water.

Place the next spread under a document projector so that everyone can see the stages of bean, rice, and pumpkin plant growth clearly. (Many students will not be familiar with slash pine or teak, so they are less important to highlight.) Because these sequences do not clearly show bean flowers or rice flowers and fruits, it may be helpful to project the photos you found earlier on your interactive whiteboard.

At this point, show the students several time-lapse videos of plants growing. Explain that the changes they are seeing in a few minutes actually occurred over several days or weeks. Ask them to compare the changes they see in the videos to the changes they see in the illustrations from *A Seed Is Sleepy*.

Now add a second column to your class data table, as shown below. Using information from the videos and *A Seed Is Sleepy*, work with your students to complete the data table.

Return to *A Seed Is Sleepy* and continue reading. When you reach the double-page spread that says, "A seed is thirsty . . . and hungry," encourage students to review the stages of plant growth by describing what the illustrations show and comparing it to the information in the class data table. The children may want to add more details or new information to the table. Continue this process as you read the rest of the book.

How Plantzilla Changes as He Grows	How a Real Plant Changes as It Grows
He starts eating real food.	It starts as a seed.
He can move on his own.	It grows into a seedling (small plant).
He shows feelings.	The plant gets bigger.
He blooms.	Flowers bloom.
He writes a letter.	Fruits grow with new seeds inside.

Teaching Tip

The page with the main text "A seed is clever" includes sophisticated information about photosynthesis. Because this part of the text is beyond the understanding of most second graders, you may want to skip it.

After reading the final page of *A Seed Is Sleepy*, ask your students if they think *awake* is a good word to describe the sunflowers in full bloom. Why or why not? Encourage them to use information in the data table to support their responses.

To review the information in the data table, divide the class into two groups: Plantzillas and Real Plants. Let the class know that you are going to randomly select cells in the data table and read the text. When the children hear you reading text from the first column, students in the Plantzillas group should raise their hands and students in the Real Plants group should point to students in the other group. When the class hears you reading text from the second column, students in the Real Plants group should raise their hands and students in the Plantzillas group should point to students in the other group.

Encouraging Students to Draw Conclusions

Give each child the Lesson 2.6 Wonder Journal Label that poses the Wonder Statement as a question: *How do plants change as they grow?* Then ask students which book, *Plantzilla* or *A Seed Is Sleepy*, they think contained the following:

- The most *complete* description of how a plant grows and changes during its life. *Are any life stages missing from one of the books? If so, why?*
- The most *accurate* description of how a plant grows and changes during its life. *Does either book take liberties with the facts? If so, why?*

To help your students synthesize what they have learned in this lesson, ask them to Turn and Talk with a classmate about how Plantzilla's growth and development is unusual. If students seem to struggle with this task, encourage them to use the data table as a guide.

When the students seem ready, work with them to write a class letter to Mortimer that compares the changes Plantzilla goes through in the story to the changes a real plant goes through as it grows. Then invite students to draw and label pictures (in their Wonder Journals) that show three changes a real plant goes through as it grows. The children may look at the data tables or the growth chart in *A Seed Is Sleepy* to generate ideas. When the students have finished their drawings, encourage them to check the validity of their ideas by sharing their pictures with one or more classmates.

Next, pass out copies of the Lesson 2.6 True/False Student Worksheet and ask students to complete it on their own. When the children are done, they may discuss their answers with a buddy and make changes to the worksheet based on their conversation.

To bring this lesson to a close, divide the class into ten groups. Give each group one of the Lesson 2.6 Plant Growth Statement Cards you pre-

Teaching Tip

To provide students with a complete record of the ideas incorporated into the class letter to Mortimer, consider typing the text and giving students copies for their Wonder Journals.

This Wonder Journal's entry shows three stages in a strawberry plant's growth.

pared earlier and invite the class to gather for a Science Circle. Explain that the statements on the cards match the ones on the worksheet they just completed. After writing the column headings "True" and "False" on a piece of chart paper, invite a group of student volunteers to come forward, read the statement on their card aloud, and use double-sided tape to attach the card to the chart paper under the appropriate heading.

After the students have provided evidence for their decision, other children should feel free to agree, disagree, or ask questions. If a discussion develops, you should help students stay focused and restate any unclear comments or ideas. When the class is in agreement, move on to another group of students. When all the Plant Growth Statement Cards are on the board, guide the class in rewriting each false statement to make it true. Then place the Plant Growth Statement Card under the "True" heading.

In this lesson, students learned that seeds can be very different from one another and from the plants they become. They also discovered that plants change in predictable ways as they grow. With these new insights, students may now begin to wonder how other kinds of plants change as they grow. They should feel free to record these new questions in their Wonder Journals.

Reinforcing the Concept

- You can extend the lesson by reading the following book pairs and discussing the content with the Wonder Statement in mind:
  —*The Sea, the Storm, and the Mangrove Tangle* by Lynne Cherry & *Seed, Soil, Sun* by Cris Peterson
  —*Plant a Little Seed* by Bonnie Christensen & *From Seed to Pumpkin* by Wendy Pfeffer
- Provide each student with a plastic cup, some potting soil, and a bean seed. Inivite them to plant their seed so they can observe a plant's various life stages as they occur. Encourage the children to

measure and record their plant's changes in height and document the changes in its overall appearance in their Wonder Journals.

- The author of *A Seed Is Sleepy* uses words like *inventive, clever,* and *adventurous* to describe seeds. Challenge students to choose one of the descriptive words from *A Seed Is Sleepy* and use it creatively to describe Plantzilla. On a left-hand page of their Wonder Journal, students should reiterate how a seed demonstrates the characteristic, and on the right-hand page, they should describe in words and/or pictures how Plantzilla demonstrates the same characteristic in a different way.

ELA Links   By now, students have learned a lot about how plants grow and change. Two different books—one fiction, one nonfiction—have played important roles in this lesson. The following questions can help students reflect on the aspects of the featured books that aroused their curiosity, generated and maintained their interest, and enhanced their understanding of the natural world.

- *What do the two books have in common?* (They both focus on the changes a plant goes through as it grows. In *A Seed Is Sleepy,* the author uses humanlike characteristics to help us understand seeds better. In *Plantzilla,* the plant has lots of human characteristics. Both books are illustrated with paintings.)
- *How are the two books different?* (*Plantzilla* tells a silly fictional story about a plant, and all the text is presented in the form of letters and postcards. *A Seed Is Sleepy* is nonfiction. It has two layers of text and provides interesting information about seeds and how they grow.)
- *Look back at the text in* Plantzilla *and* A Seed Is Sleepy. *Who is telling each story?* (In *Plantzilla,* the story is told through letters and postcards written by Mortimer, Mr. and Mrs. Henderson, Mr. Lester, and Plantzilla. In *A Seed Is Sleepy,* the author is sharing information with us.)
- *Why do you think the author decided to use letters and postcards to tell the story in* Plantzilla?
- *Can you find a few words or sentences in the two books that you especially like? Why do you like them? Which author do you think has more fun playing with language? Why?*

Lesson 2.7: How Butterflies Change as They Grow

| Clara Caterpillar by Pamela Duncan Edwards | & | Where Butterflies Grow by Joanne Ryder |

About the Books

As Clara grows, she's in the constant company of her caterpillar companions, including boastful Catisha, who constantly reminds her friends that she'll become a beautiful crimson butterfly. But when Catisha's bright colors make her the prime target of a crow, plain-Jane Clara distracts the hungry bird and then hides among some flowers. Child-friendly artwork and lively, alliterative text make *Clara Caterpillar* an entertaining and scientifically accurate choice for butterfly units as well as a celebration of the letter C.

Where Butterflies Grow offers a lovely, gentle, and scientifically accurate description of butterfly development from a hatching egg to the glorious moment when the adult takes wing. Strong sensory imagery and lush watercolors open children's eyes to one of nature's wonders.

Wonder Statement: I wonder how butterflies change as they grow.

Learning Goal

This lesson focuses on how butterflies change as they grow, a topic that has traditionally been part of the K–2 life-science curricula but is not included in the NGSS for K–2. Because some states have chosen to adapt rather than adopt the NGSS, we believe that many K–2 educators will continue to teach this concept. In this lesson, students learn that butterflies grow and change in predictable ways as part of a continuous life cycle.

Prep Steps

1. Post the Wonder Statement, *I wonder how butterflies change as they grow*, on the wall in the classroom meeting area.
2. Use Google Images to find a variety of photos of the four stages in a butterfly's life cycle—egg, caterpillar (larva), pupa, adult. Be sure to include images of cabbage white (*Pieris rapae*) and black swallowtail

(*Papilio polyxenes*) life stages. Then add the following images to your collection: other kinds of insect eggs, bee grubs, fly maggots, a ladybug larva, and pupal cases of beetles and flies.

3. Prepare a set of Yes/No/Maybe cards for each student in your class by cutting sheets of green (Yes), red (No), and yellow (Maybe) construction paper into 4-by-4-inch pieces. If you laminate the cards, you can use them over and over.

4. Make copies of the Lesson 2.7 Wonder Journal Labels in Appendix B for each child in your class and cut them out.

Engaging Students

Begin the lesson by passing out copies of the Lesson 2.7 Wonder Journal Label with the Wonder Statement written on it. After reading the Wonder Statement with the class, ask your students to add it to their Wonder Journals.

Now give each student a set of the Yes/No/Maybe cards you prepared earlier. As you project each of the images you collected in advance on the interactive whiteboard, ask students if they think the photo shows how a butterfly looks during any part of its life. If they think the answer is yes, they should hold up their green cards. If they think the answer is no, they should hold up their red cards. And if they aren't sure, they should hold up their yellow Maybe cards. You may wish to occasionally choose volunteers to explain their thinking.

Exploring with Students

Introduce *Clara Caterpillar* by opening the book to show the full front and back cover. What do your students think the book will be about? Do the front endpapers give them any additional ideas?

After reading the first page, ask a volunteer to point out the butterfly and the egg that she laid. Then ask the students: *Where is Clara?*

Show your students the image of the cabbage white egg from the collection you projected on the interactive whiteboard earlier. Then ask: *Does Clara's egg look like a real cabbage white egg? How is it similar? How is it different?*

Let the class know that all insects start their lives inside eggs. To reinforce this point, project the variety of insect egg images for a second time and identify the insects that laid them.

After reading the next two double-page spreads in which the other caterpillars talk about the egg, encourage your students to predict what will happen next in the story. After a brief class discussion, turn the page and read on.

Read the page where Clara hatches, and show your students the image of the cabbage white caterpillar from the collection you projected earlier. Let your class know that a caterpillar is one kind of larva. Other larvae include bee grubs, fly maggots, and ladybug larvae. After projecting these images for a second time, write the word *larva* on an index card and add a quick sketch to help your students remember what the word means. Then post the card under the Wonder Statement on the wall.

Encourage your class to take another look at the cabbage white caterpillar photo. Then ask: *Does Clara look like a real cabbage white larva? How is she similar? How is she different?*

After reading the next double-page spread, point out that a lot of the words in this story start with the same letter. Then ask them: *Do you know what letter that is?* If students struggle to answer this question, ask them to name all the caterpillar characters they've met so far. *What letter do all of their names start with?* Then, reread the text on the spread, emphasizing all the C sounds.

Now reread the final line one more time: "They grew into colossal caterpillars." Ask your students to predict what will happen next in the story. After a brief class discussion, turn the page and read on.

When you read the page that shows eight chrysalises on a white background, explain that while a butterfly is inside its chrysalis it is called a pupa. Let your class know that many other insects also have a pupal stage, and show them the images of fly and beetle pupal cases for a second time. Write the words *pupa* and *chrysalis* on separate index cards, and add a quick sketch to each one. Then ask a volunteer to post the card under the Wonder Statement.

After reading the next page (which shows a rabbit), ask your students which chrysalis they think holds Clara. Show them the image of the cabbage white chrysalis from the collection you projected, and ask: *Does Clara's chrysalis look like a real cabbage white's chrysalis? How is it similar? How is it different?*

Invite students to predict what will happen next in the story. After a brief class discussion, turn the page and read on.

When you finish the story, encourage the children to predict what Clara will do next. After recording their ideas on chart paper, ask them to identify the four stages in a butterfly's life cycle and use that information to begin a table, as shown below. (Be sure to leave extra room on the right, so you can add a third column later.)

How a Butterfly Changes as It Grows

Stage in Life Cycle	Clara Caterpillar	
Egg		
Caterpillar (larva)		
Pupa		
Adult		

Now look back through the story with your class and work together to fill in details about how Clara looks and acts at each stage in her life cycle. Your final table may look like this:

How a Butterfly Changes as It Grows

Stage in Life Cycle	Clara Caterpillar	
Egg	Small, white, on cabbage	
Caterpillar (larva)	Green with stripe; eats and grows	
Pupa	Inside a chrysalis	
Adult	Chrysalis cracks, and she comes out as a butterfly	

When you are done filling in the data table, ask the students if they think *Clara Caterpillar* describes how a real butterfly changes as it grows. *Does anything listed in the data table seem unrealistic?*

Now introduce *Where Butterflies Grow* by opening the book to show the full back and front cover. Then ask the following questions: *How do you think this book will be similar to* Clara Caterpillar? *How do you think it will be different? Do you think this book is fiction or nonfiction? What is your evidence?*

As you read the second double-page spread of the book, point out that the main illustration shows tiny eggs on the leaves and the close-up paintings show the eggs and a caterpillar hatching at a larger scale. Ask your class: *Who or what is the main character of this book? What do you think it would be like to be growing inside a tiny egg in the middle of a garden? How might it feel to burst out into the world?*

Show your students the image of the black swallowtail egg from the images you projected at the beginning of the lesson. Then ask: *Do the eggs in the book look like real black swallowtail eggs? Why do you think the eggs in this illustration look more similar to real eggs than the egg in* Clara Caterpillar?

Next, add a third column to your class data table. As you read the rest of the book, fill in details about how the black swallowtail looks and acts at each stage of its life cycle. Your final table may look something like the table on the next page.

As you read about the black swallowtail caterpillar, pupa, and adult, show your students the corresponding photos you collected earlier. In each case, students should notice that the artwork created by illustrator Lynne Cherry looks just like the real insect.

When you are done reading the book, ask your class how the style of the writing in *Where Butterflies Grow* is different from *Clara Caterpillar*. (It is more poetic and full of details. It helps you understand what life is like during each stage of a butterfly's life cycle.)

Teaching Tip

The entries in the sample data tables shown here are fully fleshed out and include all possible answers. You should not expect your class's tables to be as detailed, but they should include enough essential information to fully address the Wonder Statement. Providing students with copies of each data table as soon as possible after the class compiles it will allow each child to keep a record of the investigation in his or her Wonder Journal.

How a Butterfly Changes as It Grows

Stage in Life Cycle	Clara Caterpillar	Where Butterflies Grow
Egg	Small, white, on cabbage	Small, round, on parsley
Caterpillar (larva)	Green with stripe; eats and grows	Black with orange spots; eats and grows; changes "skin" and looks different; eats and grows some more
Pupa	Inside a chrysalis	Inside a chrysalis; grows long legs; wide wings covered with scales; body gets darker
Adult	Chrysalis cracks, and she comes out as a butterfly	Wings slowly unfold and become more colorful; tastes flowers with feet; sips nectar

To review the information in the data table, ask your students to count off by fours. All number ones should go to the front of the classroom. Ask them to pretend they are butterfly eggs. Number twos should stand on the right-hand side of the room. They will pretend to be caterpillars (larvae). Threes should go to the back of the room and act like pupae inside chrysalises, and fours should stand on the left-hand side of the room and pretend to be adult butterflies. After a few minutes, reassign roles so that eggs become caterpillars, caterpillars become pupa, and so on.

Students pretend to be adult butterflies.

Encouraging Students to Draw Conclusions

Give each child the Lesson 2.7 Wonder Journal Label that poses the Wonder Statement as a question: *How do butterflies change as they grow?*

Now invite your class to look back at the piece of chart paper where you recorded their predictions about what Clara would do after the story ends, and ask the following questions:

- *Based on the ending of* Where Butterflies Grow, *would you like to change or add to any of the ideas we listed earlier?*
- *What do you think the black swallowtail butterfly in* Where Butterflies Grow *will do next?*

If students do not suggest that both Clara and the black swallowtail may mate and lay eggs, guide them to that idea by asking the following questions:

- *Where does a butterfly egg come from?*
- *In the butterfly life cycle, what stage would come after the adult?*
- *In the butterfly life cycle, what stage would come before the egg?*
- *What does the word cycle mean?*

After the class discusses their ideas, divide the students into four or five small groups and present each team with this challenge: *Can you think of a way to arrange and display illustrations of a butterfly's four life stages so that people looking at them will understand that the life cycle continues on and on, without a beginning or an end?*

Students show their model of the butterfly life cycle.

While the groups brainstorm, set out a variety of art materials. When the students seem ready, invite each team to create a visual model that illustrates the never-ending nature of the butterfly life cycle.

To bring this lesson to a close, invite each group to present its solution to the challenge. Use a digital camera to photograph the visual models, so that students can add the images to their Wonder Journals as a response to the question, *How do butterflies change as they grow?*

In this lesson students learned that a butterfly goes through four stages as it grows: egg, caterpillar (larva), pupa, and adult. They also discovered that the butterfly's life cycle is continuous. With this new knowledge, students may wonder about how other animals change as they grow. They should feel free to record these new questions in their Wonder Journals.

Reinforcing the Concept

- You can extend the lesson by reading the following book pairs and discussing the content with the Wonder Statement in mind:
  —*Tadpole's Promise* by Jeanne Willis & *From Caterpillar to Butterfly* by Deborah Heiligman
  —*Butterfly House* by Eve Bunting & *Monarch and Milkweed* by Helen Frost

- The needs of a butterfly change over its life cycle. As a class, make a list of a butterfly's needs at each stage of its life. Then ask students to use this information and their imaginations to draw and label the perfect habitat for a butterfly in their Wonder Journals.

- Have students pretend they are butterflies. Use a digital camera to record them acting out and describing how it feels to go through each life stage. Then use a simple video editing program to create a class video.

- Invite your students to join you in singing the following song:

The Butterfly Song
(To The Tune of "London Bridge")

Butterflies lay their eggs,
Here and there—
On leaves and twigs.
Butterflies lay their eggs.
Then they fly away.

Caterpillars hatch from eggs.
They creep and crawl,
chomp and chew.
Caterpillars grow and grow.
Then they shed their skin.

Wrapped inside a chrysalis
Pupae change.
They grow wings.
They slip out of that chrysalis
And slowly spread their wings.

Butterflies flit and fly.
They search and seek
For a mate.
Butterflies lay more eggs.
Then they fly away.

Encourage your students to make up movements and/or hand gestures to go with the song or accompany the song with simple musical instruments. Then perform for another class.

ELA Links   By now, students have learned a lot about how butterflies grow and change. Two different books—one fiction, one nonfiction—have played important roles in this lesson. The following questions can help students reflect on the aspects of the featured books that aroused their curiosity, generated and maintained their interest, and enhanced their understanding of the natural world.

- *What do the two books have in common?* (They describe the stages of the butterfly life cycle. They both feature appealing language and watercolor illustrations.)
- *How are the two books different?* (The books look at different species of butterflies. *Clara Caterpillar* is a fun fictional story. *Where Butterflies Grow* is nonfiction. The author asks readers to imagine that they are going through the stages of a black swallowtail butterfly's life cycle.)
- *Even though* Where Butterflies Grow *is nonfiction, it uses descriptive terms like* creeper *instead of* caterpillar *or* larva. *Why do you think author Joanne Ryder made those choices? Are the descriptive terms accurate?*
- *When author Pamela Duncan Edwards was writing* Clara Caterpillar, *she decided to include a lot of alliteration—words that begin with the letter* C. *Are you glad that she made that decision? How does her decision affect the story?*

Picture Books for Grade 2 Lessons

Featured Titles

Aston, Dianna Hutts. *A Seed Is Sleepy*. San Francisco: Chronicle, 2007.
  HC 978-0-81185-520-4

Bateman, Donna M. *Out on the Prairie*. Watertown, MA: Charlesbridge, 2012.
  HC 978-1-58089-378-7

Carle, Eric. *A House for Hermit Crab*. New York: Simon & Schuster, 1991.
  HC 978-0-88708-168-2; PB 978-0-68984-894-0

Cherry, Lynne. *The Great Kapok Tree*. San Diego: Harcourt, 1990.
  HC 978-0-15200-520-7; PB 978-0-15202-614-1

Dunphy, Madeleine. *Here Is the Southwestern Desert*. Berkeley, CA: Web of Life Children's Books, 2006.
  HC 978-0-97737-957-6; PB 978-0-97737-956-9

Edwards, Pamela Duncan. *Clara Caterpillar*. New York: HarperCollins, 2001.
  PB 978-0-06443-691-5

Galbraith, Kathryn O. *Planting the Wild Garden*. Atlanta: Peachtree, 2011.
  HC 978-1-56145-563-8

Himmelman, John. *Frog in a Bog*. Watertown, MA: Charlesbridge, 2004.
  HC 978-1-57091-518-5

Kurtz, Jane, and Christopher Kurtz. *Water Hole Waiting*. New York: Greenwillow/HarperCollins, 2002.
  HC 978-0-06029-850-0

Nolen, Jerdine. *Plantzilla*. San Diego: Harcourt, 2002.
  HC 978-0-15202-412-3; PB 978-0-15205-392-5

Ryder, Joanne. *Where Butterflies Grow*. New York: Puffin, 1996.
  PB 978-0-14055-858-6

Sidman, Joyce. *Song of the Water Boatman & Other Pond Poems*. Boston: Houghton Mifflin Harcourt, 2005.
  HC 978-0-61813-547-9

Weeks, Sarah. *Catfish Kate and the Sweet Swamp Band*. New York: Atheneum, 2009.
  HC 978-1-41694-026-5

Wheeler, Eliza. *Miss Maple's Seeds*. New York: Nancy Paulsen Books/ Penguin, 2013.
  HC 978-0-39925-792-6

Supplementary Titles

Bateman, Donna M. *Deep in the Swamp*. Watertown, MA: Charlesbridge, 2007.
  HC 978-1-57091-597-0

Baylor, Byrd. *The Desert Is Theirs*. New York: Aladdin, 1987.
   PB 978-0-68971-105-3

———. *Desert Voices*. New York: Aladdin, 1993.
   PB 978-0-68971-691-1

Berkes, Marianne. *The Swamp Where Gator Hides*. Nevada City, CA: Dawn, 2014.
   HC 978-1-58469-471-7

Bunting, Eve. *Butterfly House*. New York: Scholastic, 1999.
   HC 978-0-59084-884-8.

Cannon, Janell. *Pinduli*. San Diego: Harcourt, 2004.
   HC 978-0-15204-668-2

Cherry, Lynne. *The Sea, the Storm, and the Mangrove Tangle*. New York: Farrar, Straus and Giroux, 2004.
   HC 978-0-37436-482-3

Christensen, Bonnie. *Plant a Little Seed*. New York: Roaring Brook, 2012.
   HC 978-1-59643-550-6

Dunphy, Madeleine. *Here Is the Tropical Rainforest*. Berkeley, CA: Web of Life Children's Books, 2006.
   HC 978-0-97737-951-4; PB 978-0-97737-950-7

Ering, Timothy Basil. *Necks Out for Adventure: The True Story of Edwin Wiggleskin*. Cambridge, MA: Candlewick, 2008.
   HC 978-0-76362-355-5

Frost, Helen. *Monarch and Milkweed*. New York: Atheneum, 2008.
   HC 978-1-41690-085-6

Guiberson, Brenda Z. *Rain, Rain, Rain Forest*. New York: Holt, 2004.
   HC 978-0-80506-582-4; PB 978-0-43977-469-7

Halfmann, Janet. *Star of the Sea: A Day in the Life of a Starfish*. New York: Holt, 2011.
   HC 978-0-80509-073-4

Harley, Avis. *African Acrostics: A Word in Edgeways*. Cambridge, MA: Candlewick, 2012.
   HC 978-0-76365-818-2

Heiligman, Deborah. *From Caterpillar to Butterfly*. New York: Greenwillow/HarperCollins, 1996.
   PB 978-0-06445-129-1.

Kurtz, Kevin. *A Day in the Salt Marsh*. Mount Pleasant, SC: Sylvan Dell, 2007.
   HC 978-0-97688-235-0; PB 978-1-93435-919-8

LaMarche, Jim. *The Raft*. New York: HarperCollins, 2005.
   HC 978-0-68813-977-3

Lamstein, Sarah Marwil. *Big Night for Salamanders*. Honesdale, PA: Boyds Mills, 2009.
   HC 978-1-93242-598-7

Peterson, Cris. *Seed, Soil, Sun*. Honesdale, PA: Boyds Mills, 2010.
　　HC 978-1-59078-713-7

Pfeffer, Wendy. *From Seed to Pumpkin*. New York: HarperCollins, 2004.
　　HC 978-0-75693-238-1 PB 978-0-06445-190-1

Rockwell, Anne. *Who Lives in an Alligator Hole?* New York:
　　HarperCollins, 2006.
　　PB 978-0-06445-200-7

Sayre, April Pulley. *Trout Are Made of Trees*. Watertown, MA:
　　Charlesbridge, 2008.
　　HC 978-1-58089-138-7

Sidman, Joyce. *Butterfly Eyes and Other Secrets of the Meadow*. Boston:
　　Houghton Mifflin Harcourt, 2006.
　　HC 978-0-61856-313-5

Stevens, Janet, and Susan Stevens Crummel. *The Great Fuzz Frenzy*.
　　Boston: Houghton Mifflin Harcourt, 2005.
　　HC 978-0-15204-626-2

Stewart, Melissa. *No Monkeys, No Chocolate*. Watertown, MA:
　　Charlesbridge, 2013.
　　HC 978-1-58089-287-2

Willis, Jeanne. *Tadpole's Promise*. New York: Atheneum, 2005.
　　PB 978-1-84270-426-4

Wilson, Karma. *A Frog in the Bog*. New York: Margaret K. McElderry,
　　2007.
　　HC 978-0-68984-081-4; PB 978-1-416-92727-3

Appendix A

Tables of Next Generation Science Standards (NGSS)
and Common Core State Standards
for English Language Arts (ELA)
for English Language Arts (ELA)
Addressed in *Perfect Pairs* Lessons

Table 1. NGSS Performance Expectations Addressed in Each Kindergarten Lesson

Lesson	Disciplinary Core Idea(s)	Performance Expectation
K.1 What Plants and Animals Need to Survive	**Organization for Matter and Energy Flow in Organisms** All animals need food in order to live and grow. They obtain their food from plants or from other animals. Plants need water and light to live and grow.	K-LS1-1. Use observations to describe patterns of what plants and animals (including humans) need to survive.
K.2 What Animals Eat	**Organization for Matter and Energy Flow in Organisms** All animals need food in order to live and grow. They obtain their food from plants or from other animals. Plants need water and light to live and grow.	K-LS1-1. Use observations to describe patterns of what plants and animals (including humans) need to survive.
K.3 How Animals Depend on Their Environment	**Natural Resources** Living things need water, air, and resources from the land, and they live in places that have the things they need. Humans use natural resources for everything they do.	K-ESS3-1. Use a model to represent the relationship between the needs of different plants and animals (including humans) and the places they live.
K.4 How Animals Can Change an Environment	**Biogeology** Plants and animals can change their environment.	K-ESS2-2. Construct an argument supported by evidence for how plants and animals (including humans) can change the environment to meet their needs.
K.5 How People Can Change an Environment	**Biogeology** Plants and animals can change their environment. **Human Impact of Earth Systems** Things that people do to live comfortably can affect the world around them. But they can make choices that reduce their impacts on the land, water, air, and other living things.	K-ESS2-2. Construct an argument supported by evidence for how plants and animals (including humans) can change the environment- to meet their needs.
K.6 How to Reduce Our Impact on Creatures in Land Environments	**Human Impact of Earth Systems** Things that people do to live comfortably can affect the world around them. But they can make choices that reduce their impacts on the land, water, air, and other living things.	K-ESS3-3. Communicate solutions that will reduce the impact of humans on the land, water, air, and/or other living things in the local environment.
K.7 How to Reduce Our Impact on Creatures in Water Environments	**Human Impact of Earth Systems** Things that people do to live comfortably can affect the world around them. But they can make choices that reduce their impacts on the land, water, air, and other living things.	K-ESS3-3. Communicate solutions that will reduce the impact of humans on the land, water, air, and/or other living things in the local environment.

Table 2. NGSS Performance Expectations Addressed in Each Grade 1 Lesson

Lesson	Disciplinary Core Idea(s)	Performance Expectation
1.1 How an Animal's Body Parts Help It Survive	**Structure and Function** All organisms have external parts. Different animals use their body parts in different ways to see, hear, grasp objects, protect themselves, move from place to place, and seek, find, and take in food, water and air. Plants also have different parts (roots, stems, leaves, flowers, fruits) that help them survive and grow. **Information Processing** Animals have body parts that capture and convey different kinds of information needed for growth and survival. Animals respond to these inputs with behaviors that help them survive. Plants also respond to some external inputs.	1-LS1-1. Use materials to design a solution to a human problem by mimicking how plants and/or animals use their external parts to help them survive, grow, and meet their needs.
1.2 How Animals Find and Catch Food	**Structure and Function** All organisms have external parts. Different animals use their body parts in different ways to see, hear, grasp objects, protect themselves, move from place to place, and seek, find, and take in food, water and air. Plants also have different parts (roots, stems, leaves, flowers, fruits) that help them survive and grow. **Information Processing** Animals have body parts that capture and convey different kinds of information needed for growth and survival. Animals respond to these inputs with behaviors that help them survive. Plants also respond to some external inputs.	1-LS1-1. Use materials to design a solution to a human problem by mimicking how plants and/or animals use their external parts to help them survive, grow, and meet their needs.
1.3 How Animals Protect Themselves	**Structure and Function** All organisms have external parts. Different animals use their body parts in different ways to see, hear, grasp objects, protect themselves, move from place to place, and seek, find, and take in food, water and air. Plants also have different parts (roots, stems, leaves, flowers, fruits) that help them survive and grow. **Information Processing** Animals have body parts that capture and convey different kinds of information needed for growth and survival. Animals respond to these inputs with behaviors that help them survive. Plants also respond to some external inputs.	1-LS1-1. Use materials to design a solution to a human problem by mimicking how plants and/or animals use their external parts to help them survive, grow, and meet their needs.

(continued)

Perfect Pairs: Using Fiction and Nonfiction Picture Books to Teach Life Science, K–2 by Melissa Stewart and Nancy Chesley. Copyright © 2014. Stenhouse Publishers.

Table 2. NGSS Performance Expectations Addressed in Each Grade 1 Lesson (continued)

1.4 How a Plant's Parts Help It Survive	**Structure and Function** All organisms have external parts. Different animals use their body parts in different ways to see, hear, grasp objects, protect themselves, move from place to place, and seek, find, and take in food, water and air. Plants also have different parts (roots, stems, leaves, flowers, fruits) that help them survive and grow. **Information Processing** Animals have body parts that capture and convey different kinds of information needed for growth and survival. Animals respond to these inputs with behaviors that help them survive. Plants also respond to some external inputs.	1-LS1-1. Use materials to design a solution to a human problem by mimicking how plants and/or animals use their external parts to help them survive, grow, and meet their needs.
1.5 Mimicking Plant and Animal Body Parts to Solve Problems	**Structure and Function** All organisms have external parts. Different animals use their body parts in different ways to see, hear, grasp objects, protect themselves, move from place to place, and seek, find, and take in food, water and air. Plants also have different parts (roots, stems, leaves, flowers, fruits) that help them survive and grow. **Information Processing** Animals have body parts that capture and convey different kinds of information needed for growth and survival. Animals respond to these inputs with behaviors that help them survive. Plants also respond to some external inputs.	1-LS1-1. Use materials to design a solution to a human problem by mimicking how plants and/or animals use their external parts to help them survive, grow, and meet their needs.
1.6 How Animal Parents and Young Interact	**Growth and Development of Organisms** Adult plants and animals can have young. In many kinds of animals, parents and the offspring themselves engage in behaviors that help the offspring to survive.	1-LS1-2. Read texts and use media to determine patterns in behavior of parents and offspring that help offspring survive.
1.7 How Young Animals Are Like Their Parents	**Inheritance of Traits** Young animals are very much, but not exactly, like their parents. Plants also are very much, but not exactly, like their parents.	1-LS3-1. Make observations to construct an evidence-based account that young plants and animals are like, but not exactly like, their parents.
1.8 How Adult Animals of the Same Species Can Be Different	**Variation of Traits** Individuals of the same kind of plant or animal are recognizable as similar but can also vary in many ways.	1-LS3-1. Make observations to construct an evidence-based account that young plants and animals are like, but not exactly like, their parents.

Table 3. NGSS Performance Expectations Addressed in Each Grade 2 Lesson

Lesson	Disciplinary Core Idea	Performance Expectation
2.1 How Wind, Water, and Animals Disperse Seeds	**Interdependent Relationships in Ecosystems** Plants depend on animals for pollination or to move their seeds around.	2-LS2-2. Develop a simple model that mimics the function of an animal in dispersing seeds or pollinating plants.
2.2 Understanding Habitats	**Biodiversity and Humans** There are many different kinds of living things in any area, and they exist in different places on land and in water.	2-LS4-1. Make observations of plants and animals to compare the diversity of life in different habitats.
2.3 Understanding Biomes	**Biodiversity and Humans** There are many different kinds of living things in any area, and they exist in different places on land and in water.	2-LS4-1. Make observations of plants and animals to compare the diversity of life in different habitats.
2.4 Life in Wetlands	**Biodiversity and Humans** There are many different kinds of living things in any area, and they exist in different places on land and in water.	2-LS4-1. Make observations of plants and animals to compare the diversity of life in different habitats.
2.5 Life in Grasslands	**Biodiversity and Humans** There are many different kinds of living things in any area, and they exist in different places on land and in water.	2-LS4-1. Make observations of plants and animals to compare the diversity of life in different habitats.
2.6 How Plants Change as They Grow	**Growth and Development of Organisms** Reproduction is essential to the continued existence of every kind of organism. Plants and animals have unique and diverse life cycles.	N/A
2.7 How Butterflies Change as They Grow	**Growth and Development of Organisms** Reproduction is essential to the continued existence of every kind of organism. Plants and animals have unique and diverse life cycles.	N/A

Perfect Pairs: Using Fiction and Nonfiction Picture Books to Teach Life Science, K–2 by Melissa Stewart and Nancy Chesley. Copyright © 2014. Stenhouse Publishers.

Table 4. NGSS Science and Engineering Practices Included in Each Kindergarten Lesson

Practice	K.1	K.2	K.3	K.4	K.5	K.6	K.7
1. Asking Questions and Defining Problems	X	X	X	X	X	X	X
2. Developing and Using Models	X		**X**	X	X	X	X
3. Planning and Carrying Out Investigations	X	X	X	X	X	X	X
4. Analyzing and Interpreting Data	**X**	**X**	X	X	X	X	X
5. Using Mathematics and Computational Thinking (Not targeted for K)							
6. Constructing Explanations and Designing Solutions	X	X	X	X	X	X	X
7. Engaging in Argument from Evidence	X	X	X	**X**	**X**	X	X
8. Obtaining, Evaluating, and Communicating Information	X	X	X	X	X	**X**	**X**

The targeted practice for each lesson is indicated with a bold **X**.

Table 5. NGSS Science and Engineering Practices Included in Each Grade 1 Lesson

Practice	1.1	1.2	1.3	1.4	1.5	1.6	1.7	1.8
1. Asking Questions and Defining Problems	X	X	X	X	X	X	X	X
2. Developing and Using Models	X	X	X	X	X		X	X
3. Planning and Carrying Out Investigations	X	X	X	X	X	X	X	X
4. Analyzing and Interpreting Data	X	X	X	X	X	X	X	X
5. Using Mathematics and Computational Thinking (Not targeted for Grade 1)		X						
6. Constructing Explanations and Designing Solutions					**X**	X	**X**	**X**
7. Engaging in Argument from Evidence	X	X	X	X	X	X	X	X
8. Obtaining, Evaluating, and Communicating Information	X	X	X	X	X	**X**	X	X

The targeted practices for Lessons 1.5–1.8 are indicated with bold **X**s. Lessons 1.1–1.4 focus on providing necessary background knowledge, so that students can perform the targeted engineering practice, Designing Solutions, in Lesson 1.5.

Table 6. NGSS Science and Engineering Practices Included in Each Grade 2 Lesson

Practice	2.1	2.2	2.3	2.4	2.5	2.6	2.7
1. Asking Questions and Defining Problems	X	X	X	X	X	X	X
2. Developing and Using Models	**X**	X				X	X
3. Planning and Carrying Out Investigations	X	**X**	**X**	**X**	**X**	X	X
4. Analyzing and Interpreting Data	X	X	X	X	X	X	X
5. Using Mathematics and Computational Thinking (Not targeted for Grade 2)				X	X		
6. Constructing Explanations and Designing Solutions	X	X	X	X	X	X	X
7. Engaging in Argument from Evidence	X	X	X	X	X	X	X
8. Obtaining, Evaluating, and Communicating Information	X	X	X	X	X	X	X

The targeted practice for each lesson is indicated with a bold **X**. There are no targeted practices for Lessons 2.6 and 2.7.

Table 7. Common Core State Standards for ELA Addressed in Each Kindergarten Lesson

	Standards for Reading Literature	K.1	K.2	K.3	K.4	K.5	K.6	K.7
Key Ideas and Details	1. With prompting and support, ask and answer questions about key details in a text.	X	X	X	X	X	X	X
	2. With prompting and support, retell familiar stories, including key details.						X	
	3. With prompting and support, identify characters, settings, and major events in a story.	X	X	X	X	X	X	X
Craft and Structure	4. Ask and answer questions about unknown words in a text.	X	X	X	X	X	X	X
	5. Recognize common types of texts (e.g., storybooks, poems).							
	6. With prompting and support, name the author and illustrator of a story and define the role of each in telling a story.	X	X	X	X	X	X	X
Integration of Knowledge and Ideas	7. With prompting and support, describe the relationship between illustrations in a story and the story in which they appear.	X	X	X	X	X	X	X
	8. (Not applicable to literature)							
	9. With prompting and support, compare and contrast the adventures and experiences of characters in familiar stories.							
Range of Reading and Level Text Complexity	10. Actively engage in group reading activities with purpose and understanding.	X	X	X	X	X	X	X

	Standards for Reading Informational Text	K.1	K.2	K.3	K.4	K.5	K.6	K.7
Key Ideas and Details	1. With prompting and support, ask and answer questions about key details in a text.	X	X	X	X	X	X	X
	2. With prompting and support, identify the main topic and retell key details of a text.	X	X	X	X	X	X	X
	3. With prompting and support, describe the connection between two individuals, events, ideas, or pieces of information in a text.	X	X	X	X	X	X	X
Craft and Structure	4. With prompting and support, ask and answer questions about unknown words in a text.	X	X	X	X	X	X	X
	5. Identify the front cover, back cover, and title page of a book.	X			X		X	X
	6. Name the author and illustrator of a text and define the role of each in presenting the ideas or information in a text.	X	X		X	X	X	X
Integration of Knowledge and Ideas	7. With prompting and support, describe the relationship between illustrations and the text in which they appear (e.g., what person, place, thing, or idea in the text an illustration depicts).	X		X	X	X	X	X
	8. With prompting and support, identify the reasons an author gives to support points in a text.		X		X		X	
	9. With prompting and support, identify basic similarities and differences between two texts on the same topic (e.g., in illustrations, descriptions, or procedures).	X	X	X	X	X	X	X
Range of Reading and Level Text Complexity	10. Actively engage in group reading activities with purpose and understanding.	X	X	X	X	X	X	X

Perfect Pairs: Using Fiction and Nonfiction Picture Books to Teach Life Science, K–2 by Melissa Stewart and Nancy Chesley. Copyright © 2014. Stenhouse Publishers.

Table 7. Common Core State Standards for ELA Addressed in Each Kindergarten Lesson *(continued)*

	Standards for Writing	K.1	K.2	K.3	K.4	K.5	K.6	K.7
Text Types and Purposes	1. Use a combination of drawing, dictating, and writing to compose opinion pieces in which they tell the reader a topic or the name of a book they are writing about and state an opinion or preference about the topic of the book.							
	2. Use a combination of drawing, dictating, and writing to compose informative/explanatory text in which they name what they are writing about and supply some information about the topic.	X	X	X	X	X	X	X
	3. Use a combination of drawing, dictating, and writing to narrate a single event or several loosely linked events, tell about the events in the order in which they occurred, and provide a reaction to what happened.	X	X				X	X
Production and Distribution of Writing	4. Begins in grade 3.							
	5. With guidance and support from adults, respond to questions and suggestions from peers and add details to strengthen writing as needed.	X	X		X		X	
	6. With support and guidance from adults, explore a variety of digital tools to produce and publish writing, including in collaboration with peers.							
Research to Build and Present Knowledge	7. Participate in shared research and writing projects (e.g., explore a number of books by a favorite author and express opinions about them).	X	X	X	X	X	X	X
	8. With support and guidance from adults, recall information from experiences or gather information from provided sources to answer a question.	X	X	X	X	X	X	X

	Standards for Speaking and Listening	K.1	K.2	K.3	K.4	K.5	K.6	K.7
Comprehension and Collaboration	1. Participate in collaborative conversations with diverse partners about kindergarten topics and texts with peers and adults in small and larger groups.	X	X	X	X	X	X	X
	2. Confirm understanding of a text read aloud or information presented orally or through other media by asking and answering questions about key details and requesting clarification if something is not understood.	X	X	X	X	X	X	X
	3. Ask and answer questions in order to seek help, get information, or clarify something that is not understood.	X	X	X	X	X	X	X
Presentation of Knowledge and Ideas	4. Describe familiar people, places, things, and events and, with prompting and support, provide additional detail.						X	X
	5. Add drawings or other visual displays to descriptions as desired to provide additional detail.	X	X	X	X	X	X	X
	6. Speak audibly and express thoughts, feelings, and ideas clearly.	X	X	X	X	X	X	X

Table 8. Common Core State Standards for ELA Addressed in Each Grade 1 Lesson

	Standards for Reading Literature	1.1	1.2	1.3	1.4	1.5	1.6	1.7	1.8
Key Ideas and Details	1. Ask and answer questions about key details in a text.	X	X	X	X	X	X	X	X
	2. Retell familiar stories, including key details, and demonstrate an understanding of their central message or lesson.								X
	3. Describe characters, settings, and major events in a story, using key details.	X	X	X		X	X	X	
Craft and Structure	4. Identify words or phrases in stories or poems that suggest feelings or appeal to senses.	X	X			X	X	X	X
	5. Explain major differences between books that tell stories and books that give information, drawing on a wide reading of a range of text types.	X	X	X	X	X	X	X	X
	6. Identify who is telling the story at various points in the text.	X	X			X	X	X	X
Integration of Knowledge and Ideas	7. Use illustrations and details in a story to describe its characters, setting, or events.	X	X			X	X	X	X
	8. (Not applicable to literature)								
	9. Compare and contrast the adventures and experiences of characters in stories.							X	X
Range of Reading and Level Text Complexity	10. With prompting and support, read prose and poetry of appropriate complexity for grade 1.	X	X	X	X	X	X	X	X

	Standards for Reading Informational Text	1.1	1.2	1.3	1.4	1.5	1.6	1.7	1.8
Key Ideas and Details	1. Ask and answer questions about key details in a text.	X	X	X	X	X	X	X	X
	2. Identify the main topic and retell key details of a text.	X	X			X	X	X	X
	3. Describe the connection between two individuals, events, ideas, or pieces of information in a text.	X	X	X	X	X	X	X	X
Craft and Structure	4. Ask and answer questions to help determine or clarify the meaning of words and phrases in a text.	X	X	X	X	X	X	X	X
	5. Know and use various text features (e.g., headings, tables of contents, glossaries, electronic menus, icons) to locate key facts or information in a text.	X	X			X	X		X
	6. Distinguish between information provided by pictures and other illustrations and information provided by the words in a text.	X	X			X	X	X	X
Integration of Knowledge and Ideas	7. Use illustrations and details in a text to describe its key ideas.	X	X	X	X	X	X	X	X
	8. Identify the reasons an author gives to support points in a text.	X	X	X	X	X	X		X
	9. Identify basic similarities and differences between two texts on the same topic (e.g., in illustrations, descriptions, or procedures).	X	X	X	X	X	X	X	X
Range of Reading and Level Text Complexity	10. With prompting and support, read informational texts appropriately complex for grade 1.	X	X	X	X	X	X	X	X

Perfect Pairs: Using Fiction and Nonfiction Picture Books to Teach Life Science, K–2 by Melissa Stewart and Nancy Chesley. Copyright © 2014. Stenhouse Publishers.

Table 8. Common Core State Standards for ELA Addressed in Each Grade 1 Lesson (continued)

	Standards for Writing	1.1	1.2	1.3	1.4	1.5	1.6	1.7	1.8
Text Types and Purposes	1. Write opinion pieces in which they introduce the topic or name the book they are writing about, state an opinion, supply a reason for the opinion, and provide some sense of closure.								
	2. Write informative/explanatory text in which they name the topic, supply some facts about the topic, and provide some sense of closure.	X	X	X	X	X	X	X	X
	3. Write narratives in which they recount two or more appropriately sequenced events, include some details regarding what happened, use temporal words to signal event order, and provide some sense of closure.								
Production and Distribution of Writing	4. Begins in grade 3.								
	5. With guidance and support from adults, focus on a topic, respond to questions and suggestions from peers, and add details to strengthen writing as needed.								
	6. With guidance and support from adults, use a variety of digital tools to produce and publish writing, including in collaboration with peers.								
Research to Build and Present Knowledge	7. Participate in shared research and writing projects (e.g., explore a number of "how-to" books on a given topic and use them to write a sequence of instructions).	X	X	X	X	X	X	X	X
	8. With support and guidance from adults, recall information from experiences or gather information from provided sources to answer a question.	X	X	X	X	X	X	X	X

	Standards for Speaking and Listening	1.1	1.2	1.3	1.4	1.5	1.6	1.7	1.8
Comprehension and Collaboration	1. Participate in collaborative conversations with diverse partners about grade 1 topics and texts with peers and adults in small and larger groups.	X	X	X	X	X	X	X	X
	2. Ask and answer questions about key details in a text read aloud or information presented orally or through other media.	X	X	X	X	X	X	X	X
	3. Ask and answer questions about what a speaker says in order to gather additional information or clarify something that is not understood.	X	X	X	X	X	X	X	X
	4. Describe people, places, things, and events with relevant details, expressing ideas and feelings clearly.		X		X	X	X	X	X
	5. Add drawings or other visual displays to descriptions when appropriate to clarify ideas, thoughts, and feelings.	X	X	X	X	X	X	X	X
Presentation of Knowledge and Ideas	6. Produce complete sentences when appropriate to task and situation.	X	X	X	X	X	X	X	X

Table 9. Common Core State Standards for ELA Addressed in Each Grade 2 Lesson

	Standards for Reading Literature	**2.1**	**2.2**	**2.3**	**2.4**	**2.5**	**2.6**	**2.7**
Key Ideas and Details	1. Ask and answer such questions as *who, what, where, when, why,* and *how* to demonstrate understanding of key details in a text.	X	X	X	X	X	X	X
	2. Recount stories, including fables and folktales from diverse cultures, and determine their central message, lesson, or moral.							
	3. Describe how characters in a story respond to major events and challenges.	X	X	X		X		
Craft and Structure	4. Describe how words and phrases (e.g., regular beats, alliteration, rhymes, repeated storylines) supply rhythm and meaning in a story, poem, or song.	X			X	X		X
	5. Describe the overall structure of a story, including describing how the beginning introduces the story and the ending concludes the action.	X		X				
	6. Acknowledge differences in points of view of characters, including by speaking in a different voice for each character when reading dialogue aloud.							
Integration of Knowledge and Ideas	7. Use information gained from the illustrations and words in a print or digital text to demonstrate understanding of its characters, setting, or plot.	X	X	X	X	X	X	X
	8. (Not applicable to literature)							
	9. Compare and contrast two or more versions of the same story (e.g., Cinderella stories) by different authors or from different cultures.							
Range of Reading and Level Text Complexity	10. By the end of the year, read and comprehend literature, including stories and poetry, in the grades 2–3 text complexity band proficiently, with scaffolding as needed at the high end of the range.	X	X	X	X	X	X	X

Table 9. Common Core State Standards for ELA Addressed in Each Grade 2 Lesson *(continued)*

	Standards for Reading Informational Text	**2.1**	**2.2**	**2.3**	**2.4**	**2.5**	**2.6**	**2.7**
Key Ideas and Details	1. Ask and answer such questions as *who, what, where, when, why,* and *how* to demonstrate understanding of key details in a text.	X	X	X	X	X	X	X
	2. Identify the main topic of a multiparagraph text as well as the focus of specific paragraphs within the text.							
	3. Describe the connection between a series of historical events, scientific ideas or concepts, or steps in technical procedures in a text.	X	X	X	X	X	X	X
Craft and Structure	4. Determine the meaning of words and phrases in a text relevant to a *grade 2 topic or subject area.*	X	X	X	X	X	X	X
	5. Know and use various text features (e.g., captions, bold print, subheadings, glossaries, indexes, electronic menus, icons) to locate key facts or information in a text efficiently.							
	6. Identify the main purpose of a text, including what the author wants to answer, explain, or describe.	X	X	X	X	X	X	X
Integration of Knowledge and Ideas	7. Explain how specific images (e.g., a diagram showing how a machine works) contribute to and clarify a text.	X	X	X	X	X	X	X
	8. Describe how reasons support specific points the author makes in a text.	X	X	X	X	X	X	X
	9. Compare and contrast the most important points presented by two texts on the same topic.	X	X	X	X	X	X	X
Range of Reading and Level Text Complexity	10. By the end of the year, read and comprehend informational texts, including history/social studies, science, and technical texts, in the grades 2–3 text complexity band proficiently, with scaffolding as needed at the high end of the range.	X	X	X	X	X	X	X

Table 9. Common Core State Standards for ELA Addressed in Each Grade 2 Lesson (continued)

	Standards for Writing	**2.1**	**2.2**	**2.3**	**2.4**	**2.5**	**2.6**	**2.7**
Text Types and Purposes	1. Write opinion pieces in which they introduce the topic or book they are writing about, state an opinion, supply reasons for the opinion, use linking words (e.g., *because, and, also*) to connect opinion and reasons, and provide a concluding statement or section.							
	2. Write informative/explanatory text in which they introduce a topic, use facts and definitions to develop points, and provide a concluding statement or section.							
	3. Write narratives in which they recount a well-elaborated event or short sequence of events, include details to describe actions, thoughts, and feelings, use temporal words to signal event order, and provide a sense of closure.							
Production and Distribution of Writing	4. Begins in grade 3.							
	5. With guidance and support from adults and peers, focus on a topic and strengthen writing as needed by revising and editing.							
	6. With support and guidance from adults, use a variety of digital tools to produce and publish writing, including in collaboration with peers.							
Research to Build and Present Knowledge	7. Participate in shared research and writing projects (e.g., read a number of books on a single topic to produce a report; record science observations).	X	X	X	X	X	X	X
	8. Recall information from experiences or gather information from provided sources to answer a question.	X	X	X	X	X	X	X

	Standards for Speaking and Listening	**2.1**	**2.2**	**2.3**	**2.4**	**2.5**	**2.6**	**2.7**
Comprehension and Collaboration	1. Participate in collaborative conversations with diverse partners about *grade 2 topics and texts* with peers and adults in smaller and larger groups.	X	X	X	X	X	X	X
	2. Recount or describe key ideas or details from a text read aloud or information presented orally or through other media.	X	X	X	X	X	X	X
	3. Ask and answer questions about what a speaker says in order to clarify comprehension, gather additional information, or deepen understanding of a topic or issue.	X	X	X	X	X	X	X
Presentation of Knowledge and Ideas	4. Tell a story or recount an experience with appropriate facts and relevant, descriptive details, speaking audibly in coherent sentences.							
	5. Create audio recordings of stories or poems; add drawings or other visual displays to stories or recounts of experiences when appropriate to clarify ideas, thoughts, and feelings.							
	6. Produce complete sentences when appropriate to task and situation in order to provide requested detail or clarification.	X	X	X	X	X	X	X

Perfect Pairs: Using Fiction and Nonfiction Picture Books to Teach Life Science, K–2 by Melissa Stewart and Nancy Chesley. Copyright © 2014. Stenhouse Publishers.

Appendix B

Reproducibles for *Perfect Pairs* Lessons

(The pages in Appendix B also may be printed from
www.stenhouse.com/perfect-pairs.)

Lesson K.1 Wonder Journal Labels

I wonder what plants and animals need to live and grow.

A pumpkin plant needs two things to grow. I think they are:

The Perfect Salamander Room

What do plants and animals need to live and grow?

···

I wonder what plants and animals need to live and grow.

A pumpkin plant needs two things to grow. I think they are:

The Perfect Salamander Room

What do plants and animals need to live and grow?

Perfect Pairs: Using Fiction and Nonfiction Picture Books to Teach Life Science, K–2 by Melissa Stewart and Nancy Chesley. Copyright © 2014. Stenhouse Publishers.

Lesson K.1 Venn Diagram Template

Name: _____ Date: _____

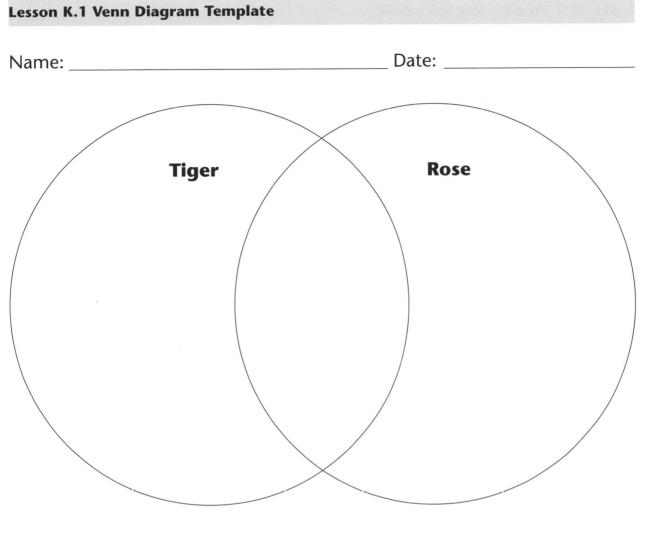

Lesson K.2 Wonder Journal Labels

I wonder what kinds of foods different animals eat.

My animal is _____. I predict it eats _____.

My food is _____. I predict a _____ eats it.

What kinds of foods do different animals eat?

A _____ (animal 1) and a _____ (animal 2)

are very different, but they both eat _____ (food).

A _____ (animal) eats _____ (food 1), but it

also eats _____ (food 2)

Perfect Pairs: Using Fiction and Nonfiction Picture Books to Teach Life Science, K–2 by Melissa Stewart and Nancy Chesley. Copyright © 2014. Stenhouse Publishers.

Lesson K.2 Animal and Food Cards

panda animal	**tick** animal	**shrew** animal
woodpecker animal	**chipmunk** animal	**bird** animal
spider animal	**toad** animal	**anaconda** animal

ostrich animal	**beetle** animal	**pelican** animal
moth animal	**aye-aye** animal	**shark** animal
rat animal	**baby whale** animal	

Perfect Pairs: Using Fiction and Nonfiction Picture Books to Teach Life Science, K–2 by Melissa Stewart and Nancy Chesley. Copyright © 2014. Stenhouse Publishers.

Lesson K.2 Animal and Food Cards *(continued)*

bamboo shoots food	**blood** food	**worm** food
acorn food	**seeds** food	**grasshopper** food
insect food	**insect** food	**jaguar** food

Lesson K.2 Animal and Food Cards *(continued)*

leaves food	**dung** food	**fish** food
nectar food	**beetle** food	**fish** food
grain food	**milk** food	

Lesson K.2 Wonder Journal Handout

I used to wonder what kinds of foods different animals eat.

Now I know that animals eat many different kinds of foods.

Some animals eat plants.

Some animals eat other animals.

Some animals eat both.

Lesson K.3 Wonder Journal Labels

I wonder how animals depend on the places where they live.

How do animals depend on the places where they live?

I wonder how animals depend on the places where they live.

How do animals depend on the places where they live?

I wonder how animals depend on the places where they live.

How do animals depend on the places where they live?

I wonder how animals depend on the places where they live.

How do animals depend on the places where they live?

Perfect Pairs: Using Fiction and Nonfiction Picture Books to Teach Life Science, K–2 by Melissa Stewart and Nancy Chesley. Copyright © 2014. Stenhouse Publishers.

Lesson K.4 Wonder Journal Labels

I wonder how animals can change an environment.

This is where I think a mole might live.

My arrow points to evidence that Mole has changed her environment.

She changed the land because she needed _____.

At Home with the Gopher Tortoise

How can animals change an environment?

Lesson K.4 Building Permit Worksheet

Name: _____ Date: _____

I am a: I live here:

I want to build: I need to build it because:

This drawing shows how I will change the environment.

Lesson K.4 Skunk Cousin Letters

As you write these letters on chart paper, prompt your students to help you fill in the blanks with the words in parenthesis.

Dear Cousin Woods Skunk,

I live near a gopher tortoise.

It dug a _____ (burrow) because _____ (It needs to stay warm in winter and cool in summer. It also needs protection from wildfires).

I _____ (like) the way the tortoise changed our environment because I can use the burrow for _____ (shelter and hunting).

Here is a picture of me inside the burrow.

From your cousin,

Forest Skunk

....

Dear Cousin Forest Skunk,

I live near a mole named Mole.

She made a _____ (pile of dirt) because _____ (she was tunneling for food).

I _____ (don't like) the way Mole changed our environment because _____ (it blocked our path to the pond).

But then Mole _____ (built a hill with a path through the middle of it). Now it's easy to get to the pond.

Here is a picture of Mole's hill.

From your cousin,

Woods Skunk

Lesson K.5 Wonder Journal Labels

....

I wonder how people can change an environment.

....

This is what the meadow would look like after people had started living there.

....

When Caroline let flowers grow in her yard, a _____ came.

When Caroline's family planted a tree, a _____ came.

When Caroline's family built a pond and added water plants, a

_____ came.

....

How can people change an environment?

....

Perfect Pairs: Using Fiction and Nonfiction Picture Books to Teach Life Science, K–2 by Melissa Stewart and Nancy Chesley. Copyright © 2014. Stenhouse Publishers.

Lesson K.5 Text for Interactive Whiteboard Slide 1

- How does it feel to stretch up toward the sun?
- What do your flowers smell like?
- What animals visit you?
- What is it like to always stay in one place day and night, rain or shine?
- What do you like most about living in the meadow?
- What do you think would happen to the meadow if people decided to live there?

Lesson K.5 Text for Interactive Whiteboard Slide 2

Kenyan Forest Story

1. This is a forest in Kenya when Wangari was young.
2. This is how the people changed the forest when Wangari was in America.
3. This is why the people of Kenya changed the forest. They thought they needed it more than trees.
4. These are the problems the people of Kenya had after the trees were cut down.
5. These are the trees that Wangari planted.
6. This is how the new trees met the needs of the people in Kenya.

Lesson K.5 Text for Interactive Whiteboard Slide 3

Meadowview Street Meadow Story

1. This is what the land probably looked like before Meadowview Street was built.
2. This is how people changed the environment.
3. This is why people changed the environment. They needed
   _____.
4. This is the problem Caroline saw on Meadowview Street.
5. This is the meadow Caroline and her family created in their yard.
6. This is why Caroline wanted a meadow on Meadowview Street. It met the needs of _____.

Lesson K.5 Concept Map

Name: _____ Date: _____

How did Wangari's trees change the environment in Kenya?

Perfect Pairs: Using Fiction and Nonfiction Picture Books to Teach Life Science, K–2 by Melissa Stewart and Nancy Chesley. Copyright © 2014. Stenhouse Publishers.

Lesson K.6 Wonder Journal Labels

I wonder how people can work together to protect living things and the land they call home.

How can people work together to protect living things and the land they call home?

I wonder how people can work together to protect living things and the land they call home.

How can people work together to protect living things and the land they call home?

I wonder how people can work together to protect living things and the land they call home.

How can people work together to protect living things and the land they call home?

Perfect Pairs: Using Fiction and Nonfiction Picture Books to Teach Life Science, K–2 by Melissa Stewart and Nancy Chesley. Copyright © 2014. Stenhouse Publishers.

Lesson K.6 Readers Theater Script

Based on **Where Once There Was a Wood** *by Denise Fleming*

Getting Started

Many reader's theater scripts have just ten or twelve parts, but this script has a role for every student in the class. The script also includes quite a few choruses read by everyone.

As written, the script includes nineteen roles. The parts vary in difficulty, to accommodate children at a variety of reading levels. If you are working with fewer than nineteen children, some students can perform two roles. If you have a large group, students can share a role.

After you have matched students with parts, ask the class to read through the script a few times. As the children practice, provide as much support and advice as needed.

Planning the Performance

When the children feel confident about their roles, ask them to think about staging. Where and how will they stand during the performance? Are there times when they should move? Should they move their drawings before or as they say their line? Would they like to make a poster with lots of houses to illustrate the last line of the reader's theater?

Consider inviting a class of younger students to your classroom for the final performance. It will give your class a sense of accomplishment, and both groups will enjoy interacting.

Lesson K.6 Readers Theater Script *(continued)*

Everyone:	**Where once . . .**
Child 1:	there was a wood
Child 2:	a meadow
Child 3:	a creek
Everyone:	**Where once . . .**
Child 4:	a red fox rested, and closed his eyes to sleep
Everyone:	**Where once . . .**
Child 5:	ferns uncurled their leaves
Child 6:	and purple violets grew
Everyone:	**Where once . . .**
Child 7:	a woodchuck left his den to catch the morning dew
Everyone:	**Where once . . .**

Lesson K.6 Readers Theater Script *(continued)*

Child 8:   the horned owl hunted

Child 9, 10, 11:   to feed her hungry brood

Everyone: **Where once . . .**

Child 12:   the heron fished

Child 13 (fish):   and speared his glittery food

Everyone: **Where once . . .**

Child 14:   the brown snake slithered and slipped out of sight

Everyone: **Where once . . .**

Child 15:   the raccoon rambled and rummaged in the night

Everyone: **Where once . . .**

Child 16:   the berries ripened

Child 17:   and waxwings came to feed

Perfect Pairs: Using Fiction and Nonfiction Picture Books to Teach Life Science, K–2 by Melissa Stewart and Nancy Chesley. Copyright © 2014. Stenhouse Publishers.

Lesson K.6 Readers Theater Script *(continued)*

Everyone:	**Where once . . .**
Child 18:	the pheasant roosted
Child 19:	and fed on nuts and seeds
Everyone:	**Where once . . .**
Child 1:	there was a wood
Child 2:	a meadow
Child 3:	a creek
Everyone:	**sit houses side by side, twenty houses deep**

Lesson K.6 Butterfly Outline

Perfect Pairs: Using Fiction and Nonfiction Picture Books to Teach Life Science, K–2 by Melissa Stewart and Nancy Chesley. Copyright © 2014. Stenhouse Publishers.

Lesson K.6 Butterfly Data Table

Butterfly	What It Needs	What People Do
Eastern tiger swallowtail	Flower nectar	Plant gardens
Mourning cloak	Sugary tree sap	Protect forests
Karner blue	Plants that grow on burned land	Let some natural wildfires burn
Hessel's hairstreak	Plants that grow in wet places	Protect swamps and marshes
Monarch	Caterpillars need plants that make cattle and sheep sick	Let the plants that monarchs eat grow in other fields
Thicket hairstreak	Plants that attack trees people use to make paper	Leave these plants alone
Mitchell's satyr	To stay safe and healthy	Laws to keep people from catching butterflies
Schaus swallowtail	To stay healthy	Stop using chemicals that hurt butterflies
Oregon silverspot	Places where there are native plants	People choose native plants to grow
Harris's checkerspot	Open fields	Create new grassy areas
Palos Verdes	Sandy thickets near the ocean	Restore these wild places

Lesson K.7 Wonder Journal Labels

....

I wonder how people can work together to protect creatures that depend

on water environments.

....

On Big Night, spotted salamanders move from _____ to

_____.

....

The boy in this story will help the salamanders cross a _____.

....

How can people work together to protect creatures that depend

on water environments?

....

People can help creatures that depend on water environments.

My evidence is:

....

Lesson K.7 *Turtle, Turtle, Watch Out!*

Name: _____ Date: _____

Turtle, Turtle, Watch Out!

Lesson 1.1 Wonder Journal Labels

....

I wonder how an animal's body parts help it live and grow.

....

How do an animal's body parts help it live and grow?

....

A _____ (animal 1) uses its tail to _____ (job 1).

But a _____ (animal 2) uses its tail to _____

(job 2).

....

A _____ (animal 1) uses its _____ (body part 1)

to find, catch, or eat food.

But a _____ (animal 2) uses its _____ (body

part 2) to find, catch, or eat food.

....

Lesson 1.1 Animal Cards*

platypus	hyena	mole
alligator	bat	hippopotamus
cricket	humpback whale	skunk
lizard	scorpion	monkey
eagle	chameleon	four-eyed fish

Lesson 1.1 Animal Cards* *(continued)*

horned lizard	**bush baby**	**chimpanzee**
blue-footed booby	**water strider**	**gecko**
mountain goat	**pelican**	**mosquito**
egg-eating snake	**anteater**	**archerfish**

* Elephant, jackrabbit, and giraffe are not included due to atypical uses of featured body parts.

Lesson 1.1 Body Part Cards

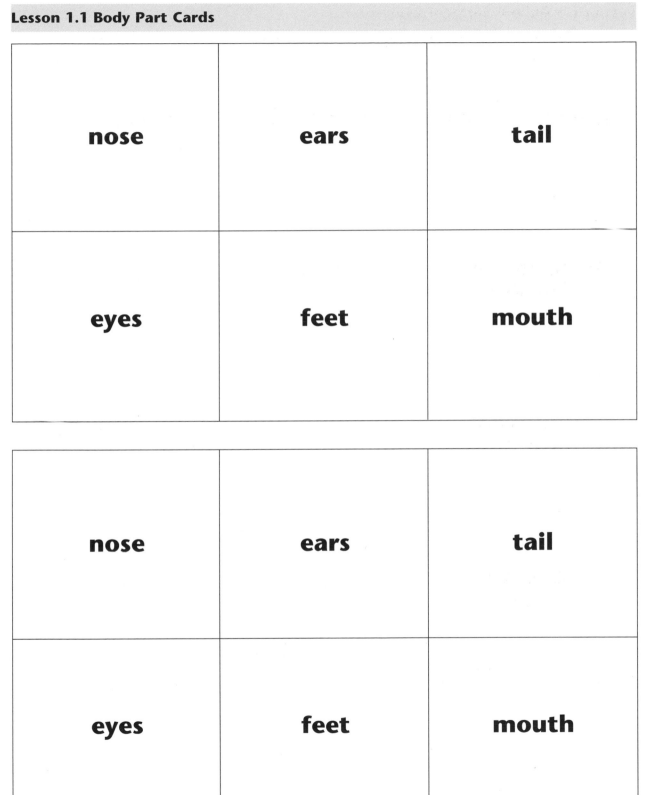

nose	ears	tail
eyes	feet	mouth
nose	ears	tail
eyes	feet	mouth

Lesson 1.2 Wonder Journal Labels

I wonder how some animals find and catch food.

A frog depends on its _____ (body part) to find food.

A frog depends on its _____ (body part) and its

_____ (body part) to catch food.

How do some animals find and catch food?

Lesson 1.2 What It Eats Cards

dirt	nectar	beetles
crabs	clams, snails	nuts
clover	snake	honey
insects, seeds, berries	fish, young deer or elk, garbage	leaves
shoots, fruits, seedpods	bamboo	grasses, bark, roots
leaves, herbs, fruit	giant squid	fish, rays

Lesson 1.2 Catches (Grabs) Food With Cards

mouth	**proboscis**	**tongue**
arms, radula	**beak**	**mouth**
teeth	**tongue, teeth**	**upper lip, tongue**
trunk	**teeth**	

Perfect Pairs: Using Fiction and Nonfiction Picture Books to Teach Life Science, K–2 by Melissa Stewart and Nancy Chesley. Copyright © 2014. Stenhouse Publishers.

Lesson 1.3 Wonder Journal Labels

I wonder how animals protect themselves from predators.

If I were a fish, I would _____ to protect myself

from predators.

How do animals protect themselves from predators?

I wonder how animals protect themselves from predators.

If I were a fish, I would _____ to protect myself

from predators.

How do animals protect themselves from predators?

Lesson 1.3 Wonder Journal Handout

I used to wonder how animals protect themselves from predators.

Now I know that animals have many ways of staying safe.

Some animals use external body parts.

Some animals use behaviors.

Some animals use both.

Lesson 1.4 Wonder Journal Labels

I wonder how a plant's parts help it live, grow, and make more plants.

When I cut open a lima-bean seed, I think I will find _____.

How do a plant's parts help it live, grow, and make more plants?

I wonder how a plant's parts help it live, grow, and make more plants.

When I cut open a lima-bean seed, I think I will find _____.

How do a plant's parts help it live, grow, and make more plants?

Lesson 1.5 Wonder Journal Labels

I wonder how people solve problems by designing things that work like plant or animal parts.

How do people solve problems by designing things that work like plant or animal parts?

I wonder how people solve problems by designing things that work like plant or animal parts.

How do people solve problems by designing things that work like plant or animal parts?

Lesson 1.5 Body Part Matching Worksheet

Name: _____ Date: _____

Directions: Draw a line between each animal body part and the kitchen gadget that works in the same way as the body part. Some animal body parts match more than one gadget.

Animal Body Part	**Kitchen Gadget**
Butterfly proboscis	Salad tongs
Pelican beak	Nut cracker
Earthworm gizzard	Salad spinner
Octopus arms	Potato masher
Parrot beak	Drinking straw
	Colander
	Pepper grinder
	Turkey baster
	Chopsticks

Lesson 1.5 Steps in the Design Process Cards

Steps in the Design Process 1. Identify a Problem 2. Identify Challenges 3. Share Ideas 4. Design 5. Build 6. Test	***Steps in the Design Process*** 1. Identify a Problem 2. Identify Challenges 3. Share Ideas 4. Design 5. Build 6. Test
Steps in the Design Process 1. Identify a Problem 2. Identify Challenges 3. Share Ideas 4. Design 5. Build 6. Test	***Steps in the Design Process*** 1. Identify a Problem 2. Identify Challenges 3. Share Ideas 4. Design 5. Build 6. Test
Steps in the Design Process 1. Identify a Problem 2. Identify Challenges 3. Share Ideas 4. Design 5. Build 6. Test	***Steps in the Design Process*** 1. Identify a Problem 2. Identify Challenges 3. Share Ideas 4. Design 5. Build 6. Test

Lesson 1.5 Design Task Worksheet for TEAM 1

Design Problem: You need to water a vegetable garden, but the garden hose is full of holes and you can't get to the store to buy a new one.

Plant/Animal Part and Use Data Table

Plant/Animal Part	How It Is Used
Tree trunk	Carries water from the tree's roots to its leaves
Tree roots	Soak up water
Mole nose	Has sensors that help a mole avoid getting lost in underground tunnels
Anteater tongue	Sticks way out to catch food
Gecko fcet	Walk up walls and across ceilings, so a gecko can find food and escape from enemies

. . . .

Lesson 1.5 Design Task Worksheet for TEAM 2

Design Problem: You need to clean up a wad of gum stuck to the ceiling before your mom gets home.

Plant/Animal Part and Use Data Table

Plant/Animal Part	How It Is Used
Tree trunk	Carries water from the tree's roots to its leaves
Tree roots	Soak up water
Mole nose	Has sensors that help a mole avoid getting lost in underground tunnels
Anteater tongue	Sticks way out to catch food
Gecko feet	Walk up walls and across ceilings, so a gecko can find food and escape from enemies

Lesson 1.5 Design Task Worksheet for TEAM 3

Design Problem: You need to get a bouncy ball that is trapped under a dresser.

Plant/Animal Part and Use Data Table

Plant/Animal Part	How It Is Used
Tree trunk	Carries water from the tree's roots to its leaves
Tree roots	Soak up water
Mole nose	Has sensors that help a mole avoid getting lost in underground tunnels
Anteater tongue	Sticks way out to catch food
Gecko feet	Walk up walls and across ceilings, so a gecko can find food and escape from enemies

Lesson 1.5 Design Task Worksheet for TEAM 4

Design Problem: You need to clean up a spill, but you don't have paper towels or a sponge.

Plant/Animal Part and Use Data Table

Plant/Animal Part	How It Is Used
Tree trunk	Carries water from the tree's roots to its leaves
Tree roots	Soak up water
Mole nose	Has sensors that help a mole avoid getting lost in underground tunnels
Anteater tongue	Sticks way out to catch food
Gecko feet	Walk up walls and across ceilings, so a gecko can find food and escape from enemies

Perfect Pairs: Using Fiction and Nonfiction Picture Books to Teach Life Science, K–2 by Melissa Stewart and Nancy Chesley. Copyright © 2014. Stenhouse Publishers.

Lesson 1.5 Design Task Worksheet for TEAM 5

Design Problem: You need to find your way around a dark place without a flashlight, candles, or anything else that produces light.

Plant/Animal Part and Use Data Table

Plant/Animal Part	How It Is Used
Tree trunk	Carries water from the tree's roots to its leaves
Tree roots	Soak up water
Mole nose	Has sensors that help a mole avoid getting lost in underground tunnels
Anteater tongue	Sticks way out to catch food
Gecko feet	Walk up walls and across ceilings, so a gecko can find food and escape from enemies

Lesson 1.6 Wonder Journal Labels

....

I wonder how some animal parents help their young grow up.

....

How do some animal parents help their young grow up?

....

An animal parent's behaviors can help its young survive in the world.

My evidence is:

....

A young animal's behaviors can help it survive in the world.

My evidence is:

....

Lesson 1.7 Wonder Journal Labels

....

I wonder how young animals are like their parents.

....

This is what I think a young bluebird looks like:

....

How are young animals like their parents?

....

Young animals look like their parents in some ways.

My evidence is:

....

Young animals look different from their parents in some ways.

My evidence is:

....

Lesson 1.7 Bluebird Similarity Data Tables

Adult	Hatchling
Blue head and back feathers	Pink skin with fuzzy down feathers
Blue wing and tail feathers	Pink skin with fuzzy down feathers
Rusty chest feathers	Pink skin with fuzzy down feathers
White belly feathers	Pink skin with fuzzy down feathers
Eyes open	Eyes shut
Beak	✓
Two legs, feet with three toes	✓

Adult	Chick
Blue head and back feathers	Spotted head and back feathers
Blue wing and tail feathers	✓
Rusty chest feathers	Spotted chest feathers
White belly feathers	✓
Eyes open	✓
Beak	✓
Two legs, feet with three toes	✓

···

Adult	Hatchling
Blue head and back feathers	Pink skin with fuzzy down feathers
Blue wing and tail feathers	Pink skin with fuzzy down feathers
Rusty chest feathers	Pink skin with fuzzy down feathers
White belly feathers	Pink skin with fuzzy down feathers
Eyes open	Eyes shut
Beak	✓
Two legs, feet with three toes	✓

Adult	Chick
Blue head and back feathers	Spotted head and back feathers
Blue wing and tail feathers	✓
Rusty chest feathers	Spotted chest feathers
White belly feathers	✓
Eyes open	✓
Beak	✓
Two legs, feet with three toes	✓

Perfect Pairs: Using Fiction and Nonfiction Picture Books to Teach Life Science, K–2 by Melissa Stewart and Nancy Chesley. Copyright © 2014. Stenhouse Publishers.

Lesson 1.8 Wonder Journal Labels

I wonder how adult animals of the same kind can be different from one another.

How can adult animals of the same kind be different from one another?

I wonder how adult animals of the same kind can be different from one another.

How can adult animals of the same kind be different from one another?

Lesson 1.8 Venn Diagram Template

Name: _____ Date: _____

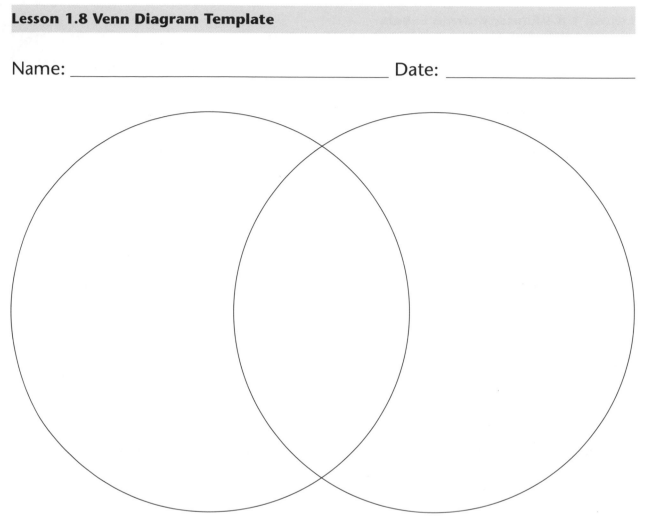

Lesson 2.1 Wonder Journal Labels

I wonder how wind, water, and animals help some seeds move to new places.

How do wind, water, and animals help some seeds move to new places?

I wonder how wind, water, and animals help some seeds move to new places.

How do wind, water, and animals help some seeds move to new places?

I wonder how wind, water, and animals help some seeds move to new places.

How do wind, water, and animals help some seeds move to new places?

Lesson 2.2 Wonder Journal Labels

I wonder why living things need a habitat.

Why do living things need a habitat?

A water boatman lives near the _____ of a _____

because that habitat has everything the insect needs to survive.

My evidence is:

A hermit crab lives on the _____ of a _____

because that habitat has everything the crab needs to survive.

My evidence is:

Lesson 2.2 Ocean Floor Critter Cards

A. This ocean animal protects its "soft spot" by keeping most of its body inside a shell it finds on the ocean floor. When it outgrows the shell, it finds another one.

B. As this ocean critter crawls on rocks, it grazes on slimy green algae and other kinds of food. When it feels scared, it curls up inside a shell it made itself.

C. This living thing attaches itself to the ocean floor. It lives in shallow water, so it can soak up enough sunlight to make food.

D. This colorful ocean critter has to attach itself to a hard surface, such as the seafloor. It can reach out in all directions to catch tiny ocean animals in the water or on the ocean bottom.

E. This five-armed ocean animal has a tricky name because it isn't really a fish. It crawls along the ocean floor in search of oysters, clams, and other tasty treats.

F. This living thing is no bigger than the eraser on the end of a pencil. It attaches itself to a solid surface and builds a hard skeleton around its soft body. Then it catches even tinier critters as they swim by.

G. This ocean critter moves across the ocean floor on spiky spines. It spends its days searching for mussels, sponges, and other small creatures to eat.

Lesson 2.3 Wonder Journal Labels

I wonder how a rain forest is different from a desert.

This is what I think a desert looks like.

How is a rain forest different from a desert?

I wonder how a rain forest is different from a desert.

This is what I think a desert looks like.

How is a rain forest different from a desert?

I wonder how a rain forest is different from a desert.

This is what I think a desert looks like.

How is a rain forest different from a desert?

Lesson 2.3 Concept Map

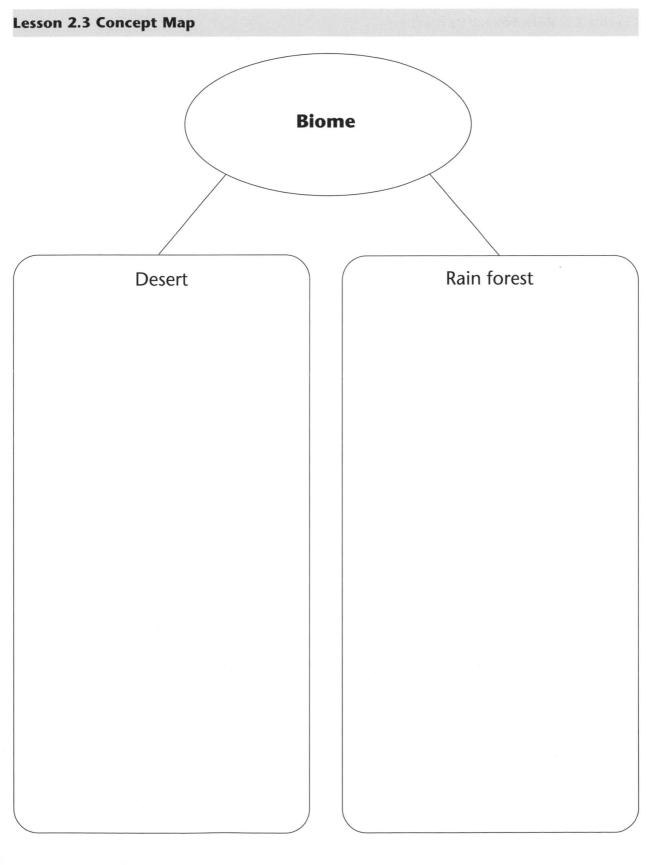

Biome

Desert

Rain forest

Lesson 2.3 Rain Forest Cards

emerald tree boa	three-toed sloth	scarlet macaw
tapir	bees	kapok tree
coati	tree porcupine	toucan
ocelot	poison arrow frog	squirrel monkey
jaguar	anteater	iguana

Lesson 2.3 Desert Cards

saguaro cactus	**red-tailed hawk**	**collared lizard**
prickly-pear cactus	**ringtail**	**black-tailed jackrabbit**
chuckwalla	**roadrunner**	**kit fox**
desert tortoise	**bobcat**	**badger**
round-tailed ground squirrel	**coyote**	**gopher snake**

Lesson 2.3 Sample Poem

I see a butterfly,

here in the Amazon rain forest.

It is big, blue, and black.

It is flying near a kapok tree.

It is one of many kinds of butterflies.

I wonder if it is afraid of a jaguar.

Lesson 2.4 Wonder Journal Labels

....

I wonder what lives in different kinds of wetlands.

....

What lives in different kinds of wetlands?

....

Based on the books we've read, there seems to be a greater diversity of

insects in a _____ than in a _____.

My evidence is:

....

Based on the books we've read, there seems to be a greater diversity of

reptiles in a _____ than in a _____.

My evidence is:

....

Based on the books we've read, there seems to be a greater diversity of

plants in a _____ than in a _____.

My evidence is:

....

Lesson 2.4 Readers Theater Script

Based on Frog in a Bog *by John Himmelman*

Getting Started

Many reader's theater scripts have just ten or twelve parts, but this script has a role for every student in the class. The script also includes choruses read by everyone.

As written, the script includes twenty-four plant and animal parts and a narrator role. The parts vary in difficulty, to accommodate children at a variety of reading levels. If you are working with fewer than twenty-five children, some students can perform two roles. If you have a large group, two or more students can share the narrator role.

After you have matched students with parts, ask the class to read through the script a few times. As the children practice, provide as much support and advice as needed.

Planning the Performance

When the children feel confident about their roles, ask them to think about staging. Where and how will they stand during the performance? Are there times when they should move? Should they move their drawings before or as they say their line?

Consider inviting a class of younger students to your classroom for the final performance. It will give your class a sense of accomplishment, and both groups will enjoy interacting.

Lesson 2.4 Readers Theater Script *(continued)*

Narrator:	Look! A frog. [Point.]
Frog:	*Ribbit!* Watch me jump around the bog. I start out on a fern . . .
Fern:	That's me. [Wave.]
Frog:	. . . and land in soft moss.
Moss:	That's me. [Wave.]
Narrator:	Look! Two mosquitoes.
Mosquitoes 1 & 2:	The frog scared us, so we're flying away. [Flap arms.]
Mosquito 1:	I land on a sundew. Uh-oh.
Sundew:	That's me. [Wave.] I'm a meat-eating plant, and I'm hungry.
Everyone:	**Bye-bye mosquito.**
Mosquito 2:	I'm the lucky mosquito. I land on a horsetail.
Horsetail:	That's me. [Wave.] I must be popular today. There's a dragonfly on me, too.
Dragonfly:	I've got my eye on a deee-licious butterfly. See it? [Point.]
Everyone:	**Over on that steeplebush plant?**
Steeplebush:	That's me. [Wave.] Butterflies love the sweet nectar inside my flowers.
Butterfly:	Mmmm. Nectar. What a tasty treat!

Lesson 2.4 Readers Theater Script *(continued)*

Steeplebush:	Hey! What's happening? Ouch! That hurts.
Narrator:	Look! A muskrat. [Point.] It's trampling you.
Muskrat:	Get out of my way! I'm a muskrat, and I'm bigger than you.
Everyone:	**Watch out, mole cricket, or you'll get smooshed!**
Mole cricket:	Yikes! That was a close call. Thanks for the warning.
Everyone:	**Watch out, ducks. The muskrat is headed your way.**
Muskrat:	I'm going for a swim in the middle of the bog.
Duck 1 & 2:	*Oo-eek, oo-eek!* Time to fly!
Narrator:	Look! A turtle. [Point.]
Turtle:	That's me. [Wave.] Oh my, what's that?
Everyone:	**A fly just landed on your nose.**
Turtle:	He-he. It tickles.
Fly:	Too much wiggling. Time to fly! I'll land over there. [Point.]
Everyone:	**Oh no! Not on the pitcher plant. It's a trap.**
Fly:	A what?
Pitcher plant:	Too late. That foolish fly is my meal now.
Narrator:	Look! A kingbird. [Point.] It's on that leatherleaf plant.

Perfect Pairs: Using Fiction and Nonfiction Picture Books to Teach Life Science, K–2 by Melissa Stewart and Nancy Chesley. Copyright © 2014. Stenhouse Publishers.

Lesson 2.4 Readers Theater Script *(continued)*

Kingbird:	Too bad about that fly. It looked yummy. Time to fly!
Leatherleaf:	Thank goodness! That big bird was awfully heavy.
Narrator:	Look! A hawk. [Point.] It's flying away from that tamarack tree.
Tamarack tree:	That's me. I'm tall and strong. When a hawk sits on me, it can see the whole bog.
Hawk:	*Kee-ahh! Kee-ahh!* I'll swoop down and grab that kingbird.
Everyone:	**Watch out, kingbird. Here comes a hungry hawk.**
Kingbird:	Don't worry about me. I'll chase that hawk away.
Narrator:	Look! A bird-watcher. [Point.] She's exploring the bog.
Bird-watcher:	Yuck! This cranberry tastes bad.
Cranberry:	*Boing! Boing! Ouch!* Where am I?
Narrator:	Poor little cranberry. You landed on the ground.
Cranberry:	Look! A ground cricket. [Point.] It's jumping through the air.
Ground cricket:	Wheee!
Frog:	Gulp.
Everyone:	**Just another day in the bog.**

Lesson 2.4 Sample Slide: Bog Animals Vs. Swamp Animals

Bog Animals	**Swamp Animals**
Frog (Spring peeper)	Catfish
Mosquitoes	Newt
Dragonfly	Bees?
Butterfly	Alligator
Muskrat	Snake
Mole cricket	Skeeter
Ducks	Spider
Turtle	Owl
Fly	Skink
Kingbird	Skunk
Hawk	Worm
Ground cricket	
Water strider	
Katydid	
Tree cricket	
Red-spotted newt	
Water snake	
Green frog	
Yellow warbler	
Red-winged blackbird	
Northern waterthrush	

Lesson 2.4 Sample Slide: Bog Plants Vs. Swamp Plants

Bog Plants	**Swamp Plants**
Fern	Grassy plants
Moss	Trees
Sundew	Cattails
Horsetail	
Steeplebush	
Pitcher plant	
Leatherleaf	
Tamarack tree	
Cranberry	
Horned bladderwort	
Bog club moss	
Grass pink	
Bulrush	
Sensitive fern	
Nutsedge	
Labrador tea	
Marsh fern	

Lesson 2.4 Concept Map

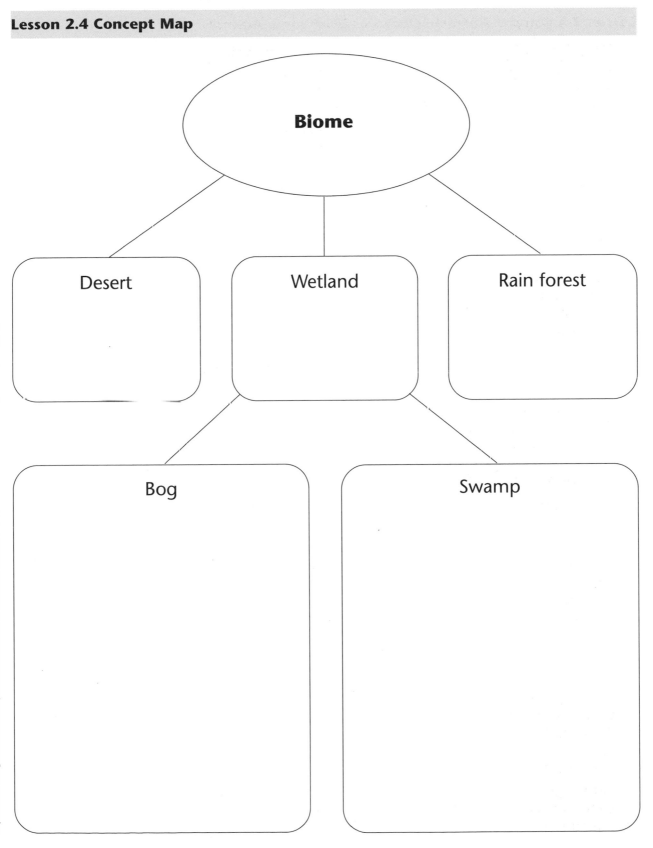

Lesson 2.5 Wonder Journal Labels

I wonder what lives in different kinds of grasslands.

What lives in different kinds of grasslands?

I wonder what lives in different kinds of grasslands.

What lives in different kinds of grasslands?

I wonder what lives in different kinds of grasslands.

What lives in different kinds of grasslands?

I wonder what lives in different kinds of grasslands.

What lives in different kinds of grasslands?

Lesson 2.5 Concept Map

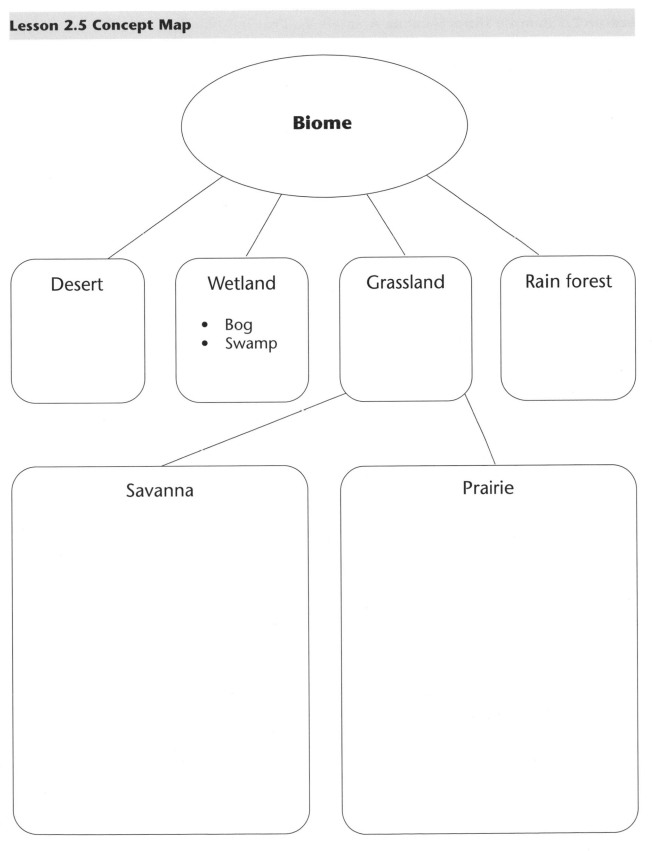

Lesson 2.5 Sample Slide: Savanna Animals Vs. Prairie Animals

Savanna Animals
Frog
Crickets
Vervet monkeys
Hippopotamuses
Birds
Insects
Zebras
Wildebeest
Crocodile
Lion
Elephants
Giraffe

Prairie Animals
Bison
Pronghorn
Meadowlark
Prairie dog
Grasshopper
Sharp-tailed grouse
Beetles
Howdy owl
Rattlesnake
Coyote
Great Plains toad

Lesson 2.5 Sample Slide: Savanna Plants Vs. Prairie Plants

Savanna Plants
Grass
Acacia tree

Prairie Plants
Snakeroot
Long grasses
Various wildflowers
Grama grass
Daisies
Yucca
Primrose
Clover

Perfect Pairs: Using Fiction and Nonfiction Picture Books to Teach Life Science, K–2 by Melissa Stewart and Nancy Chesley. Copyright © 2014. Stenhouse Publishers.

Lesson 2.5 Plants on Savannas and Prairies Worksheet

Please glue the correct word on each line.

1. Different kinds of plants live on _____ and

   _____.

2. There seems to be a greater diversity of _____ on the

   prairie.

3. There are colorful _____ on the prairie, but not on the

   savanna.

4. _____ grows on savannas and prairies.

flowers	savannas	grass	prairies	plants

Lesson 2.5 Animals on Savannas and Prairies Worksheet

Please glue the correct word on each line.

1. _____ and _____ live on savannas and

   prairies.

2. There seems to be a greater diversity of _____ living

   on the savanna.

3. _____ live on both savannas and prairies.

4. There is a _____ on the savanna and a _____

   on the prairie. They are both amphibians.

prey	insects	large animals	toad	predators	frog

Perfect Pairs: Using Fiction and Nonfiction Picture Books to Teach Life Science, K–2 by Melissa Stewart and Nancy Chesley. Copyright © 2014. Stenhouse Publishers.

Lesson 2.5 Sample Bison Postcard

Wildebeest Herd
Savanna Grassland
Kenya, Africa

Dear Wildebeest,

I live on a prairie grassland. My habitat is special because

Your Friend,

_____ Bison

Lesson 2.5 Sample Wildebeest Postcard

Bison Herd
Prairie Grassland
Kansas, United States

Dear Bison,

I live on a savanna grassland. My habitat is special because

_____

_____

_____

_____

_____

Your Friend,

_____ Wildebeest

Lesson 2.6 Wonder Journal Labels

I wonder how plants change as they grow.

How do plants change as they grow?

I wonder how plants change as they grow.

How do plants change as they grow?

I wonder how plants change as they grow.

How do plants change as they grow?

I wonder how plants change as they grow.

How do plants change as they grow?

Lesson 2.6 True/False Student Worksheet

Name: _____ Date: _____

Plants start life as seeds. _____True _____False	To get a big tomato, you must plant a big tomato seed. _____True _____False
All seeds look pretty much the same. _____True _____False	A plant's appearance changes as it grows. _____True _____False
All plants look pretty much the same. _____True _____False	As a plant grows, it forms fruits first and then flowers. _____True _____False
All plants act pretty much the same. _____True _____False	Seeds form inside a fruit. _____True _____False
Seeds get bigger as they grow into plants. _____True _____False	The correct sequence of stages in a plant's life is: seed, fruit, flower, seedling. _____True _____False

Lesson 2.6 Plant Growth Statement Cards

Plants start life as seeds.	To get a big tomato, you must plant a big tomato seed.
All seeds look pretty much the same.	A plant's appearance changes as it grows.
All plants look pretty much the same.	As a plant grows, it forms fruits first and then flowers.
All plants act pretty much the same.	Seeds form inside a fruit.
Seeds get bigger as they grow into plants.	The correct sequence of stages in a plant's life is: seed, fruit, flower, seedling.

Lesson 2.7 Wonder Journal Labels

I wonder how butterflies change as they grow.

How do butterflies change as they grow?

I wonder how butterflies change as they grow.

How do butterflies change as they grow?

I wonder how butterflies change as they grow.

How do butterflies change as they grow?

I wonder how butterflies change as they grow.

How do butterflies change as they grow?

Bibliography of Picture Books in *Perfect Pairs* Lessons

Aliki. *My Five Senses.* New York: HarperCollins, 1989.
   PB 978-0-06445-083-6

Alter, Anna. *Disappearing Desmond.* New York: Knopf, 2010.
   HC 978-0-37586-684-5

Arnold, Caroline. *A Warmer World.* Watertown, MA: Charlesbridge, 2007.
   HC 978-1-58089-266-7; PB 978-1-58089-267-4

Arnosky, Jim. *Gobble It Up! A Fun Song About Eating!* New York: Scholastic, 2008.
   HC 978-0-43990-362-2

Aston, Dianna Hutts. *A Seed Is Sleepy.* San Francisco: Chronicle, 2007.
   HC 978-0-81185-520-4

Baker, Keith. *No Two Alike.* San Diego: Beach Lane Books, 2011.
   HC 978-1-44241-742-7

Barretta, Gene. *Neo Leo: The Ageless Ideas of Leonardo da Vinci.* New York: Holt, 2009.
   HC 978-0-80508-703-1

Bateman, Donna M. *Deep in the Swamp.* Watertown, MA: Charlesbridge, 2007.
   HC 978-1-57091-597-0
———. *Out on the Prairie.* Watertown, MA: Charlesbridge, 2012.
   HC 978-1-58089-378-7

Baylor, Byrd. *The Desert Is Theirs.* New York: Aladdin, 1987.
   PB 978-0-68971-105-3

———. *Desert Voices*. New York: Aladdin, 1993.
  PB 978-0-68971-691-1

Beaty, Andrea. *Iggy Peck, Architect*. New York: Abrams, 2007.
  HC 978-0-81091-106-2

Berkes, Marianne. *The Swamp Where Gator Hides*. Nevada City, CA: Dawn, 2014.
  HC 978-1-58469-471-7

Biedrzycki, David. *Ace Lacewing, Bug Detective*. Watertown, MA: Charlesbridge, 2008.
  PB 978-1-57091-684-7

Brown, Peter. *The Curious Garden*. New York: Little, Brown, 2009.
  HC 978-0-31601-547-9

Bruchac, Joseph, and James Bruchac. *Turtle's Race with Beaver*. New York: Puffin, 2005.
  PB 978-0-14240-466-9

Bunting, Eve. *Butterfly House*. New York: Scholastic, 1999.
  HC 978-0-59084-884-8.

Buzzeo, Toni. *Just Like My Papa*. New York: Disney-Hyperion, 2013.
  HC 978-1-42314-263-8

———. *Stay Close to Mama*. New York: Disney-Hyperion, 2012.
  HC 978-1-42313-482-4

Campbell, Sarah C. *Wolfsnail: A Backyard Predator*. Honesdale, PA: Boyds Mills, 2008.
  HC 978-1-59078-554-6

Cannon, Janell. *Pinduli*. San Diego: Harcourt, 2004.
  HC 978-0-15204-668-2

Carle, Eric. *A House for Hermit Crab*. New York: Simon & Schuster, 1991.
  HC 978-0-88708-168-2; PB 978-0-68984-894-0

Cherry, Lynne. *The Great Kapok Tree*. San Diego: Harcourt, 1990.
  HC 978-0-15200-520-7; PB 978-0-15202-614-1

———. *The Sea, the Storm, and the Mangrove Tangle*. New York: Farrar, Straus and Giroux, 2004.
  HC 978-0-37436-482-3

Christensen, Bonnie. *Plant a Little Seed*. New York: Roaring Brook, 2012.
  HC 978-1-59643-550-6

Cole, Henry. *Jack's Garden*. New York: Greenwillow, 1997.
  HC 978-0-68813-501-0; PB 978-0-68815-283-3

———. *On Meadowview Street*. New York: Greenwillow, 2007.
  HC 978-0-06056-481-0

Cronin, Doreen. *Diary of a Fly*. New York: HarperCollins, 2007.
  HC 978-0-06000-156-8

Davies, Nicola. *Bat Loves the Night*. Cambridge, MA: Candlewick, 2004.
  HC 978-0-75696-561-7; PB 978-0-76362-438-5

———. *Dolphin Baby!* Somerville, MA: Candlewick, 2012.
HC 978-0-76365-548-8

———. *Just Ducks!* Cambridge, MA: Candlewick, 2012.
HC 978-0-76365-936-3

dePaola, Tomie. *Oliver Button Is a Sissy*. San Diego: Harcourt, 1979.
HC 978-0-15257-852-7; PB 978-0-15668-140-7

Dunphy, Madeleine. *At Home with the Gopher Tortoise: The Story of a Keystone Species*. Berkeley, CA: Web of Life Children's Books, 2010.
HC 978-0-97775-396-3; PB 978-0-97775-395-6

———. *Here Is the Southwestern Desert*. Berkeley, CA: Web of Life Children's Books, 2006.
HC 978-0-97737-957-6; PB 978-0-97737-956-9

———. *Here Is the Tropical Rainforest*. Berkeley, CA: Web of Life Children's Books, 2006.
HC 978-0-97737-951-4; PB 978-0-97737-950-7

Edwards, Pamela Duncan. *Clara Caterpillar*. New York: HarperCollins, 2001.
PB 978-0-06443-691-5

Ehlert, Lois. *Mole's Hill*. San Diego: Harcourt, 1998.
HC 978-0-61309-930-1; PB 978-0-15201-890-0

Ering, Timothy Basil. *Necks Out for Adventure: The True Story of Edwin Wiggleskin*. Cambridge, MA: Candlewick, 2008.
HC 978-0-76362-355-5

Fleming, Candace. *Papa's Mechanical Fish*. New York: Farrar, Straus and Giroux, 2013.
HC 978-0-37439-908-5

Fleming, Denise. *Where Once There Was a Wood*. New York: Holt, 2000.
PB 978-0-80506-482-7

Fromental, Jean-Luc. *365 Penguins*. New York: Abrams, 2006.
HC 978-0-81094-460-2; PB 978-0-06058-703-1

Frost, Helen. *Monarch and Milkweed*. New York: Atheneum, 2008.
HC 978-1-41690-085-6

Galbraith, Kathryn O. *Planting the Wild Garden*. Atlanta: Peachtree, 2011.
HC 978-1-56145-563-8

Goodman, Emily. *Plant Secrets*. Watertown, MA: Charlesbridge, 2009.
HC 978-1-58089-204-9; PB 978-1-58089-205-6

Gravett, Emily. *Dogs*. New York: Simon & Schuster, 2010.
HC 978-1-41698-703-1

Guiberson, Brenda Z. *Rain, Rain, Rain Forest*. New York: Holt, 2004.
HC 978-0-80506-582-4; PB 978-0-43977-469-7

Halfmann, Janet. *Star of the Sea: A Day in the Life of a Starfish*. New York: Holt, 2011.
HC 978-0-80509-073-4

Harley, Avis. *African Acrostics: A Word in Edgeways*. Cambridge, MA: Candlewick, 2012.
HC 978-0-76365-818-2

Hatkoff, Juliana, Isabella Hatkoff, and Craig Hatkoff. *Winter's Tail: How One Little Dolphin Learned to Swim Again*. New York: Scholastic, 2009.
HC 978-0-54512-335-8; PB 978-0-54534-830-0

Hauth, Katherine B. *What's for Dinner? Quirky, Squirmy Poems from the Animal World*. Watertown, MA: Charlesbridge, 2011.
HC 978-1-57091-471-3; PB 978-1-57091-472-0

Heiligman, Deborah. *From Caterpillar to Butterfly*. New York: Greenwillow/HarperCollins, 1996.
PB 978-0-06445-129-1

Heos, Bridget. *What to Expect When You're Expecting Joeys: A Guide for Marsupial Parents (and Curious Kids)*. Minneapolis, MN: Millbrook, 2011.
HC 978-0-76135-858-9

Himmelman, John. *Frog in a Bog*. Watertown, MA: Charlesbridge, 2004.
HC 978-1-57091-518-5

James, Simon. *Baby Brains and RoboMom*. Somerville, MA: Candlewick, 2008.
HC 978-0-76363-463-6

Jenkins, Steve. *Never Smile at a Monkey*. Boston: Houghton Mifflin, 2009.
HC 978-0-61896-620-2

———. *What Do You Do When Something Wants to Eat You?* Boston: Houghton Mifflin, 2001.
HC 978-0-61335-590-2; PB 978-0-61815-243-8

———. *What Do You Do with a Tail Like This?* Boston: Houghton Mifflin, 2003.
HC 978-0-61825-628-0

Jenkins, Steve, and Robin Page. *Time to Eat*. Boston: Houghton Mifflin, 2011.
HC 978-0-54725-032-8

Kirby, Pamela F. *What Bluebirds Do*. Honesdale, PA: Boyds Mills, 2009.
HC 978-1-59078-614-7

Kurtz, Jane. *Do Kangaroos Wear Seatbelts?* New York: Dutton, 2005.
HC 978-0-52547-358-9

Kurtz, Jane, and Christopher Kurtz. *Water Hole Waiting*. New York: Greenwillow/HarperCollins, 2002.
HC 978-0-06029-850-0

Kurtz, Kevin. *A Day in the Salt Marsh*. Mount Pleasant, SC: Sylvan Dell, 2007.
HC 978-0-97688-235-0; PB 978-1-93435-919-8

LaMarche, Jim. *The Raft*. New York: HarperCollins, 2005.
HC 978-0-68813-977-3

Lamstein, Sarah Marwil. *Big Night for Salamanders*. Honesdale, PA: Boyds Mills, 2009.
HC 978-1-93242-598-7

Lionni, Leo. *Swimmy*. New York: Knopf, 1994.
HC 978-0-39481-713-2; PB 978-0-39482-620-2

Markle, Sandra. *Finding Home*. Watertown, MA: Charlesbridge, 2010.
HC 978-1-58089-123-3

———. *Hip-Pocket Papa*. Watertown, MA: Charlesbridge, 2010.
HC 978-1-57091-708-0

———. *Little Lost Bat*. Watertown, MA: Charlesbridge, 2006.
PB 978-1-57091-657-1

———. *A Mother's Journey*. Watertown, MA: Charlesbridge, 2005.
HC 978-1-57091-621-2; PB 978-1-57091-622-9

Mazer, Anne. *The Salamander Room*. Boston: Houghton Mifflin, 2000.
HC 978-0-78073-945-1; PB 978-0-67986-187-4

McDermott, Gerald. *Monkey: A Trickster Tale from India*. Boston: Harcourt, 2011.
HC 978-0-15216-596-3

Nolen, Jerdine. *Plantzilla*. San Diego: Harcourt, 2002.
HC 978-0-15202-412-3; PB 978-0-15205-392-5

Peterson, Cris. *Seed, Soil, Sun*. Honesdale, PA: Boyds Mills, 2010.
HC 978-1-59078-713-7

Pfeffer, Wendy. *From Seed to Pumpkin*. New York: HarperCollins, 2004.
HC 978-0-75693-238-1; PB 978-0-06445-190-1

———. *Wiggling Worms at Work*. New York: HarperCollins, 2003.
HC 978-0-06028-448-0; PB 978-0-06445-199-4

Rockwell, Anne. *Who Lives in an Alligator Hole?* New York: HarperCollins, 2006.
PB 978-0-06445-200-7

Roth, Susan L., and Cindy Trumbore. *The Mangrove Tree: Planting Trees to Feed Families*. New York: Lee and Low, 2011.
HC 978-1-60060-459-1

Rotner, Shelley, and Sheila M. Kelly. *Shades of People*. New York: Holiday House, 2010.
HC 978-0-82342-191-6; PB 978-0-82342-305-7

Ryder, Joanne. *The Snail's Spell*. New York: Scholastic, 1991.
HC 978-0-81246-361-3; PB 978-0-14050-891-8

———. *Where Butterflies Grow*. New York: Puffin, 1996.
PB 978-0-14055-858-6

Sarcone-Roach, Julia. *Subway Story*. New York: Knopf, 2011.
HC 978-0-37585-859-8

Sayre, April Pulley. *Dig, Wait, Listen: A Desert Toad's Tale*. New York: Greenwillow, 2001.
HC 978-0-68816-614-4

———. *Trout Are Made of Trees*. Watertown, MA: Charlesbridge, 2008.
    HC 978-1-58089-138-7

———. *Turtle, Turtle, Watch Out!* Watertown, MA: Charlesbridge, 2010.
    HC 978-1-58089-148-6; PB 978-1-58089-149-3

———. *Vulture View*. New York: Holt, 2007.
    HC 978-0-80507-557-1

Schaefer, Lola. *Just One Bite*. San Francisco: Chronicle, 2010.
    HC 978-0-81186-473-2

Schanzer, Rosalyn. *How Ben Franklin Stole the Lightning*. New York:
    HarperCollins, 2002.
    HC 978-0-68816-993-0

Schwartz, David M., and Yael Schy. *Where in the Wild? Camouflaged
    Creatures Concealed . . . and Revealed*. San Francisco, CA: Tricycle,
    2007.
    HC 978-1-58246-207-3; PB 978-1-58246-399-5

Sidman, Joyce. *Butterfly Eyes & Other Secrets of the Meadow*. Boston:
    Houghton Mifflin Harcourt, 2006.
    HC 978-0-61856-313-5

———. *Song of the Water Boatman & Other Pond Poems*. Boston:
    Houghton Mifflin Harcourt, 2005.
    HC 978-0-61813-547-9

Stevens, Janet, and Susan Stevens Crummel. *The Great Fuzz Frenzy*.
    Boston, MA: Houghton Mifflin Harcourt, 2005.
    HC 978-0-15204-626-2

Stewart, Melissa. *No Monkeys, No Chocolate*. Watertown, MA:
    Charlesbridge, 2013.
    HC 978-1-58089-287-2

———. *A Place for Butterflies*. Atlanta: Peachtree, 2006.
    HC 978-1-56145-357-3; PB 978-1-56145-571-3

———. *A Place for Fish*. Atlanta: Peachtree, 2011.
    HC 978-1-56145-562-1

Stewart, Sarah. *The Gardener*. New York: Farrar, Straus and Giroux, 1997.
    HC 978-0-37432-517-6

Weeks, Sarah. *Catfish Kate and the Sweet Swamp Band*. New York:
    Atheneum, 2009.
    HC 978-1-41694-026-5

Wheeler, Eliza. *Miss Maple's Seeds*. New York: Nancy Paulsen
    Books/Penguin, 2013.
    HC 978-0-39925-792-6

Willis, Jeanne. *Tadpole's Promise*. New York: Atheneum, 2005.
    PB 978-1-84270-426-4

Wilson, Karma. *Bear Wants More*. New York: Margaret K. McElderry,
    2003.
    HC 978-0-68984-509-3

————. *A Frog in the Bog.* New York: Margaret K. McElderry, 2007.
   HC 978-0-68984-081-4; PB 978-1-41692-727-3

Winter, Jeanette. *Wangari's Trees of Peace: A True Story from Africa.* San
   Diego: Harcourt, 2008.
   HC 978-0-15206-545-4

Wong, Janet S. *Dumpster Diver.* Somerville, MA: Candlewick, 2007.
   HC 978-0-76362-380-7

Wood, Douglas. *No One But You.* Somerville, MA: Candlewick, 2011.
   HC 978-0-76363-848-1

————. *What Dads Can't Do.* New York: Simon & Schuster, 2000.
   HC 978-0-68982-620-7

————. *What Moms Can't Do.* New York: Simon & Schuster, 2001.
   HC 978-0-68983-358-8

Yolen, Jane. *Eloise's Bird.* New York: Philomel, 2010.
   HC 978-0-39925-292-1

Ziefert, Harriet. *One Red Apple.* Maplewood, NJ: Blue Apple Books, 2009.
   HC 978-1-93470-667-1

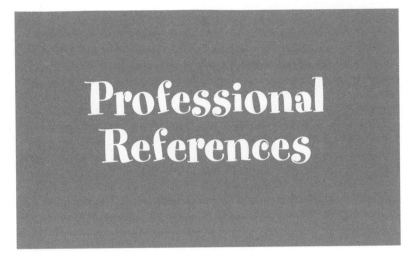

Professional References

AAAS (American Association for the Advancement of Science). 1993. *Benchmarks for Science Literacy*. New York: Oxford University Press.

Bybee, Roger. 2011. "Scientific and Engineering Practices in K–12 Classrooms: Understanding a Framework for K–12 Science Education." *Science and Children*, December.

———. 2013. "The Next Generation Science Standards and the Life Sciences." *Science and Children*, February.

Bybee, Roger, Joseph A. Taylor, April Gardner, Pamela Van Scotter, Janet Carlson Powell, Anne Westbrook, and Nancy Landes. 2006. *The BSCS 5-E Instructional Model: Origins and Effectiveness. A Report Prepared for the Office for Science Education, National Institutes for Health*. Colorado Springs, CO: BSCS. Available online at http://science.education.nih.gov/houseofreps.nsf/b82d55fa138783c2852572c9004f5566/$FILE/Appendix%20D.pdf.

Camp, Deanne. 2000. "It Takes Two: Teaching with Twin Texts of Fact and Fiction." *The Reading Teacher* 53(5): 400–408.

Driver, Rosalind, Ann Squires, Peter Rushworth, and Valerie Wood-Robinson. 2001. *Making Sense of Secondary Science: Research into Children's Ideas*. London and New York: Routledge and Falmer.

Keeley, Page. 2008. *Science Formative Assessment*. Thousand Oaks, CA: Corwin.

Marek, Edmund A., and Ann M. L. Cavallo. 1997. *The Learning Cycle: Elementary School Science and Beyond*. Portsmouth, NH: Heinemann.

Michaels, Sarah, Andrew W. Shouse, and Heidi A. Schweingruber. 2008. *Ready, Set, Science!: Putting Research to Work in K–8 Science Classrooms*. Washington, DC: National Academies Press.

National Governors Association and Council of Chief State School Officers. *Common Core State Standards Initiative: English Language Arts Standards.* http://www.corestandards.org/ELA-Literacy/. Access date: May 19, 2014. (Note: It is important to refer to standards on the website, as language there is continually updated.)

NRC (National Research Council). 1996. *National Science Education Standards.* Washington, DC: National Academies Press.

———. 2012. *A Framework for K–12 Science Education: Practices, Crosscutting Concepts, and Core Ideas.* Washington, DC: National Academies Press.

NGSS Lead States. *Next Generation Science Standards: For States, By States.* http://www.nextgenscience.org/. Access date: May 19, 2014. (Note: It is important to refer to standards on the website, as language there is continually updated.)

Pratt, Harold. 2012. *The NSTA Reader's Guide to a Framework for Science Education: Practices, Crosscutting Concepts, and Core Ideas.* Arlington, VA: NSTA.

Stewart, Melissa. 2010. "Perfect Pairs: Teaching Science Through Literature." *Science Books & Films,* May: 108–112.

Taberski, Sharon. 2014. "Fact & Fiction: Read Aloud." *Scholastic Teachers.* http://www2.scholastic.com/browse/article.jsp?id=3344.

Worth, Karen, Jeff Winokur, Sally Crissman, Martha Winokur, and Martha Davis. 2009. *The Essentials of Science and Literacy: A Guide for Teachers.* Portsmouth, NH: Heinemann.

Credits

Lesson K.1: *Book cover*, copyright © 1991 by Alfred A. Knopf, an imprint of Random House Children's Books; from *The Salamander Room* by Anne Mazer. Used by permission of Alfred A. Knopf, an imprint of Random House Children's Books, a division of Random House LLC. All rights reserved. From *From Seed to Pumpkin* by Wendy Pfeffer, illustrated by James Graham Hale. Copyright © 2004. Used by permission of HarperCollins Publishers.

Lesson K.2: From *Gobble It Up!* by Jim Arnosky. Copyright © 2008 by Jim Arnosky. Published by Scholastic Press. Used by permission. Cover from *Time to Eat* by Steve Jenkins and Robin Page. Copyright © 2011 by Steve Jenkins and Robin Page. Reprinted by permission of Houghton Mifflin Harcourt Company. All rights reserved.

Lesson K.3: From *Just Ducks!* Text copyright © 2012 by Nicola Davies. Illustrations copyright © 2012 by Salvatore Rubbino. Reproduced by permission of the publisher, Candlewick Press, Somerville, MA, on behalf of Walker Books, London. Used by permission. From *Hip-Pocket Papa* written by Sandra Markle, illustrated by Alan Marks. Copyright © 2010 by Sandra Markle and Alan Marks. Used with permission by Charlesbridge Publishing, 85 Main St., Watertown, MA 02472, (617) 926-0329, www.charlesbridge.com.

Lesson K.4: Cover from *Mole's Hill* by Lois Ehlert. Copyright © 1998 by Lois Ehlert. Reprinted by permission of Houghton Mifflin Harcourt Company. All rights reserved. From *At Home with the Gopher Tortoise: The Story of a Keystone Species*, written by Madeleine Dunphy, illustrated by Michael Rothman. Copyright © 2010 by Madeleine Dunphy and Michael Rothman. Published by Web of Life Children's Books. Used by permission.

Lesson K.5: From *On Meadowview Street*, written and illustrated by Henry Cole. Copyright © 2007. Used by permission of HarperCollins Publishers. From *Wangari's Trees of Peace: A True Story from Africa* by Jeanette Winter. Copyright ©

2008 by Jeanette Winters. Reprinted by permission of Houghton Mifflin Harcourt Company. All rights reserved.

Lesson K.6: From *Where Once There Was a Wood* © 1996 by Denise Fleming. Reprinted by permission of Henry Holt & Company, LLC. All rights reserved. From *A Place for Butterflies*, Second Edition, written by Melissa Stewart, illustrated by Higgins Bond. Copyright © 2014 by Melissa Stewart and Higgins Bond. Published by Peachtree Publishers. Used by permission.

Lesson K.7: From *Big Night for Salamanders*, written by Sarah Marwil Lamstein, illustrated by Carol Benioff. Copyright © 2010 by Sarah Marwil Lamstein and Carol Benioff. Published by Boyds Mills Press. Used by permission. From *Turtle, Turtle, Watch Out!*, written by April Pulley Sayre, illustrated by Annie Patterson. Copyright © 2010 by April Pulley Sayre and Annie Patterson. Used with permission by Charlesbridge Publishing, 85 Main St., Watertown, MA 02472, (617) 926-0329, www.charlesbridge.com.

Lesson 1.1: From *The Snail's Spell* by Joanne Ryder, illustrated by Lynne Cherry. Used by permission of Penguin Group (USA) LLC. All rights reserved. Cover from *What Do You Do with a Tail like This?* by Steve Jenkins. Copyright © 2001 by Steve Jenkins. Reprinted by permission of Houghton Mifflin Harcourt Company. All rights reserved.

Lesson 1.2: From *A Frog in the Bog*, written by Karma Wilson, illustrated by Joan Rankin. Copyright © 2007 by Karma Wilson and Joan Rankin. Published by Margaret K. McElderry Books/Simon & Schuster. Used by permission. From *Just One Bite* written by Lola Schaefer, illustrated by Geoff Waring. Copyright © 2010 by Lola Schafer and Geoff Waring. Published by Chronicle Books. Used by permission.

Lesson 1.3: *Book Cover*, copyright © 1963, 1991 by Alfred A. Knopf, an imprint of Random House Children's Books; from *Swimmy* by Leo Lionni. Used by permission of Alfred A. Knopf, an imprint of Random House Children's Books, a division of Random House LLC. All rights reserved. Cover from *What Do You Do When Something Wants to Eat You?* by Steve Jenkins. Copyright © 2003 by Steve Jenkins. Reprinted by permission of Houghton Mifflin Harcourt Company. All rights reserved.

Lesson 1.4: From *Jack's Garden*, written and illustrated by Henry Cole. Copyright © 1997. Used by permission of HarperCollins Publishers. From *Plant Secrets*, written by Emily Goodman, illustrated by Phyllis Limbacher Tildes. Copyright © 2009 by Emily Goodman and Phyllis Limbacher Tildes. Used with permission by Charlesbridge Publishing, 85 Main St., Watertown, MA 02472, (617) 926-0329, www.charlesbridge.com.

Lesson 1.5: From *Iggy Peck, Architect*, by Andrea Beaty, illustrated by David Roberts. Illustrations copyright © 2007 David Roberts. Published by Abrams Books for Young Readers. Used by permission. From *Winter's Tail: How One Little Dolphin Learned to Swim Again*, written and photographed by Juliana Hatkoff, Isabella Hatkoff, and Craig Hatkoff. Copyright © 2011 by Juliana Hatkoff, Isabella Hatkoff, and Craig Hatkoff. Published by Scholastic Press. Used by permission.

Index

Page numbers followed by an *f* indicate figures.

A

Agreement Circle activity, 208–210

Animal Cards
- How an Animal's Body Parts Help it Survive (1.1), 94, 99–100, 283–284
- What Animals Eat (K.2), 36–38, 261–264

Animal Lunch Quilt, 109–110

Animal Photo Cards, 215–218, 221

animals. *See also* diet of animals
- How Adult Animals of the Same Species Can be Different (1.8), 156–162, 247
- How an Animal's Body Parts Help it Survive (1.1), 93–102, 246
- How Animal Parents and Young Interact (1.6), 138–146, 247
- How Animals Can Change an Environment (K.4), 54–61, 245
- How Animals Depend on Their Environment (K.3), 45–53, 245
- How Animals Find and Catch Food (1.2), 103–111, 246
- How Animals Protect Themselves (1.3), 112–118, 246
- How Butterflies Change as They Grow (2.7), 231–238, 248
- How to Reduce Our Impact on Creatures in Land Environments (K.6), 72–79, 245
- How to Reduce Our Impact on Creatures in Water Environments (K.7), 80–86, 245
- How Wind, Water, and Animals Disperse Seeds (2.1), 169–177, 248
- How Young Animals are Like Their Parents (1.7), 147–155, 247
- Life in Grasslands (2.5), 214–223, 248
- Life in Wetlands (2.4), 200–213, 248
- Mimicking Plant and Animal Body Parts to Solve Problems (1.5), 128–137, 247
- seeds and pollination and, 16
- Understanding Biomes (2.3), 188–199, 248
- Understanding Habitats (2.2), 178–187, 248
- What Animals Eat (K.2), 36–44, 245
- What Plants and Animals Need to Survive (K.1), 25–35, 245

Animals on Savannas and Prairies Worksheet, 215, 221, 322

arguments from evidence
- How Animals Can Change an Environment (K.4), 54–61
- How People Can Change an Environment (K.5), 62–71
- science and engineering practices and, 18, 249

At Home with the Gopher Tortoise (Dunphy), 54–61

B

bar graphs, 172

Big Night for Salamanders (Lamstein), 80–86

Bingo game, 52–53

biogeology
- How Animals Can Change an Environment (K.4), 54–61, 245
- How People Can Change an Environment (K.5), 62–71, 245

biomes. *See also* environment; habitats
- Life in Wetlands (2.4), 200–213
- overview, 17
- Understanding Biomes (2.3), 188–199, 248

Bluebird Similarity Data Tables, 151, 300. *See also* data tables

Body Part Cards, 94, 99–100, 285

Body Part Matching Worksheet, 129, 130–131, 293
body parts
  How an Animal's Body Parts Help it Survive (1.1),
    93–102, 246
  How Animals Find and Catch Food (1.2), 103–111
  How Animals Protect Themselves (1.3), 112–118
  Mimicking Plant and Animal Body Parts to Solve
    Problems (1.5), 128–137, 247
Bog Animal Sticky Notes, 201, 207–208
Bog Animals Vs. Swamp Animals, 201, 207–209, 316
Bog Plants Vs. Swamp Plants, 207, 209–211, 316
bogs, 200–213
booklets, 211, 212f
booksellers
  AbeBooks, 7
  Alibris, 7
  Amazon.com, 7
  bookstores, 7
  Powell's Books, 7
Building Permit Worksheet, 54, 59–60, 59f, 268
butterflies
  How Butterflies Change as They Grow (2.7),
    231–238, 248
  How to Reduce Our Impact on Creatures in Land
    Environments (K.6), 72–79, 245, 278, 279
Butterfly Data Table, 76. See also data tables
Butterfly Outline, 77, 278

C

Catches (Grabs) Food With Cards, 108–109, 288
Catfish Kate and the Sweet Swamp Band (Weeks), 200–213
cause and effect, 15. See also crosscutting concepts
Clara Caterpillar (Edwards), 231–238
Clarification Statements, 15–16
Commit and Toss activity, 189–190
Common Core State Standards for English Language Arts
  list of, 250–256
  Next Generation Science Standards (NGSS) and, 10–11
  science-themed fiction and nonfiction picture books
    and, 5
  supporting, 18–21, 20f
communicating information, 18, 249
Concentration game
  How Plants Change as They Grow (2.6), 225–226,
    225f
  How to Reduce Our Impact on Creatures in Water
    Environments (K.7), 82
Concept Map
  How People Can Change an Environment (K.5), 63,
    67, 272
  Life in Grasslands (2.5), 215, 218–219, 218f, 319
  Life in Wetlands (2.4), 201, 205, 205f, 317
  Understanding Biomes (2.3), 191–192, 194, 194f, 307
conclusions. See drawing conclusions
constructing explanations. See explanations
crosscutting concepts, 15, 16

D

data analysis and interpretation, 18, 249
  What Animals Eat (K.2), 36
  What Plants and Animals Need to Survive (K.1), 25
data tables
  investigative process and, 9, 10, 12, 13, 20, 21
  within specific lessons
    How Adult Animals of the Same Species Can be
      Different (1.8), 157, 158–161
    How an Animal's Body Parts Help it Survive (1.1),
      95–99, 98f
    How Animal Parents and Young Interact (1.6),
      140–143
    How Animals Can Change an Environment (K.4),
      56–58
    How Animals Depend on Their Environment
      (K.3), 48, 49
    How Animals Find and Catch Food (1.2),
      108–109, 111
    How Animals Protect Themselves (1.3), 115–117
    How a Plant's Parts Help it Survive (1.4), 122–124,
      123f
    How Butterflies Change as They Grow (2.7),
      232–235
    How People Can Change an Environment (K.5),
      65–67
    How Plants Change as They Grow (2.6), 226–228
    How to Reduce Our Impact on Creatures in Land
      Environments (K.6), 75–76, 279
    How to Reduce Our Impact on Creatures in Water
      Environments (K.7), 81, 82–84
    How Wind, Water, and Animals Disperse Seeds
      (2.1), 171–174
    How Young Animals are Like Their Parents (1.7),
      148–151, 300
    Mimicking Plant and Animal Body Parts to Solve
      Problems (1.5), 129, 131–133, 135, 295–297
    Understanding Habitats (2.2), 179–184, 185–186
    What Animals Eat (K.2), 36–37, 39–40, 43
    What Plants and Animals Need to Survive (K.1),
      29, 30, 31–32
defense strategies. See protection; survival
defining problems, 18, 249
desert biomes, 188–199. See also biomes
Desert Cards, 189, 196, 309
Design Task Worksheets, 129, 135–136, 295–297
diet of animals. See also animals
  How Animals Find and Catch Food (1.2), 103–111, 246
  overview, 16
  What Animals Eat (K.2), 36–44, 245
dioramas, 198
Disciplinary Core Ideas (DCIs). See also Performance
  Expectations, NGSS
  How Adult Animals of the Same Species Can be
    Different (1.8), 156
  How an Animal's Body Parts Help it Survive (1.1), 93

How Animals Find and Catch Food (1.2), 103
How Animals Protect Themselves (1.3), 112
incorporating, 17
list of, 245–248
Mimicking Plant and Animal Body Parts to Solve
    Problems (1.5), 128–129
NGSS Performance Expectation (PE) and, 16
overview, 15, 16
diversity of life
    Life in Grasslands (2.5), 220–221, 220*f*, 222–223
    Life in Wetlands (2.4), 209–210
    overview, 17
    Understanding Biomes (2.3), 188
    Understanding Habitats (2.2), 178
Dogs (Gravett), 156–162
domain-specific language, 9
drawing conclusions.
    overview, 9–10
    Wonder Journals and, 12

E

Earth and Space Sciences PEs, 15, 16. *See also*
    Performance Expectations, NGSS
Education Development Center (EDC), 8–10, 9*f*, 10*f*
ELA standards. *See* Common Core State Standards for
    English Language Arts
engaging students, 9. *See also* investigative process
engineering practices, 15, 17–18, 249
English Language Arts (ELA) standards. *See* Common
    Core State Standards for English Language Arts
English language learners, 14
environment. *See also* biomes; habitats
    How Animals Can Change an Environment (K.4),
        54–61, 245
    How Animals Depend on Their Environment (K.3),
        45–53, 245
    How People Can Change an Environment (K.5),
        62–71, 245
    How to Reduce Our Impact on Creatures in Land
        Environments (K.6), 72–79, 245
    How to Reduce Our Impact on Creatures in Water
        Environments (K.7), 80–86, 245
    Life in Grasslands (2.5), 214–223, 248
    Life in Wetlands (2.4), 200–213, 248
    Understanding Biomes (2.3), 188
    Understanding Habitats (2.2), 178
evaluating information, 18, 249
explanations, 18, 249
    Mimicking Plant and Animal Body Parts to Solve
        Problems (1.5), 128
    How Young Animals Are Like Their Parents (1.7), 147
    How Adult Animals of the Same Species Can Be
        Different (1.8), 156
exploration
    overview, 9
    Wonder Journals and, 12

F
fables
    Understanding Biomes (2.3), 199
    Understanding Habitats (2.2), 187
fiction books. *See also* fiction-nonfiction book pairs
    combining with science instruction, 4
    obtaining the books needed, 7
    pairing with nonfiction books, 4–5
fiction-nonfiction book pairs, 4–5, 8. *See also* fiction
    books; nonfiction books
5-E Learning Cycle model, 8–10, 9*f*, 10*f*
Food Cards, 36–38, 261–264
A Framework for K-12 Science Education (NRC, 2012), 18
Frog in a Bog (Himmelman), 200–213
A Frog in the Bog (Wilson), 103–111
From Seed to Pumpkin (Pfeffer), 25–35

G
gadgets, 130–131, 135–136, 136*f*
Gobble It Up! A Fun Song About Eating (Arnosky), 36–44
grasslands, 214–223, 248
The Great Kapok Tree (Cherry), 188–199
guided journal entries, 12. *See also* Wonder Journals

H
Habitat Real Estate Ads activity, 184–186
habitats. *See also* biomes; environment
    How an Animal's Body Parts Help it Survive (1.1), 101
    How to Reduce Our Impact on Creatures in Land
        Environments (K.6), 72–79
    How to Reduce Our Impact on Creatures in Water
        Environments (K.7), 80
    Life in Grasslands (2.5), 214–223, 248
    Life in Wetlands (2.4), 200–213, 248
    overview, 17
    Understanding Biomes (2.3), 188
    Understanding Habitats (2.2), 178–187, 248
Haiku poetry, 222. *See also* poetry
handwriting, 13
Here is the Southwestern Desert (Dunphy), 188–199
Hip-Pocket Papa (Markle), 45–53
A House for Hermit Crab (Carle), 178–187
human impact of earth systems
    How People Can Change an Environment (K.5),
        62–71, 245
    How to Reduce Our Impact on Creatures in Land
        Environments (K.6), 72–79, 245
    How to Reduce Our Impact on Creatures in Water
        Environments (K.7), 80–86, 245

I
Iggy Peck, Architect (Beaty), 128–137
informational text, 18
information, obtaining
    How to Reduce Our Impact on Creatures in Land
        Environments (K.6), 72–79

information, obtaining *(continued)*
How to Reduce Our Impact on Creatures in Water Environments (K.7), 80–86
inquiry, 17–18
interactive bulletin board, 211
investigations, planning and carrying out
Life in Grasslands (2.5), 214–223
Life in Wetlands (2.4), 200–213
Understanding Biomes (2.3), 188–199
Understanding Habitats (2.2), 178–187
investigative process
overview, 8–10, 9*f*, 10*f*
science and engineering practices and, 249
Wonder Journals and, 12

J

Jack's Garden (Cole), 119–127
journals. *See* Wonder Journals
Just Ducks! (Davies), 45–53
Just Like My Papa (Buzzeo), 147–155
Just One Bite (Schaefer), 103–111

L

land environments. *See also* environment
How Animals Can Change an Environment (K.4), 54–61, 245
How Animals Depend on Their Environment (K.3), 45–53, 245
How People Can Change an Environment (K.5), 62–71, 245
How to Reduce Our Impact on Creatures in Land Environments (K.6), 72–79, 245
Life in Grasslands (2.5), 214–223
Understanding Biomes (2.3), 188
learning goals
reinforcing, 10
Wonder Statements and, 8
learning styles, 10
Lessons for Grade 1
How Adult Animals of the Same Species Can be Different (1.8), 156–162, 247, 249, 252–253, 301, 302
How an Animal's Body Parts Help it Survive (1.1), 93–102, 246, 249, 252–253, 282, 283–284, 285
How Animal Parents and Young Interact (1.6), 138–146, 247, 249, 252–253, 298
How Animals Find and Catch Food (1.2), 103–111, 246, 249, 252–253, 286, 287, 288
How Animals Protect Themselves (1.3), 112–118, 246, 249, 252–253, 289, 290
How a Plant's Parts Help it Survive (1.4), 119–127, 247, 249, 252–253, 291
How Young Animals are Like Their Parents (1.7), 147–155, 247, 249, 252–253, 299, 300
Mimicking Plant and Animal Body Parts to Solve Problems (1.5), 128–137, 247, 249, 252–253, 292, 293, 294, 295–297
Lessons for Grade 2
How Butterflies Change as They Grow (2.7), 231–238, 248, 249, 254–256, 328
How Plants Change as They Grow (2.6), 224–230, 248, 249, 254–256, 325, 326, 327
How Wind, Water, and Animals Disperse Seeds (2.1), 169–177, 248, 249, 254–256, 303
Life in Grasslands (2.5), 214–223, 248, 249, 254–256, 318, 319, 320, 321, 322, 323, 324
Life in Wetlands (2.4), 200–213, 248, 249, 254–256, 311, 312–315, 316, 317
Understanding Biomes (2.3), 188–199, 248, 249, 254–256, 306, 307, 308, 309, 310
Understanding Habitats (2.2), 178–187, 248, 249, 254–256, 304, 305
Lessons for Kindergarten
How Animals Can Change an Environment (K.4), 54–61, 245, 249, 250–251, 267, 268, 269
How Animals Depend on Their Environment (K.3), 45–53, 245, 249, 250–251, 266
How People Can Change an Environment (K.5), 62–71, 245, 249, 250–251, 270, 271, 272
How to Reduce Our Impact on Creatures in Land Environments (K.6), 72–79, 245, 249, 250–251, 273, 274–277, 278, 279
How to Reduce Our Impact on Creatures in Water Environments (K.7), 80–86, 245, 249, 250–251, 280, 281
What Animals Eat (K.2), 36–44, 245, 249, 250–251, 260, 261–264, 265
What Plants and Animals Need to Survive (K.1), 25–35, 245, 249, 250–251, 258, 259
life cycles. *See also* animals; plants
butterfly life cycles, 18, 231–238, 248
plant life cycles, 18, 224–230, 248
Life Sciences PEs, 15–16. *See also* Performance Expectations, NGSS
listening, 20–21
Little Lost Bat (Markle), 138–146

M

Matching Game, 37–38
Match Me activity, 34–35
mathematics, 18, 249
Miss Maple's Seeds (Wheeler), 169–177
model development and use
How Animals Depend on Their Environment (K.3), 45–53
How Wind, Water, and Animals Disperse Seeds (2.1), 169–177
science and engineering practices and, 18, 249
Mole's Hill (Ehlert), 54–61

N

Next Generation Science Standards (NGSS). *See also* Performance Expectations, NGSS
  Common Core State Standards for English Language Arts and, 10–11
  investigative process and, 8–10
  overview, 15–18, 17*f*
  science-themed fiction and nonfiction picture books and, 5
  Wonder Journals and, 11–13
  Wonder Statements and, 8
NGSS Performance Expectations (PEs). *See* Performance Expectations, NGSS
nonfiction books. *See also* fiction-nonfiction book pairs
  combining with science instruction, 4
  obtaining the books needed, 7
  overview, 2–3
  pairing with fiction books, 4–5
notebooks, science. *See* Wonder Journals
No Two Alike (Baker), 156–162

O

obtaining information, 18, 249
obtaining the books needed, 7
Ocean Floor Critter Cards, 183–184, 305
ocean habitats, 178–187. *See also* habitats
On Meadowview Street (Cole), 62–71
open-ended journal entries, 12–13. *See also* Wonder Journals
open response questions on standardized tests, 5
Out on the Prairie (Bateman), 214–223

P

parents, animal. *See also* animals
  How Animal Parents and Young Interact (1.6), 138–146, 247
  How Young Animals are Like Their Parents (1.7), 147–155, 247
patterns. *See also* crosscutting concepts
  NGSS Performance Expectations (PEs) and, 15
  What Animals Eat (K.2), 36–44
  What Plants and Animals Need to Survive (K.1), 25–35
PE Clarification Statements, 15–16
Performance Expectations, NGSS. *See also* Next Generation Science Standards (NGSS)
  investigative process and, 9–10
  overview, 15–18, 17*f*
  science and engineering practices, 15, 17–18, 249
Performance Expectations addressed in lesson goals
  1-LS1-1
    appendix table of PEs, 246–247
    How an Animal's Body Parts Help It Survive (1.1), 93
    How Animals Find and Catch Food (1.2), 103
    How Animals Protect Themselves (1.3), 112
    How a Plant's Parts Help It Survive (1.4), 119, 120
    Mimicking Plant and Animal Body Parts to Solve Problems (1.5), 128, 129
  1-LS1-2
    appendix table of PEs, 247
    How Animal Parents and Young Interact, (1.6), 138
  1-LS3-1, 17
    appendix table of PEs, 247
    How Adult Animals of the Same Species Can Be Different (1.8), 156
    How Young Animals Are Like Their Parents (1.7), 147
  2-LS2-2, 16
    appendix table of PEs, 248
    How Wind, Water, and Animals Disperse Seeds (2.1), 169
  2-LS4-1, 17
    appendix table of PEs, 248
    Life in Grasslands (2.5), 214
    Life in Wetlands (2.4), 200
    Understanding Biomes (2.3), 188
    Understanding Habitats (2.2), 178
  K-ESS2-2
    appendix table of PEs, 245
    How Animals Can Change an Environment (K.4), 54
    How People Can Change an Environment (K.5), 62
  K-ESS3-1
    appendix table of PEs, 245
    How Animals Depend on Their Environment (K.3), 45
  K-ESS3-3
    appendix table of PEs, 245
    How to Reduce Our Impact on Creatures in Land Environments (K.6), 72
    How to Reduce Our Impact on Creatures in Water Environments (K.7), 80
  K-LS1-1, 15–16
    appendix table of PEs, 245
    What Animals Eat (K.2), 36
    What Plants and Animals Need to Survive (K.1), 25
PEs. *See* Performance Expectations, NGSS
Physical Sciences PEs, 15. *See also* Performance Expectations, NGSS
Plant Growth Statement Cards, 225, 228–229, 327
Place for Butterflies, A (Stewart), 72–79
Planting the Wild Garden (Galbraith), 169–177
plants
  How a Plant's Parts Help it Survive (1.4), 119–127, 247
  How Plants Change as They Grow (2.6), 224–230, 248

plants *(continued)*

How Wind, Water, and Animals Disperse Seeds (2.1), 169–177, 248

Life in Grasslands (2.5), 214–223, 248

Life in Wetlands (2.4), 200–213, 248

Mimicking Plant and Animal Body Parts to Solve Problems (1.5), 128–137, 247

plant life cycles, 18

seeds and pollination and, 16

Understanding Biomes (2.3), 188–199, 248

Understanding Habitats (2.2), 178–187

What Plants and Animals Need to Survive (K.1), 25–35

Plant Secrets (Goodman), 119–127

Plants on Savannas and Prairies Worksheet, 215, 220, 220f, 321

Plantzilla (Nolen), 224–230

poetry

How a Plant's Parts Help it Survive (1.4), 126

Life in Grasslands (2.5), 222

Understanding Biomes (2.3), 196–197, 197f, 310

Understanding Habitats (2.2), 178–187

pond habitats, 178–187. *See also* habitats

prairies, 214–223

protection. *See also* survival

How an Animal's Body Parts Help it Survive (1.1), 93–102

How Animals Protect Themselves (1.3), 112–118, 246

pyramid diorama, 198

Q

questions

asking and answering, 18, 19, 20–21

Common Core State Standards for English Language Arts and, 18, 19, 20–21

science and engineering practices and, 18, 249

Science Dialogues and Science Circles and, 14

Understanding Biomes (2.3), 197

Wonder Journals and, 12

R

rain forest biomes, 188–199. *See also* biomes

Rain Forest Cards, 189, 196, 308

Readers Theater Script

How to Reduce Our Impact on Creatures in Land Environments (K.6), 73–75, 274–277

Life in Wetlands (2.4), 201, 202, 312–315

recalling information, 19

rhyme

Life in Grasslands (2.5), 217

Life in Wetlands (2.4), 206, 212–213

S

The Salmander Room (Mazer), 25–35

Sample Bison Postcard, 215, 221–222, 323

Sample Wildebeest Postcard, 215, 221–222, 324

savannas, 214–223

Savanna Vs. Prairie Animals slide, 215, 219–222, 320

Savanna Vs. Prairie Plants slide, 219–222, 320

scaffolding, 9

science center

How Animals Depend on Their Environment (K.3), 53

How Wind, Water, and Animals Disperse Seeds (2.1), 176

How Young Animals are Like Their Parents (1.7), 153

Science Circles

How Adult Animals of the Same Species Can be Different (1.8), 161

How a Plant's Parts Help it Survive (1.4), 125

How Plants Change as They Grow (2.6), 229

How Wind, Water, and Animals Disperse Seeds (2.1), 174

overview, 14

Understanding Biomes (2.3), 195–196

What Plants and Animals Need to Survive (K.1), 31–32

Science Dialogues

Common Core State Standards for English Language Arts and, 20–21

How an Animal's Body Parts Help it Survive (1.1), 100

How Animals Can Change an Environment (K.4), 58–59

How Animals Find and Catch Food (1.2), 109

How Animals Protect Themselves (1.3), 116

How People Can Change an Environment (K.5), 69

How to Reduce Our Impact on Creatures in Land Environments (K.6), 78

overview, 14

What Plants and Animals Need to Survive (K.1), 30

science inquiry, 17–18

science notebooks. *See* Wonder Journals

science practices, 15, 17–18, 249

Seed Is Sleepy, A (Aston), 224–230

seeds. *See also* plants

How a Plant's Parts Help it Survive (1.4), 119–127, 247

How Plants Change as They Grow (2.6), 224–230, 248

How Wind, Water, and Animals Disperse Seeds (2.1), 169–177, 248

Seeds Move game, 176

Skunk Cousin Letters

How Animals Can Change an Environment (K.4), 269

overview, 60–61, 60f

The Snail's Spell (Ryder), 93–102

science and engineering practices and, 18, 249

Song of Water Boatman & Other Pond Poems (Sidman), 178–187

songs, 237–238

Sorting Game, 38

speaking, 20–21

spelling, 13

Stages of Inquiry model, 8–10, 9f, 10f

standardized tests, 5

standards. *See* Common Core State Standards for English Language Arts; Next Generation Science Standards (NGSS)

Steps in the Design Process Cards
  Mimicking Plant and Animal Body Parts to Solve Problems (1.5), 294
  overview, 129

structure and function, 15. *See also* crosscutting concepts

survival
  How an Animal's Body Parts Help it Survive (1.1), 93–102, 246
  How Animal Parents and Young Interact (1.6), 138–146, 145f, 247
  How Animals Protect Themselves (1.3), 112–118, 246
  How a Plant's Parts Help it Survive (1.4), 119–127, 247
  What Plants and Animals Need to Survive (K.1), 25–35, 245

Swamp Animal Sticky Notes, 201, 207–208

swamps, 200–213

Swimmy (Lionni), 112–118

T

Time to Eat (Jenkins & Page), 36–44

True/False Student Worksheet, 225, 228–229, 326

Turn and Talk activity
  How an Animal's Body Parts Help it Survive (1.1), 99
  How Animals Find and Catch Food (1.2), 109
  How People Can Change an Environment (K.5), 68
  How Plants Change as They Grow (2.6), 228
  How to Reduce Our Impact on Creatures in Land Environments (K.6), 77
  How to Reduce Our Impact on Creatures in Water Environments (K.7), 84
  Life in Wetlands (2.4), 204–205
  Understanding Biomes (2.3), 195

Turtle, Turtle, Watch Out! (Sayre), 80–86

Turtle, Turtle, Watch Out! Worksheet, 81, 281

Twenty Questions game, 26–27

V

Venn diagrams. *See also* Venn Diagram Template
  How Adult Animals of the Same Species Can be Different (1.8), 161
  What Plants and Animals Need to Survive (K.1), 26, 32–34

Venn Diagram Template. *See also* Venn diagrams
  How Adult Animals of the Same Species Can be Different (1.8), 157, 161, 302
  What Plants and Animals Need to Survive (K.1), 26, 33, 258

vocabulary
  How Animal Parents and Young Interact (1.6), 142
  How Animals Can Change an Environment (K.4), 57
  How Animals Depend on Their Environment (K.3), 48
  How Animals Protect Themselves (1.3), 114
  How People Can Change an Environment (K.5), 66
  How Plants Change as They Grow (2.6), 227
  How to Reduce Our Impact on Creatures in Land Environments (K.6), 75
  How to Reduce Our Impact on Creatures in Water Environments (K.7), 83
  How Wind, Water, and Animals Disperse Seeds (2.1), 171
  Life in Grasslands (2.5), 216
  Life in Wetlands (2.4), 206
  scaffolding and, 9
  Understanding Biomes (2.3), 193
  Understanding Habitats (2.2), 180
  What Animals Eat (K.2), 39

Vocabulary Cards, 8f

W

Wangari's Trees of Peace: A True Story from Africa (Winter), 62–71

water environments. *See also* environment
  How to Reduce Our Impact on Creatures in Water Environments (K.7), 80–86, 245
  Life in Wetlands (2.4), 200–213

Water Hole Waiting (Kurtz & Kurtz), 214–223

wetlands, 200–213, 248

What Bluebirds Do (Kirby), 147–155

What Dads Can't Do (Wood), 138–146

What Do You Do When Something Wants to Eat You? (Jenkins), 112–118

What Do You Do with a Tail Like This? (Jenkins), 93–102

What It Eats Cards, 107, 287

Where Butterflies Grow (Ryder), 231–238

Where Once There Was a Wood (Fleming), 72–79

Winter's Tail: How One Little Dolphin Learned to Swim Again (Hatkoff, Hatkoff, & Hatkoff), 128–137

Wonder Journal Labels
  How Adult Animals of the Same Species Can be Different (1.8), 157, 160, 301
  How an Animal's Body Parts Help it Survive (1.1), 94, 99, 100–101, 282
  How Animal Parents and Young Interact (1.6), 139, 143, 144, 298
  How Animals Can Change an Environment (K.4), 55, 56–58, 267
  How Animals Depend on Their Environment (K.3), 46, 49–50, 266
  How Animals Find and Catch Food (1.2), 105–107, 109, 286
  How Animals Protect Themselves (1.3), 113, 289

Wonder Journal Labels *(continued)*
    How a Plant's Parts Help it Survive (1.4), 120, 124, 291
    How Butterflies Change as They Grow (2.7), 232, 236, 328
    How People Can Change an Environment (K.5), 63, 64, 68, 270
    How Plants Change as They Grow (2.6), 225, 228–229, 325
    How to Reduce Our Impact on Creatures in Land Environments (K.6), 73, 76, 273
    How to Reduce Our Impact on Creatures in Water Environments (K.7), 81, 83, 84, 280
    How Wind, Water, and Animals Disperse Seeds (2.1), 170, 174, 303
    How Young Animals are Like Their Parents (1.7), 148, 152, 299
    Life in Grasslands (2.5), 215, 219–220, 318
    Life in Wetlands (2.4), 201, 207, 209–210, 311
    Mimicking Plant and Animal Body Parts to Solve Problems (1.5), 129, 134, 292
    Understanding Biomes (2.3), 189, 195, 306
    Understanding Habitats (2.2), 179, 184–185, 304
    What Animals Eat (K.2), 37, 41, 260
    What Plants and Animals Need to Survive (K.1), 26, 29, 31, 258
Wonder Journals
    discussion of, 11–13
    entries, 12–13
    overview, 11–13, 12*f*, 13*f*
    Science Dialogues and Science Circles and, 14
    setting up, 13
Wonder Statements
    investigative process and, 9–10
    overview, 8, 8*f*
writing, 12–13

Y
Yes/No/Maybe cards
    How Animal Parents and Young Interact (1.6), 143–144
    How Butterflies Change as They Grow (2.7), 232
young animals. *See also* animals
    How Animal Parents and Young Interact (1.6), 138–146, 247
    How Young Animals are Like Their Parents (1.7), 147–155, 247